English Local
The Leicester ʎ
a Departmental Ƅ
and History 1948-1998

Compiled and edited by
Margery Tranter, Ken Hawker, John Rowley,
and Mike Thompson

Introduced by
Charles Phythian-Adams

ISBN 0-9533105-3-1

Published by
Friends of the Department of English Local History
Registered Charity No. 1073528

1999

Published by the
Friends of the Department of English Local History
1999

The objective of the Friends is to promote the study of Local History

Further information is available from the Secretary of the Friends
c/o Department of English Local History,
5, Salisbury Road, Leicester, LE1 7QR

ISBN 9533105 3 1

Printed by Central Reprographic Unit
University of Leicester

CONTENTS

PREFACE

Founded in 1989, publishing its own annual *Newsletter* ever since, and now numbering some 300 members, in 1997 The Friends of the Department of English Local History set up a Jubilee Committee to mark the fiftieth anniversary of the department with both a day of events (5 December 1998) and the publication of this work. Any profits from the sale of this book, therefore, will be used towards the creation of student bursaries or to make other special provision in support of the work of the department.

Apart from the brief history of the department and its concerns that introduces the body of this work, the bibliography of writings which the latter represents comprises a considerable expansion of, and in the light of the developing historiography of the subject, some inevitable adaptation of, the content and organization of an earlier similar publication which was produced to mark the department's thirtieth anniversary in 1978. Compiled largely by Margery Tranter, for many years the department's Honorary Research Associate, and introduced and shaped by Alan Everitt, *English Local History at Leicester 1948-1978: A Bibliography of Writings by Members of the Department of English Local History, University of Leicester,* 1981, listed 1,217 items. This represented a prodigious research effort by Margery Tranter in particular, and it has been she who has continued to update our records almost ever since. On her relinquishment of this onerous task, and spurred on by the Secretary of the Friends, Derek Shorthouse, the good work was then taken over by Ken Hawker with help from Alan Tennant, who circulated past and present members of the department in order to maximise coverage of their publications. With some small input from the present writer on subject classification, sequencing, and conventions, the most burdensome task, that of entering onto a database all material additional to that on Margery Tranter's disk, fell on the capable shoulders of John Rowley. Subsequent editing and proof-reading were undertaken by Mike Thompson and Ken Hawker. The credits to be apportioned, therefore, should be shared primarily by Margery Tranter in company with Ken Hawker, John Rowley and Mike Thompson.

Even with all the care that has been taken, where either error or omission still cries out for remedy, it is hoped that readers will assist us by pointing out how the record should be corrected. Experience shows, however, that accuracy is best achieved where authors themselves keep the department updated from time to time, as we hope they will continue to do in the future.

In the meantime all those involved in this project would like to thank everyone who has responded so readily to their enquiries. The present writer also wishes to record here his widely-shared appreciation both of all the work done by Harold Fox in connection with the evolution of The Friends since its inception, and of Pauline Whitmore, whose keyboard skills have triumphed over the hand-written versions of this preface and what immediately follows, is also to be thanked most warmly.

Charles Phythian-Adams

LIST OF ABBREVIATIONS

A-S.Eng.	*Anglo-Saxon England*
A.H.	*Amateur Historian*
A.H.R.	*Agricultural History Review*
A.J.	*Ampleforth Journal*
Ag.H.	*Agricultural History*
Ant.Jnl.	*Antiquaries Journal*
Arch.	*Archives*
Arch.Camb.	*Archaeologia Cambrensis*
Arch.Cant.	*Archaeologia Cantiana*
Arch.Jnl.	*Archaeological Journal*
B.A.R.	*British Archaeological Reports*
B.H.S.	*University of Birmingham Historical Journal*
B.T.R.	*British Transport Review*
CAMPOP	Cambridge Group for the Study of Population and Social Structure
C.&C.	*Cake and Cockhorse*
Carm.Ant.	*Carmarthenshire Antiquity*
Carm.H.	*Carmarthen Historian*
C.C.T.	The Churches Conservation Trust
Cer.	*Ceredigion*
C.N.H.S.S.	*Croydon Natural History and Scientific Society*
C.N.H.S.S.Arch.	*Croydon Natural History and Scientific Society - Archaeology*
C.O.R.A.L.	The Conference of Regional and Local Historians
C.U.H.U.L.	Centre for Urban History, University of Leicester
D.C.N.Q.	*Devon and Cornwall Notes and Queries*
D.E.L.H.	Department of English Local History, University of Leicester
D.H.	*Devon Historian*
D.R.	*Downside Review*
E.H.R.	*English Historical Review*
Ec.H.R.	*Economic History Review*
E.S.R.C.	Economic and Social Research Council
Ess.R.	*Essex Review*
G.A.L.	*Gloucestershire and Avon Life*
Gen.Mag.	*Genealogists' Magazine*
Geog.Jnl.	*Geographical Journal*
Geog.Mag..	*Geographical Magazine*
GIMMS	Geographic Information Mapping and Management System
Glam.C.M.	*Glamorgan County Magazine*
Glam.H.	*Glamorgan Historian*
H.	*History*
H.M.S.O.	*Her Majesty's Stationery Office*
H.S.	*History Studies*
H.T.	*History Today*
H.W.	*History Workshop*
I.A.	*Industrial Archaeology*
I.A.R.	*Industrial Archaeology Review*
J.E.L.	*Journal of Education for Librarianship*

J.E.P.N.S.	*Journal of the English Place-Name Society*
J.Hist.Geog.	*Journal of Historical Geography*
J.L.	*Journal of Librarianship*
J.Mod.H.	*Journal of Modern History*
J.P.S.	*Journal of Peasant Studies*
J.Soc.Arch.	*Journal of the Society of Archivists*
J.T.H.	*Journal of Transport History*
L.	*Libri*
L.A.B.	*Lancashire Archaeological Bulletin*
L.H.	*The Local Historian*
L.P.S.	*Local Population Studies*
Leics.H.	*Leicestershire Historian*
Lincs.H.	*Lincolnshire Historian*
Lincs.H.A.	*Lincolnshire History and Archaeology*
Lit.Hist.	*Literature and History*
M.D.A.	Museum Documentation Association
M.S.R.G.	Medieval Settlement Research Group
M.H.	*Midland History*
Med.Aev.	*Medium Aevum*
Med.Arch.	*Medieval Archaeology*
N.A.	*Norfolk Archaeology*
N.A.L.S.H.N.	*Newark Archaeological and Local History Society Newsletter*
N.H.	*Northern History*
N.L.W.J.	*National Library of Wales Journal*
N.P.P.	*Northamptonshire Past and Present*
N.S.	*New Society*
n.s.	*New series*
N.S.J.F.S.	*North Staffordshire Journal of Field Studies*
O.D.&C.	*Out of Doors and Countrygoer*
O.G.S.	Ontario Genealogical Society
O.W.R.	*Old West Riding*
Ox.	*Oxoniensia*
P.&P.	*Past and Present*
P.-Med.Arch.	*Post-Medieval Archaeology*
P.Camb.A.S.	*Proceedings of the Cambridge Antiquarian Society*
P.D.A.S.	*Proceedings of the Devon Archaeological Society*
P.D.N.H.A.S.	*Proceedings of the Dorset Natural History and Archaeological Society*
P.S.I.A.	*Proceedings of the Suffolk Institute of Archaeology*
R.C.H.M.	Royal Commission on Historical Monuments
R.H.E.S.C.	*Rural History: Economy, Society, Culture*
R.M.	*Railway Modeller*
R.W.	*Record of Witney*
S.A.C.	*Surrey Archaeological Collections*
S.A.N.H.	*Somerset Archaeology and Natural History*
S.C.H.	*Studies in Church History*
S.C.M. Press	*Student Christian Movement Press*
S.H.A.	*Society for Historical Archaeology*
S.H.C.G.	*Social History Curators' Group Journal*
S.O.A.S.	School of Oriental and African Studies

S.P.M.A.	*Society for Post-Medieval Archaeology*
S.Y.H.	*South Yorkshire Historian*
T.B.G.A.S.	*Transactions of the Bristol and Gloucestershire Archaeological Society*
T.B.W.A.S.	*Transactions of the Birmingham and Warwickshire Archaeological Society*
T.D.A.	*Transactions of the Devon Association*
T.E.S.	*Times Educational Supplement*
T.H.	*Textile History*
T.H.A.S.	*Transactions of the Hunter Archaeological Society*
T.H.E.S.	*Times Higher Educational Supplement*
T.H.L.C.	*Transactions of the Historical Society of Lancashire and Cheshire*
T.L.A.S.	*Transactions of the Leicestershire Archaeological and Historical Society*
T.L.M.A.S.	*Transactions of the London and Middlesex Archaeological Society*
T.L.S.	*Times Literary Supplement*
T.R.H.S.	*Transactions of the Royal Historical Society*
T.S.A.S.	*Transactions of the Shropshire Archaeological Society*
T.T.S.	*Transactions of the Thoroton Society*
U.H.N.L.	*Urban History Newsletter*
U.H.Y.B.	*Urban History Yearbook*
V&A	Victoria and Albert Museum
V.S.	*Victorian Studies*
W.H.R.	*Welsh History Review*
Y.A.J.	*Yorkshire Archaeological Journal*

PART I

THE DEPARTMENT OF ENGLISH LOCAL HISTORY (1948-1998): CONTEXTS AND EVOLUTION [1]

I

When in 1948 the then University College of Leicester saw fit to invest W.G. Hoskins with what became known as the Department of English Local History, the College could not claim to be the first institution of higher education formally to recognise local history as an academic activity. Designated posts in the subject had long been earmarked by other centres of learning like Reading, Exeter, London, or Hull; whilst the VCH had been edited from the Institute of Historical Research since 1933. The novelty of the Leicester decision lay rather in the establishment of a specifically independent *department* and in a definition of its concerns so as to embrace all England. It is a little known fact, indeed, that, despite H.P.R. Finberg's creation as the first-ever Professor of English Local History in 1963, when W.G. Hoskins returned to Leicester as Professor in 1965, the title of his chair did not even include the words `local history'. As Head of the *Department* of English Local History, his was in fact the Hatton Chair of *English* History. While his distinguished successor, Alan Everitt, resumed the former title, a point had been emphasised. The stance of the department was not to be regionally based (though practically all members of the department have sought in different ways to further the study of both Leicestershire and Rutland). Its concerns were to be nationwide and, given the variety of its provincial perspectives, therefore comparative.

Leicester caught a wave. The thirties and forties, in which William Hoskins had developed his approach, whilst in fact lecturing mainly on economics at the University College, were a time when, not least during the war, nostalgia for England, its landscapes, and its historic buildings of all kinds had been increasingly expressed. Over those decades, such sentiments were perhaps best encapsulated in the long-running Batsford British Heritage Series to which, in 1949, Hoskins himself contributed his *Midland England*.

---

[1] See endnotes to Part I.

This was a volume that included anticipations of much of his later local historical output and, like others of his publications at that time, contained superb photographs of the English countryside taken by F.L. Attenborough, the Principal of the University College. Hoskins was not alone in his concerns nor in the fluency and passion with which he communicated them: this was a time when people so different as Geoffrey Grigson, John Betjeman, John Summerson and others were also achieving reputations in their various ways. Especially relevant to the specifically historical aspects of this process was the appearance in 1941 of a modern local-historical classic, *Tudor Cornwall: Portrait of a Society*, by A.L. Rowse, the text and proofs for which were checked by an Oxford protégé of his, a remarkable young scholar, Jack Simmons.

Both Hoskins - by birth and upbringing - and Simmons - through his mother's family - were Devonians; both were regular contributors to *Devon and Cornwall Notes and Queries*, Hoskins since 1929, Simmons from 1940 (and, incidentally, H.P.R. Finberg from 1942). Both Hoskins and Simmons were therefore obvious choices to join a glittering team of historians and others named above under the Cornish leadership of A.L. Rowse, to broadcast in 1947 or 1948 on 'The West in English History' (a book of which title followed in 1949). Above all both Hoskins and Simmons shared a zest for the visual exploration and analysis of England's past. It was a remarkable conjunction of circumstances in 1947, therefore, that found Jack Simmons appointed to the first Chair of History at a University College which was headed by Principal Attenborough, and distinguished by a scholar of such fast-growing reputation as William Hoskins. It was in addition an institution that, thanks to the generosity of a Leicester businessman, Thomas Hatton, had long before been gifted a valuable library collection of some 2,000 volumes of local histories, including many of the classics in original editions, from across the country. The creation of the department - as an entity separate from Simmons' own Department of History - was the direct outcome in the following year.

In 1948 it was possible for an historian of vision, like Jack Simmons, to entitle his Inaugural Lecture 'Local, National and Imperial History', having himself worked at all three levels. The growing appreciation of an academically acceptable interconnection between nation and locality in particular also strongly marked the concerns of other scholars of general reputation who exerted a direct influence on the work of the department or on appointments to it in the first decade or so of its existence: not only A.L. Rowse but also, and especially, F.M. Stenton (whose *Anglo-Saxon England* had appeared in 1943) who supported the appointment of H.P.R. Finberg; and R.H. Tawney, who also sponsored Finberg, advised Hoskins on the content and title of *The Midland Peasant* (1957), supervised Joan Thirsk's Ph.D. thesis, introduced her 1953 Occasional Paper on *Fenland Farming* and supported Alan Everitt. The long benign shadow cast on the early intellectual development of the department by the interests of these last two great men can now be readily appreciated in retrospect.

The first phase of the new department's existence (1948-1965), when research and publishing (with some light teaching and supervising duties) were its primary concerns, needs to be understood against a time when the intelligent lay reader was prone to evince a closer interest in the history of his country than is the case today, as the current popularity of such readable authors as Sir Arthur Bryant and Sir Winston Churchill then demonstrated. Moreover, with the coronation in 1953 of Elizabeth II (for which, incidentally, H.P.R. Finberg in another, typographical, guise designed the printing of the *Coronation Service*), deep historical resonances were sounded. A new Elizabethan age was then said to be dawning, a view that had been much buttressed by the republication in 1952 of John Neale's immensely popular *Elizabeth I*; by the appearance in 1950 (with two further impressions in 1951) of A.L. Rowse's superb *England of Elizabeth* (for which Simmons and Hoskins both furnished material on the provinces); and the year before that by the publication, with its wealth of local illustration, of *The Elizabethan House of Commons*, also by J.E. Neale, for whose *festschrift* in 1961 (as an `associate') Hoskins later contributed an essay on `The Elizabethan Merchants of Exeter'.

The enthusiasm for national history was echoed at local levels. A revived sense of English identification with the countryside was a distinct feature of the period of post-war austerity. For the Festival of Britain in 1951, indeed, a series of 13 `About Britain Guides' (ten of which were devoted to England) specifically sponsored by the Festival Office and under the general editorship of Geoffrey Grigson, included two slim Midland volumes by Hoskins. Three years later there appeared the immensely readable *Lost Villages of England* by Maurice Beresford of the University of Leeds, thus signalling the emergence of a new major figure onto the local historical scene. In August 1955 Hoskins's own evocative study of the continuous evolution of the countryside, *The Making of the English Landscape* was published,

3

accompanied around then by companion studies of Cornwall, Lancashire and Gloucestershire, the last by Hoskins's successor as Reader in charge of the department, H.P.R. Finberg. By 1963 *Lost Villages* was reaching its fourth impression, and *The Making* its fifth. Today it is easy to forget the degree to which academics were then communicating directly and in a popular way with the general public, and not only through writing, not only through the great growth in the number of Adult Education classes, but also through radio broadcasting and the subsequent wide circulation of the printed version in *The Listener*, or later through the writing of handbooks to National Parks or Shell Guides. Hoskins's path-breaking essay on `The Rebuilding of Rural England 1570-1640', which first appeared in *Past and Present* in 1953, was re-vamped for *History Today* in 1955.

In every respect the time was ripe for the academic development of English Local History. Coincidentally but appropriately, perhaps, in the context of the royal succession, it was Hoskins's (largely republished) *Essays in Leicestershire History* of 1950, with their heavy slant towards the *sixteenth* century, that heralded his arrival as a pioneer on the wider academic stage. A year later, when Joan Thirsk was appointed Senior Research Fellow in Agrarian History in the department to work at Hoskins's suggestion on Lincolnshire farming, she too began by concentrating on the Tudor period. Before that she had been engaged to write the section on agrarian history between 1540 and 1950 for the *Victoria History of the County of Leicester*, now newly resurrected from oblivion through the combined efforts of, amongst others, Jack Simmons and W.G. Hoskins (the latter becoming editor for volume II, 1954), but sharing that responsibility with Richard McKinley for vols III, IV) with some supportive funding from the University College. With Rodney Hilton from Birmingham University supplying the chapter on medieval agrarian history this became a landmark volume in the modern analytical development of the VCH.

But if in these ways, the new department was beginning to signal the application of new techniques to the understanding of the Midlands, simultaneously those associated with it were also making an equally innovative mark on the study of Devon. 1951 saw the publication of Finberg's *Tavistock Abbey*, significantly subtitled `A Study in the Social and Economic History of Devon', on the merits of which he succeeded Hoskins as Reader and Head of the Department when Hoskins moved to Oxford. A year later a volume of complementary and methodologically pioneering essays by each man appeared under the title *Devonshire Studies*. To cap it all, in 1954 Hoskins then published what has rightly become the classic county history of the twentieth century, *Devon*, this being the second volume in an ambitious, but sadly never fully realised, *New Survey of England* conceived by none other than Jack Simmons.

By then, of course, Hoskins had been replaced by Finberg in the department and Joan Thirsk had also joined it. At this time too a sequence of highly gifted postgraduate students began to pass through it like Margaret Spufford, Cyril R. Hart, Rosamund Faith, C.E. Hart, Esther Moir and Moelwyn Williams, whose subsequent influential publications grace this bibliography. Above all, it was a time for major initiatives that would have long-standing repercussions for the nature and direction of the department's future.

The first two of these innovations were not unconnected. In 1952 Finberg, very appropriately, took the opportunity to publicise his introductory lecture on the nature of local history as he saw it - *The Local Historian and his Theme* - by using it to launch a series of Department of English Local History Occasional Papers. These were to be published by the then newly-formed Leicester University Press until its eventual sale. Four series in all, and a total of 36 papers with one volume of three Collected Papers and a substantial introduction, were the outcome down to 1991. The Papers represented not only a vehicle for the department's own thinking (since its inception each Head, for example, has contributed two or three, and a number of staff members and students one), but also an outlet for academics unconnected with the department whose interests chimed in with its own. Such distinguished scholars have included Claire Cross; G.H. Martin; C.F. Slade; Thomas Gordon Barnes; K.J. Allison together with M.W. Beresford and J.G. Hurst; J.S. Morrill; and Christopher Dyer.

The second Occasional Paper in the first series was also by Finberg and this time on the field that he was beginning to make his own, *The Early Charters of Devon and Cornwall* (1953). This was clearly the spring-board for his later full-length *Studies in Early English History* series which opened with Eric John's *Land Tenure in Early England* (1960). The following volume by Finberg on *The Early Charters of the Midlands*, ushered in a sequence of regional volumes, a number by his pupil, Cyril R. Hart (who had also contributed several Occasional Papers on the same documentary theme), which sought initially to gazetteer and, where relevant, highlight the evidence of charter boundaries, for example, in the corpus of surviving Anglo-Saxon charters. The series was completed, appropriately, by one of Britain's leading place-name scholars, Dr Margaret Gelling, whose edition of *The Early Charters of the Thames Valley* appeared in 1979. The series as a whole has since been resurrected under the wider label, *Studies in the Early History of Britain*, under the general editorship of Professor Nicholas Brooks of the University of Birmingham.

A third Finbergian initiative followed from the formation of *The British Agricultural History Society* in 1953 and the accompanying launch of *The Agricultural History Review* which was edited from the start by him through to 1964 when he was succeeded for eight years by Joan Thirsk. This further scheme comprised nothing less than the projected compilation of *The Agrarian History of England and Wales* through from pre-history to the eve of the Second World War (eventually, in ten volumes). In 1956 an Advisory Committee was established under the chairmanship of R.H. Tawney, including such figures as Stuart Piggott, M.M. Postan, H.C. Darby, and J.D. Chambers, as well as Beresford, Finberg, Hilton, Hoskins, Thirsk and many others. As a result Finberg became the general editor and Joan Thirsk - who had completed her book on *English Peasant Farming* - was given the responsibility of editing the first volume to appear, volume IV, to cover the period 1500-1640. On his death she also succeeded Finberg as general editor. To help the contributors to this daunting project Margaret Midgley was attached until 1965 to the department as Research Assistant in Agrarian History (with funding from the Nuffield Foundation) to collect materials from record offices throughout the land. In 1957 Alan Everitt too was appointed as Research Assistant, having won the John Nichols prize the previous year (with his essay on *The County Committee of Kent in the Civil War* being published as an Occasional Paper). Three years later he was made Research Fellow in Urban History in order to research his chapter in the *Agrarian History* on `The Marketing of Agricultural Produce'. The appearance in 1967 of volume IV as a 920 page tome was thus very much a departmental achievement, two-fifths of it being written, and all of it edited, in-house. It is not too much to say that this particular volume (and especially the chapters within it by Thirsk on `Farming Regions' and Everitt on `Farm Labourers' and marketing) comprised the single most seminal contribution to English local history this century (yet the *History* as a whole would take another 33 years to complete largely under the general editorship of Joan Thirsk). For the department, however, the finalization of volume IV signalled the close of a twenty-year Golden Age of unhampered and astonishingly productive research.

II

In 1965 H.P.R. Finberg retired, and the tireless Jack Simmons took on the task of identifying possible successors to the Chair to which the former had at last been elected a year earlier. And so it was that in 1965 Hoskins returned to a very different Leicester to the one he had left, and Joan Thirsk in turn departed to take up his vacated Readership at Oxford. Alan Everitt alone survived from the former dispensation.

Hoskins was given the chance to remodel the department as a research *and* teaching department to which end he would be able to increase the staffing to six in order to create the first M.A. course of its kind in the country (he subsequently envisaged raising the total to twelve so as to be able to teach a full undergraduate degree). There would be four research staff, the professor and three research fellows with limited teaching duties, and two lecturers. Between them they would cover the entire syllabus of the new course. The topographical element Hoskins split between himself and the new Senior Lecturer, Peter Eden, who came from writing most of the Royal Commission on Historic Monuments volume on *The County of Cambridge, II, North-East Cambridgeshire* (1972), where he had pioneered the inclusion of a topographical discussion for each settlement. Peter would do the general lecture course and some of the field trips. William Hoskins would take others and both teach a selected region (Devon originally) and lead the field course to which others would also contribute. Peter was also expected to share the teaching of Vernacular Architecture with the new Senior Research Fellow in that subject, Michael Laithwaite who had been working on buildings for the Oxfordshire VCH. Alan Everitt was now promoted to Lecturer and he and William shared between them much of the two courses on 'Urban and Rural Communities' (essentially current areas of staff research interest post 1500) and 'The Methods and Materials' of English Local History (similarly post 1500). Alan also taught an examinable course on Early Modern palaeography, and Richard McKinley, fresh from editing volume V of the Leicestershire VCH (1964) and now the first Marc Fitch Research Fellow, taught the compulsory course on medieval palaeography. In 1966, the first year of the M.A. course (which was tried out on but one student!), an Oxford

7

postgraduate student of Hoskins, the present writer, was also appointed Junior Research Fellow in Urban History for three years partly to contribute to the document-led elements of the course.

At the same time three major new departmental research projects were initiated. The first, which was never completed because of Hoskins's retirement, makes fleeting and unprovenanced appearances in his *Fieldwork in Local History* and, more extensively, in one of his later television programmes. The aim was a group, multi-disciplinary project which would have exploited the skills of the geographer, the topographer, the buildings expert and the local historian in investigating a stretch of the northern and north-eastern littoral of Norfolk. It involved not only William Hoskins and Peter Eden (whose home was at Salthouse) but also Adrian Robinson from Leicester's Department of Geography (who, under another hat, was a frequent collaborator with his colleague Roy Millward, the author of the Lancashire volume in Hoskins's county series of the *Making of the English Landscape*).

The second initative resulted from the lucky chance that the University of Southampton had turned down the opportunity of mutually funding a new research fellowship with the Marc Fitch Fund. Marc Fitch, antiquary and genealogist, had set up a Fund with family money to help the study and publication of subjects in the Humanities. Its board of highly influential advisers included, *inter alia*, Francis Steer (erstwhile archivist of the Essex and Sussex Record Offices and of New College, Oxford) and Sir Anthony Wagner (author of many works on heraldry and, in 1960, of *English Genealogy*, and subsequently Garter King of Arms). Their interests overlapped with those of Hoskins who had written a prescient article in 1947 on `Leicestershire yeoman families and their pedigrees'. It was out of these shared concerns, therefore, that the Surnames Survey was established at Leicester in 1965 - with funding split between the university and the Fund. As is well known, under Richard McKinley coverage included Norfolk and Suffolk, the West Riding of Yorkshire (by George Redmonds), Oxfordshire, Lancashire and Sussex; and since 1988, under David Postles, it has already comprehended Devon and Leicestershire and Rutland.

The third project was passed on to Peter Eden from Francis Steer. This huge task involved the compilation of a *Dictionary of Land Surveyors and Local Cartographers of Great Britain and Ireland 1550-1850* and it took Peter Eden until 1976 to finalize it with help from

Avril Thomas (and others). So important were the foundations laid, albeit incomplete, that more recently Dr Sarah Bendall of Merton College, Oxford, has revised and immensely enlarged the original *Dictionary* for publication in 1997 by the British Library as a tool not only for investigations into topography but also for the historical understanding of the rise of a whole new profession.

In the meantime the department was moving - physically. In 1965 it had temporarily shared some of the space in the Geography department in the Bennett Building; in 1966 it was removed to Princess Road, and in 1967 to 7 Salisbury Road. Moreover, the new Attenborough Tower was already being envisaged, to the eighteenth floor of which - as far from the Leicestershire mud as it would be possible to get - the department would eventually be shifted in 1970. It was too much for Hoskins. A battle for even the most elementary equipment or furnishing had to be fought on each occasion and at the precise stage in which, thanks to one-off capital funding, the department was both beginning to build up its own considerable collection of maps whether new, old, or photostats, and to advise on increasing the university's main library holding in the subject (to an extent unparalleled outside Oxford, Cambridge and London) in addition to launching its new course. As is well known, his *Who's Who* entry recorded that he `retired in despair'.

Once again the department was reorganized. In 1968 Alan Everitt took the Hatton Chair of English Local History, I was appointed lecturer, and David Hey became the Junior Research Fellow in Agrarian History. Peter Eden, Michael Laithwaite and Richard McKinley remained in their former posts. The selected region now taught by Peter was changed to East Anglia (and subsequently to Kent under Alan Everitt); `Methods and Materials' together with `Urban and Rural Communities' were now largely divided between Alan Everitt and myself (with help from David Hey), a condition of my appointment being that the department's teaching in both these respects should be immediately pushed back from 1500 as far as the Anglo-Saxon period. For the first time, therefore, the department's course could be said to be chronologically comprehensive (at least down to the era of the Victorian city). It was still a very intensively taught course, but in those days so little research had been done, that teaching had to be based largely on case-study work by the lecturers. Then as now there was no general textbook on the continuous development of local society and reading lists comprehending up-to-date approaches were inevitably skimpy.

With the move to the Attenborough Building, however, a large modern new map room (with an inner sanctuary for the collections of antiquarian maps and topographical prints dating back to Finberg's day) and a very small reference library meant that many of the basic tools of the trade were now instantly to hand. The map collection itself had been largely built up by Peter Eden but, following her completion of the M.A. course in 1975, when she embarked on her long career in the department as honorary research assistant, cartographer, proof-reader, bibliographer, scholar and sage counsellor, it was the indefatigable Margery Tranter who reduced the map collection to order, catalogued it, and, with Muriel Phillips (who acted as departmental secretary from 1966 to 1987), regularly stock-checked it. Margery was the first, and for some 15 years the only, unpaid volunteer out of several more recently who have helped (`saved' might be a more accurate word) a department which, despite both its resources and its role, has never had the advantage of either a full-time technician or a draughtsman.

As early as 1974 the Hoskins staffing edifice began to crumble when the first of many financial squeezes started to bite. David Hey moved to a permanent post at Sheffield University and was replaced for three years as Research Fellow in Agrarian History by Cicely Howell before that post was lost. Michael Laithwaite's senior fellowship in Vernacular Architecture came to an end, also in 1974, just as some of his major long-term research projects were reaching fruition, and, although Peter Eden perpetuated the teaching of this subject, he too retired in 1976 so the much-prized Vernacular Architecture course (one of the department's major attractions) was lost permanently. Peter was replaced as lecturer in topography by Harold Fox - an erstwhile pupil of H.C. Darby and one who had already corrected one of Cyril Hart's charter boundary interpretations and helped Finberg in mapping saltways - but only on a three year, conditionally renewable, basis. By then Alan Everitt had had to take over the Selected Region which was now taught more systematically than ever before - over two terms plus the week's fieldcourse -to make up for the gap left by the loss of Vernacular Architecture. Alan naturally taught Kent and the prodigious amount of original research and fieldwork he put into this was of course also to provide him with a mass of material for future publication. When I started to alternate Cumberland with Kent from 1978 I discovered how right he was when he said that preparing the selected region in the department - with full chronological coverage along Leicester lines - was one of the most valuable, albeit demanding, learning experiences a Leicester local historian could expect to get. (Harold, who subsequently introduced Devon, would confirm this.) In the meantime we had had to cease servicing an undergraduate Special Subject taught over *five* terms for, and with a few staff of, the History department. As one member of English Local History after another left, the writer had found himself for a time teaching an additional 120 hours a year for another department. And worse was to follow. Plagued by repeated bouts of ill health and an excruciating back problem, Alan Everitt took early retirement in 1982 just as Harold Fox's second three-year cycle as lecturer was coming up for renewal. With great self-sacrifice, Alan negotiated a deal whereby Harold's post would be made permanent in place of his. Without that, the loss of the established Chair (let alone the withdrawal of its holder's brilliant and original mind from our academic debates) would have spelled the end of the department. Even so, numbers now comprised but a Senior Lecturer, a Lecturer, the Marc Fitch Fellow (whose teaching and administrative contributions were very strictly rationed) and, for three years, an associate teacher (Alan) who continued to help with parts of `Methods and Materials' and `Urban and Rural Communities' but who had had to surrender up the supervision of all his research students to the rest of us. For most day-to-day purposes the core staffing had sunk effectively to two: Harold and myself. It was an impossible situation, alleviated only in part by the presence of Sue Wright as ESRC Post-Doctoral Research Fellow (1984-1988). When, finally, Richard McKinley was on the eve of retirement, the Marc Fitch Fund with extraordinary generosity agreed for training purposes to overlap him with his successor, Margaret Camsell (1984-1988). As it happened the part of her post that was funded by the university was now required to be split between us and the Department of History!

Eventually the tide began to turn. With David Postles' appointment to head the Surname Survey, the Marc Fitch Fund helpfully increased their proportion of the funding of his post very considerably, thus largely emancipating the fellowship from further division with outside bodies. After two fruitless efforts, moreover, application for a `New Blood' post extra to the university's own established UGC funding bore fruit. All attempts to reinstate Vernacular Architecture having failed, a bid for a post in Regional Popular Culture now succeeded against very considerable national competition. The result was one of Tony Wrigley's outstanding Cambridge pupils, Keith Snell, whose prize-winning *Annals of the Labouring Poor* had just appeared. In 1987-8, moreover, Dr Marc Fitch, founder of the Marc Fitch Fund, being still concerned about the department's continuing need for support and wishing to find a place for the safeguarding of the Fund's extensive library (which also included Francis Steer's personal library) on the sale of its headquarters, agreed to an ingenious plan with the then Vice-Chancellor, Maurice Shock. The university would provide two contiguous semi-detached Victorian villas in Salisbury Road to which the department could be moved and the library relocated, whilst the Fund would pay both for the structural alterations necessary to knock the houses into one and for the total refurbishment and furnishing of this new property. For its adornment, Marc Fitch personally provided several family treasures. In 1989, accordingly, Marc Fitch House was formally opened by Major General His Grace the Duke of Norfolk, Chairman of the Fund. Now resident at numbers 3 and 5 Salisbury Road it meant in fact that the department had returned to the house next door to no.7, the one it had vacated when it moved to the Attenborough Tower some 20 years earlier.

New initiatives became possible. First, the M.A. course could now be taught on both a one-year twice-a-week basis, plus field-trips and a fieldcourse, and also on a once-a-week part-time basis over two years on either Monday mornings or Thursday evenings plus the same extras. A very successful and wholly restructured course based on taking two out of four chronological options (including therefore the possibility of taking either medieval or early modern palaeography) which thus gave a chance of greater depth of study had, however, to be completely redesigned when modular-based teaching was adopted by Leicester. Even this course is due to be changed with forthcoming staff changes; at present, however, it involves two core courses - Regional Societies: pre-Modern and Modern (with Skills and Approaches); and two out of three optional modules: Landscape History, and pre-Modern or Modern Regional Cultures; *plus* regular field trips and the field-course. These last two features, indeed, together with the regular seminar programme, represent all that remains of the original M.A. structure. (This is not to mention other teaching provision made for students largely from Archaeology). In a second major initiative, Keith Snell with co-editors Tom Williamson and Liz Bellamy from UEA launched *Rural History*, the second successful international journal to be substantially edited from the department. Then, third, there were the major research grant applications which were lent weight by the nature of the department's new facilities: from ESRC for Harold Fox's work on the medieval estates of Winchester and Glastonbury (in which Chris Thornton assisted); from the British Academy for Keith Snell's bibliography of the regional novel (which added Linda McKenna as research assistant to our number); and from Leverhulme and ESRC for his project on the geography of religious allegiance (which led to the addition successively of Paul Ell, a former M.A. student, and Alasdair Crockett as Research Fellow, but now of Nuffield College, Oxford). Most recent of all has been the Special Leverhulme Fellowship (in conjunction with the Aurelius Charitable Trust) held by Graham Jones for his work on medieval cults of saints.

Even with a changing constellation of research assistants and honorary research assistants - including Lydia Pye who is voluntarily cataloguing the library; Ken Smith who helps in the library and draws many of our maps; Mike Thompson who, as successor to Rosie Keep, now edits the Friends' *Newsletter* (founded, like the `Friends' themselves, by Harold Fox) amidst other help, not least in the later production stages of this bibliography; and Celia Swainson who is steadily cataloguing a growing collection of local guide books dating back to the nineteenth century - even with all this largely voluntary help, the department still lacks technical back-up for its map room and nowadays, of course, computers, whilst the library has to be run by a member of staff, and very successfully too, by Harold Fox. And inevitably, the department is still continuing to augment its holdings by purchase or gift. The Marc Fitch Library, now comprising over 14,000 items, for example, has been generously kept `alive' by The Aurelius Charitable Trust (and it now also includes John Hurst's unique collection of offprints *etc.* concerning Medieval Villages across Europe); the map collection has grown to 10,350 maps both old and new. We also hold 2000 topographical prints; nearly 8,000 pamphlets, church and other local guides including the collections of Jack Simmons, Gordon Forster, Francis Steer and Eleanor Vollans; a collection of 1,728 plate photographs taken by Principal F.L. Attenborough; 3,500 colour and black and white slides donated by W.G. Hoskins, G.H. Martin and Maurice Beresford; and nearly 900 photographic prints. Above all the archive, now stored in 130 archive boxes, has hugely grown with the addition of papers emanating from Finberg, Hoskins, Everitt, McKinley, Cyril Hart, Francis Steer, and Susan Wright, together with papers surrounding the establishment of the *Journal of Historical Geography*, and those connected with W.E. Tate or Anthony Walsh (1913 1993) of Cumbria (kindly donated by Professor Chris Wrigley).

In all these circumstances, since we moved into Marc Fitch House, Pauline Whitmore, our faithful departmental secretary, has had to act effectively as house-supervisor, in addition to all her numerous other duties. Margery Tranter still assists in countless ways and not least with regard to organizing the re-photographing of the Attenborough photographs (now available for scrutiny on the Internet along with those taken by Hoskins) and the electronic cataloguing of the map room, and archive. Thanks to her we were able to apply successfully for substantial funding for a cataloguer first from the British Academy and, second from the British Library, with matching support from the Aurelius Charitable Trust on each occasion. With her personally-designed database and with the in-putting (and archiving) by Bruce McGarva who joined us in this capacity in 1994, most of the department's holdings, apart from the Library, have now been catalogued electronically, and should become available for consultation publicly through JANET before long.

It is clear that the department would not have come through without the support of its assistants both paid and unpaid. The former, however, are inevitably bound by their short-term contracts of usually no more than three years maximum. By 1997, increasing bureaucracy and administrative chores imposed from above, moreover, consumed, on my estimation, the time equivalent of 1.25 permanent staff member's workload per year out of current staff total of four, a total that has since dropped to three. When consulting the bibliography of writings by those who have passed through the department, over the last fifty years, it will be appropriate to remember that the total of staff `stayers', those who have remained for *more* than three years, amounts to only twelve.

III

The second phase in the department's existence has therefore to be set against what Alan Everitt has described as the accompanying `explosion' of local (and, indeed, general) historical activity in general. Local and agrarian history had not emerged in isolation. Increasingly evident was the `new' social history practised most influentially, so far as academic local historians were then concerned, by Asa Briggs, by Peter Laslett and Tony Wrigley of the Cambridge Group for the (quantitative) Study of Population and Social Structure (CAMPOP); by Keith Thomas of Oxford with his exhortation to historians to adopt anthropological approaches; by E.P. Thompson and the Warwick social history school; and by Raphael Samuel and the History Workshop with its emphasis on working-class oral history. Alternatively there was the cool, dispassionate approach of historical geographers, many of them the intellectual heirs of H.C. Darby.

Above all, this was a time of ever-increasing specialisation and subject fissiparation. Areas that a generalist local historian of Hoskins's calibre might have hoped to have encompassed were now becoming technical fields in their own rights. As with Agrarian History, Urban History (many aspects of which Hoskins himself had pioneered before his retirement), for example, was already emerging strongly as an independent area of study before 1970. By then, in the Department of History at Leicester itself, Geoffrey Martin had already earned himself a reputation as an historian of the medieval borough and Jack Simmons had evolved a visual approach to the understanding of Victorian Leicester. Well before 1960 when it was published, indeed, Jim Dyos's path-breaking *Victorian Suburb: A Study of the Growth of Camberwell*, had originally been intended to become one of this department's Occasional Papers. Out of his work, with its emphasis on the nineteenth-century urbanising process and its physical impact, and his organizing abilities, developed the far-flung Urban History group (but always focused on the then Department of Economic History) with its own annual conference, twice-yearly *Newsletter* and eventually *Yearbook*. An early-modern dimension was added both by the publication in 1972 of *Crisis and Order in English Towns*, edited by Peter Clark and Paul Slack, with contributors, like the present writer, who were either pupils of Hoskins (who wrote a generous foreword acknowledging the new sophistication of the subject) or those who had been influenced by his work; and in 1973 by *Perspectives in Urban History* edited by Alan Everitt which also signalled numerous fresh avenues many of them pioneered by him or others in this department. With the creation of the Centre for Urban History at Leicester and its subsequent development in the hands of Peter Clark into an international forum for the subject, friendly complementarity rather than rivalry between the Department and the Centre has been the logical outcome.

Other areas of interest directly relevant to local history have also been refined into specialist fields often with their own journals and frequently focused on local case-studies of their subjects. The heady days of university expansion witnessed the flowering of medieval and post-medieval archaeology, field-archaeology, landscape studies, industrial archaeology, transport history (another specifically Leicester speciality), vernacular architecture, folk-life studies, historical ecology, a more topographical approach to place-name analysis, historical demography, dialect studies, oral history and gender studies, not to mention increasing signs of chronological specialisation in more conventional areas of academic history, and the opening up of ever more thematic approaches (to topics like crime), together with a growing sophistication with regard to the possibilities and limitations of old and new classes of document.

Against these exciting and challenging developments must also be set the astonishing proliferation of what might be described as institutionalised local history. With the opening up of local record offices, with the greater provision of local history sections in local libraries, and with the dynamic expansion in the numbers of museums and heritage sites since the mid-sixties, a huge well of public interest had been tapped not least within the related area of family history. The points of contact between the layman and the academic have also multiplied. Communication has been sustained above all by the British Association for Local History (which since 1982 has perpetuated the work of the Standing Conference for Local History in which both Finberg and Thirsk were active) and by the continuing success of its journal, *The Local Historian*. Another widely-read periodical has been *Local Population Studies* (published since 1968 in association with the Nottingham University Department of Adult Education) which arose out of the policy of CAMPOP to engage amateurs across the country in the collection of data from parish registers. Not only have Adult Education classes in the subject proliferated across the country, but two centres in particular have fielded regular, well-attended and influential conferences; at Cambridge (Madingley Hall) and at Oxford (Rewley House, since known as Kellogg College), both also now providing qualifications in the subject. Since 1978, moreover, under the inspiration of Dr John Marshall, and through its *Journal of Local and Regional Studies*, teachers of regional and local history in higher and further education have been serviced by the Conference of Regional and Local Historians (CORAL). At regional levels, the most significant journals in the field have been: *Northern History*, published since 1965 by the History Department of the University of Leeds; *Midland History*, published from the University of Birmingham since 1971; and *Southern History* founded in 1979 with particularly significant in-put from the Universities of Kent and Sussex. Other universities have fostered their own *foci* or centres, like Nottingham under the inspiration of Alan Rodgers with its *Bulletin for Local History Tutors: East Midlands Region* or the Local History Centre at

Keele. More specific in their regional approach have been the newer centres: for North-Western Studies at Lancaster University; for East Anglian Studies at the University of East Anglia/Norwich); for South-Western Historical Studies at Exeter University; and now, even a North-East England History Institute sustained by the six north-eastern universities. All this is not to mention the Borthwick Institute at York; the Rural History Centre at Reading University; the Centre for English Cultural Tradition and Language at the University of Sheffield; and the Centre for Metropolitan History at the Institute of Historical Research.

Over some 35 years, therefore, local and regional history has become a major academic industry into which numerous amateurs are also drawn together with their own original insights. There can be barely a university in the country which does not now furnish some sort of course in the subject. That this has been the case can be ascribed at least in part to the influence of Hoskins and the early work of the Leicester department, including the standard set by its innovatory M.A. course as conceived by him. It is only by appreciating this accompanying radical shift in the academic environment, however, that the second phase in the intellectual evolution of the department itself may sensibly be understood.

The implication of these developments was that the days in which the department had interacted (then almost uniquely) *both* with the world of historical scholarship in general *and* with the informed public (a connection which Joan Thirsk has successfully sustained) were being displaced by an increasingly complex and formalised world of local history in which distinct levels of activity were emerging: a growing popular audience which liked to participate; an expanding adult education service equipped to meet much of that demand through both teaching and popular publication; an explosion of regionalised historical publications by fellow academics especially in other provincial universities; and the department itself with its now established national, and therefore inter-provincially comparative, remit. Regrettably, even for the eight years in which its staff numbers rose to and stayed at six, it rapidly became impracticable for its members to involve themselves any longer at the more popular end of this activity. To that extent a degree of polarisation within the overall field inexorably developed. Rather than acting, as it once had, as a kind of filter between the world of academic history and the general public, in company with many of those working in the newly emergent centres of regional activity in other universities, the department came to operate more as a filter between ever-more specialised fields of academic history and the whole range of people or institutions actually *teaching* or *communicating* local history to the general public (including museums).

As this situation gradually developed the department's own interests became both broader in terms of thematic coverage (as a direct result of more staff and a steady output of newly qualified local historians), and also increasingly concerned with relating localities to wider trends or contexts. In doing so the department sought only to fulfil its peculiar remit as a body devoted to the comparative understanding of the local histories of England and its subdivisions, rather than to the multiplication of specific local histories. It is important to stress that such work has never been intended to be prescriptive in what it indicates. Always it has been hoped that it might simply be both suggestive and helpful to those working in more restricted spatial ways who might wish to locate their studies thematically or contextually at sub-national levels.

IV

This is not the place to do more than touch on the various ways in which the department's thinking has broadly developed since its earlier days. The bibliography, which embraces some 3,000 items in all by those once, or still, attached to the department, speaks for itself. Some observations are called for, nevertheless.

Perhaps an initial point might be that since the Hoskins days of *Local History in England* (1959) and *Fieldwork in Local History* (1967), the Leicester tradition has not in fact set its face against novices or non-academics. For guidance to such an audience, on the subject itself, on sources and approaches and techniques, it is only necessary to recall here Iredale's *Local History Research and Writing*, Ravensdale's *History on Your Doorstep*, Peter Edward's *Farming: Sources for the Local Historian*, or Hey's influential full-length works on family and local history in general which culminated in his edited *Oxford Companion to Local and Family History* (to which the department contributed) and its offshoot, his own *Oxford Dictionary*. A related and highly significant development over the last two decades in particular has been the way in which the subject has also been communicated, often brilliantly, by the Museum world. It is no accident that local history in museums now earns a separate entry in this Jubilee bibliography - a connection that reaches back to the days before 1980 when part of the M.A. course was taken by students from Museum Studies.

But it has been on analysis that the department has built its reputation for being what John Whyman has recently described in the *Agricultural History Review* as `the great think tank' of the subject; and in that regard a number of interrelated general directions emerge in the writings of the last fifty years. Appropriately the first and most fundamental has been the continued local historical pursuit of what H.P.R. Finberg originally and famously described as the re-enactment of `the Origin, Growth, Decline, and Fall of a Local Community' or of what W.G. Hoskins also thought of in similar terms, as a local `society'. Certainly we forget at our peril the latter's enjoinder in his Inaugural that `in the last resort the local historian should be trying to restore the fundamental unity of human history which the ever-increasing mountain of available records has caused to be fragmented into a score of specialisms' (even if few of us now feel so bold as to pursue such histories through from origins to extinction). On that basis mention should be made here of studies - whether books or theses - of particular places as well as of districts (whether rural or urban-focused) that have sought both to re-fabricate the past and to tease out wider problems or developments which are more subtle than undifferentiated national trends. Of rural community studies, for example, there have been not only Hoskins's own classic investigation into the long history of Wigston Magna itself, but also early-modern studies - some of them highly influential - of Wrangle in the Lincolnshire fenland (West), of the Shropshire woodland community of Myddle (Hey), of the contrasted societies occupying the chalk lands, claylands and fenlands of Spufford's Cambridgeshire, as well as an exploration of medieval Kibworth Harcourt in common-field Leicestershire between 1280 and 1700 by Howell. Coastal communities too have been exceptionally well analysed by Pawley at Skidbrooke-with-Saltfleethaven, Lincolnshire, between 1300 and 1600, and by Storm at early-modern Robin Hood's Bay. Equally innovative was James Moir's outstanding, and sadly still unpublished, thesis, on a Herefordshire squatter community as part of a wider local social process in the late eighteenth and early nineteenth centuries. More recently there has been a remarkable group of technically accomplished studies of medieval Somerset communities under the direction of Harold Fox: Rimpton (Thornton), Polden Hill manors (Thompson), and Brent (Harrison); and, more briefly, on Ditcheat and Pilton by Fox himself.

19

At wider levels a number of Leicester scholars have made the multi-faceted study of an entire district or region very much their own as Hoskins did Devon and Leicestershire in particular. For medieval Devon, however, his - and Finberg's - views are now being fundamentally revised in the light of detailed study into an ever-increasing range of agrarian (and urban) matters by Fox, especially in his major contributions to the *Agrarian History, Volume III, 1348-1500*. Kent in the eighteenth and nineteenth centuries, the seventeenth, and for the Anglo-Saxon period, has been stamped with the imprint of Alan Everitt; Buckinghamshire by Michael Reed; and over many years (even before he became associated with the department) Shropshire by Barrie Trinder. The Forest of Dean will long be associated with the name of C.E. Hart, Glamorgan with Moelwyn Williams, and above all perhaps, Yorkshire, and more particularly Hallamshire, with David Hey. These last two scholars represent the outstanding examples of *regional* historians (with interests that are spatially directed and thematically and chronologically multi-dimensional) to have emerged from the evolving Leicester tradition.

Urban communities too have received full-length, all-round attention. Especially to be remarked in a department where the agrarian context of the pre-industrialized world is strongly emphasised, is that more has been done here than elsewhere in the study of different market towns. For the middle ages there have been, for example, Newton's pioneering study of Thaxted; Peberdy's recent long view of Henley-on-Thames and its relation to the London food-market in particular; and David Postles's short but suggestive analysis of Loughborough. Also for Leicestershire there have been two fine early-modern studies: of Melton Mowbray as part of a local market system (Fleming), and of Lutterworth in a more immediate agricultural context (Goodacre). Carter has illuminated seventeenth-century St Ives, Trinder Victorian Banbury, and Cox nineteenth- and twentieth-century Croydon. Far from last is Nix's study of the ports of Barnstaple and Bideford in the later eighteenth/early nineteenth centuries. At a higher urban level, medieval and early modern Stamford has received close attention from Teall, and two theses have in turn covered Maldon through from 1500 to the later eighteenth century (Petchey and J.R. Smith). Major centres as geographically diverse as Exeter (Hoskins), Coventry (Phythian-Adams), Carlisle (Stedman), Norwich (Pound), Ipswich (Reed), Sheffield (Hey), and Gloucester (Christmas), have received perhaps the most detailed and systematic coverage of all for periods reaching from the later middle ages through to the nineteenth century. The department's urban concerns have thus been more considerable than is sometimes supposed.

If `communities' and `regions' have been treated in some 35 considerable studies, the stances adopted in these have been increasingly informed by an unceasing curiosity about, and revision of, the basic syntax of the subject which is most easily dealt with here from three marginally different (but in terms of authors, frequently overlapping) angles: the sophistication of existing concerns; innovatory approaches; and the overall search for the most appropriate spatial dimensions to the subject. It is these aspects of our shared pursuit which continue to make the intellectual life of the department so stimulating. First, then, are the ways in which the presumptions that underlie the so-called `Leicester approach' are being moved on. Most fundamental here is the landscape, the object of increasing scrutiny by our archaeologically-focused associates like Clive Hart, Paul Courtney and Jonathan Kissock. Especially noteworthy, perhaps, have been those highly suggestive investigations that have integrated such fieldwork with detailed documentary work as in Ravensdale's fenland study, Schumer's Wychwood and Warner's Suffolk greens. The chronology of settlement, of course, has concerned the department ever since Hallam's work on the new lands of Elloe, but it has been Everitt's systematic disentangling of the early settlement patterns of Kent that have helped profoundly to improve our early knowledge, and Fox is now in the process of illuminating the later appearance of fishing villages. The problems of continuity from Roman Britain have concerned not only Finberg but also Phythian-Adams and, more widely, Everitt whose identification of `seminal places' in his book on early Kent is especially suggestive. The question of origins has even wider implications: the early origins of the common fields being questioned by Thirsk and closely analysed by Fox; the origins of the village being discussed in Fox, ed.; the origins of the manor by Faith and, for its development in different terrains, Everitt; the origins of minster territories by Hall; and the origins of towns whether regionally (Finberg) or as `primary' towns (Everitt) or kings *tuns* (Phythian-Adams and Bourne); all these questions reach to the roots of our subject. Then there are the *processes* that need elucidation: inheritance and the transmission of land (Thirsk, Faith, Spufford, Howell); the early beginnings of service in husbandry (Fox); the processes of seasonal settlement (Fox); fluctuations in urban fortunes (Phythian-Adams; Reed) including Alan Everitt's `lost markets'; marketing and trade patterns and outlets (Everitt, Bone, Peter Edwards); *intra-* and *inter*-regional communications and transport: on horseback (Thirsk); by packhorse (Hey), carrier's cart (Everitt), coastal shipping as well as by land (Trevor Hill), or railway (Jenkins); agricultural improvement and specialisation

21

since the later Middle Ages (Thirsk); proto-industrialization, ever since Joan Thirsk's path-breaking essay on `Industries in the countryside' (Hey; Snell); and both craft-specialisation from the late seventeenth-century onwards and the extent of craft survival into the later nineteenth (Everitt). And finally there are those provincially significant categories of people who were first `re-instated' by Alan Everitt in particular: the farm labourers, the innholders, the country carriers, the evangelicals and, above all perhaps (because of their role in what Peter Borsay elsewhere subsequently dubbed `the English Urban Renaissance'), the so-called `pseudo-gentry'. To these could be added Fox's medieval *garciones*, Hey's packmen, Spufford's chapmen and `village scribes', while attention has been drawn by Phythian-Adams to the conciliators, or `redders', in situations of late-medieval violent confrontation. Gender studies have been encouraged by Snell. These are but some of their own concerns which Leicester local historians have often brought anew to the attention of national historians.

In addition to extending as it were the existing vocabulary and grammar of the subject have been those methodological innovations that have added wholly new dimensions to our understanding of it, albeit in the sense of formerly unperceived fresh challenges now to be undertaken rather than as finally accepted resolutions. Foremost here was the use of buildings as evidence of society and social and cultural change. The breakthrough had been Hoskins's *Past and Present* article in 1953 on `the great rebuilding' and his `Excursus on Peasant Houses and Interiors, 1400-1800' in *The Midland Peasant,* but the exploitation of this kind of evidence in conjunction with careful documentary research subsequently has owed most to Michael Laithwaite's seminal essays on the buildings of the two towns of Burford and Totnes. More recent has been Colum Giles's exemplary analysis of the social significances of West Yorkshire houses.

Another innovation was the unprecedented light that ever since 1965 has been shone on the significance of personal names when these are studied regionally for what they can tell us about the family, cultural change, physical mobility and regional variations. Thanks most recently to David Postles's continuation of Richard McKinley's pioneering work, the results of analysis by the Surname Survey for earlier periods are now beginning to interest an international audience, while David Hey is currently systematically researching the population of twentieth-century Sheffield in this respect.

A third innovation was the introduction of sub-anthropological approaches to the elucidation of community social structures through the evidence of ritual, its calendrical patterns, and body language (Phythian-Adams, Hufford), which also has attracted some European attention. Fourth has been the widening of Leicester's concerns to encompass religious as well as `economic' man, and in doing so to suggest different patterns of religious loyalties both conformist and nonconformist on the ground. Pioneering work here owes most to Everitt, Hey and Spufford for the early modern period onwards and Postles for the medieval, whilst highly sophisticated new statistical tools and mapping methods mark the recent work of Snell, Ell and Crockett for the period 1676 to 1851. Another cultural aspect, fifthly, has been a growing appreciation that folkloric evidence may properly be used by local historians in their pursuit of *mentalité* down to quite recent times (Phythian-Adams; Snell) as it has been by James Moir and David Hey. For earlier periods, sixthly, the department has long been interested in the evidence of church dedications (Lloyd, Kay, Everitt), but more recently much more ambitious attempts have been made to exploit *all* known medieval dedications over the west and east Midlands. The resulting reconstruction of a systematic chronology bids fair to change our ideas on regional cultural loyalties in the Middle Ages (G. Jones) and in other cases - in Cumbria - even to suggest cultural `edges' (Phythian-Adams). Seventh is the attention that has been drawn by Margaret Spufford to both the reading matter and the clothing of the seventeenth-century rural poor. Eighth, are the new ways in which regional novel-writing may be used as a form of cultural index (Everitt, unpublished; Snell) not least in changing perceptions of regionalism itself. Closely related, lastly, are the attempts now being made to construct cognitive maps of definable areas using less sophisticated traditions of story-telling reaching back even to quite early times (Phythian-Adams).

Such a list by no means exhausts the range of innovatory work that has marked the last few decades: one thinks, for example, of Susan Wright's success in opening up the use of Easter Books as a hitherto untapped source for household structure, or of the new work on immigrant minorities whether Asian (Davis) or Caribbean (Garrison), or Gypsy (Snell unpublished). And that is not to mention Susan Wright's work on women in early-modern Salisbury or Joan Thirsk's resurrection of so many female local historians who, until now, have - as it were - been buried historiographically. One remembers too the unveiling of what look, at first sight, like predictable areas of study for more modern times, but which turn out on closer examination to contain much that is unexpected: Joyce Miles's work on fashions of house- and street-naming, and Peter Scott's analysis, with its resonances for understanding modern suburban identities, of the interesting reasons behind the naming of Middlesex railway stations. How could anyone be bored midst this ferment of ideas?

The final `direction' to be discussed here leads to the very heart of local historical concerns: the identification of the spatial arenas in which social, economic and cultural interactions should be most meaningfully understood. The debate on these matters is likely always to be inconclusive, but in the meantime, whatever their ultimate limitations, certain frames of reference have furnished at least intermediate findings of great value especially when these have been set in comparative contexts. Thus Hoskins placed his `community' studies in county contexts that were then taken to be representative of the Highland/Lowland zone dichotomy. While he never realised the ambition, moreover, he was also hoping in 1965 to set `communities' in the contexts of local ecosystems, though how these were to be defined was unfortunately never worked out before his retirement. Alternatively, Joan Thirsk and Alan Everitt sought initially to locate local `communities' in the contexts of specific agricultural regions (largely defined by geology and inventory evidence) that frequently straddled county boundaries, the shire nevertheless being allowed to comprise some sort of outer limit to the market area of the chief town when that was measured by carrier connections. Out of the agricultural region, and especially the perceived differences between forest and `felden', of course, Alan Everitt sophisticated the idea of the *pays*, taking it as an indicator of the presence of a form of local `society' (as opposed to community) with a predominant working culture and a variety of other social characteristics peculiar to it. This has probably represented the single most fertile idea yet to emerge from the department, to the extent indeed that its current members are sometimes perceived - somewhat misleadingly - as primarily concerned with the practice of a form of historical ecology. The concept of the *pays*, however, has undoubtedly helped our understanding of both the early chronology of settlement and the incidence of lordship in the landscape, the strength or weakness of the latter being regarded as significant factors in explaining highly variable later patterns of adherence to either the established church or to some form of religious dissent. The *pays* has been used both to characterise and to investigate differently located communities (Hey, Spufford) and it has also been studied in its

24

own right - especially the wolds (Everitt and Fox) and common heathlands (Everitt forthcoming).

More formal arrangements on the ground, however, still exert a pull. One of the earlier attempts to reconstruct a pre-Scandinavian territory, for example, was a reconsideration of Rutland's beginnings as a territorial entity by the present writer, while over many years the territories and shires of the Danelaw have received extended treatment by Cyril R. Hart. Alan Everitt has studied the early organization of Kent and in one of his early pioneering works galvanised seventeenth-century studies with his brilliant portrayal of the gentry of Kent as possessing a sense of county identity or `community'. He has also seen the county town as a form of focus. It is no accident too that David Hey, now the great cause of regional studies in others (in consequence of his Longmans series), regards the most instructive form of region as being composed usually of county groups.

At the other extreme, society has also been seen as arranging itself informally so that different patterns of relationship result *between* settlements locally. Fox, for example, has identified the significant social distance separating the central cottager village of late medieval Sidbury in Devon from the dispersed farmsteads of the principal tenants. In Goodacre's innovative study of Lutterworth after 1500, by contrast, the interaction between unenclosed rural settlements and enclosed (sometimes deserted) settlements in its general vicinity was also studied in relation to the town itself, so indicating remarkable shifting patterns of economic interdependence over an entire local area. Building considerably on earlier suggestions made by the writer, Mary Carter has shown how St Ives, Huntingdonshire between 1630 and 1740 can only be understood for most purposes as the core of a whole `urban society' that embraces numerous rural settlements nearby. Over much the same period, David Hey's Sheffield with its adjacent metal-working dependencies in the surrounding countryside comprises an even larger example of the same interlocking of a formally-defined urban focus within a rural penumbra that cannot be divorced in social terms from its core. In the countryside itself it may be that kinship interconnections between core families set up patterns of `dynastic' neighbourhood as in early modern Nottinghamshire (Mitson) - interconnecting many parishes - that may become increasingly restricted occupationally in later times as in nineteenth-century south-east Surrey (Lord).

Attention has also been directed to the possibility that it might sometimes be possible to identify social `edges' across which little intermarriage takes place and especially across the watershed rims of the greater drainage basins into which England is divided. The spatial coincidence within such physical contexts of groupings of counties sharing regionalised urban networks looking towards navigable river outlets has led this writer to propose the concept of the `cultural province', sometimes separated from its neighbour by a `frontier valley', as the widest sensible setting for more localised studies. In doing so he has also sought to suggest that local historians should perhaps be paying more attention to the influences on such `provinces' of their nearer cultural neighbours whether within the British archipelago or in Europe. The origins of later Cumbria have been examined in such a context and attention has also been drawn to the sense of provincial identity preserved in the continuing relationship of twelfth-century Lincolnshire to Scandinavia.

Leicester local historians have not been daunted by wider spatial contexts still. Indeed it has seemed quite natural to take their interests even to national levels in some cases. Both Finberg (*The Formation of England*) and Hoskins (*The Age of Plunder*) explored their prime areas of chronological interest as periods of English history. In addition to her crucial contributions to *The Agrarian History* and numerous essays on a range of agrarian matters, especially innovation of various kinds, Joan Thirsk has also now applied her accumulated wisdom to the subject of *Alternative Agriculture* in England since the mid-fourteenth century. In her Oxford Ford lectures by contrast, *Economic Policy and Projects*, she had introduced the idea of a much earlier period for the emergence of consumerism in this country than had previously been thought. Reference has already been made to the nationwide treatment of horse-trading by Peter Edwards, and to Margaret Spufford's reconstructions of the spread of cheap fiction and of `the great reclothing' throughout rural England. Michael Reed has written about *The Georgian Triumph* and *The Age of Exuberance* and has gone on to examine nothing less than *The Landscape of Britain*.

Such coverage also marks some of the present department's widening interests in the local histories of England as a whole. While comparative regional studies still thrive, especially in connection with the West Country (Fox), the present emphasis in the department illustrates

26

how its concerns have developed nationally since its creation. Today the Surnames Survey is expanding its attack on early naming patterns, from county units of investigation to whole onomastic regions, in order that the survey should be finalised across the whole country by the time of David Postles's retirement many years ahead. Graham Jones is well advanced in his ambitious project of producing a nationwide electronic atlas of medieval saints' cults which should furnish us with the most intimate spatial measure yet possible of local cultural attachments at that period. In addition comparative work being conducted by him in Catalonia is probably leading to an even more ambitious attempt to extend the project into Europe on a team basis. His work, moreover, should in some ways complement the now completed survey of religious allegiance in both England and Wales, between 1676 and 1851, which has been computer-mapped in a highly sophisticated way, by registration district, across the entire country by Keith Snell, Paul Ell and Alasdair Crockett. Even more extensive geographically is Keith Snell's exhaustive bibliography of the regional novel in Britain and Ireland, the appearance of which early in the new millennium has been heralded by a volume of essays on the subject. Finally, a concise history of provincial England in its British and European contexts, from 410 to 2000, by the present writer is also now under way, an exercise that may link in with current concerns for the nature of English identity.

V

It is perhaps reasonable to claim that 50 years of focused activity by a tiny band of scholars and a growing body of pupils has opened up unsuspected vistas into the variegated history of the English and the countrysides which they have shaped. Of course there are themes not yet explored (but a glance at the bibliography should indicate the full range of topics so far covered); of course there are dimensions of the provincial past that students of the nation state would rather have seen emphasised; and of course those associated with Leicester are far from being the only contributors to this ever-expanding field.

But whether or not the `Leicester approach' (which is now discussed and compared with the work of the *Annales* school as part of the set curricula in M.A. courses both in England and the Republic of Ireland) is the right one, English Local History may at last be seen to have gradually developed over the last half century into a fully-fledged academic subject in its own right *and* within its own terms of reference. As such it has also become the object of increasing interest abroad. It has been no coincidence that staff have been invited to contribute to conferences and to publish widely at international levels in the U.S.A., Russia, France, Italy, Denmark, Sweden and Japan. Recent visiting Fellows have come from Japan, Australia and Venezuela.

For the department it is a matter of pride that two of its staff (W.G. Hoskins and Joan Thirsk) have received the CBE for services to local history or to agricultural history and local history; that three have been elected Fellows of the British Academy (W.G. Hoskins, Joan Thirsk and Alan Everitt, not to mention one erstwhile student, Margaret Spufford); that four of its ex-students have become professors in their own rights: three in England (Michael Reed, David Hey, Margaret Spufford), and one (Bruce Elliott) in Canada; and that in both the last two Research Selectivity Exercises it was rated with Economic and Social History as 5a. Above all, despite ever-increasing bureaucratic pressures, the department itself has remained faithful to at least the ideal of a university as a centre for the acquisition and propagation of learning and for the ceaseless pursuit of truth unfettered by commercially motivated funding. We can only hope that such aspirations will not be dashed as the department enters the predictably turbulent financial waters of the new millennium.

Charles Phythian-Adams
November 1998

Postscript. In the 1999 New Year's Honours lists, Professor Emeritus Jack Simmons was awarded the OBE for services to railway history and local history.

Endnotes:

This essay concentrates exclusively on the history of the *department* and its developing approach to local history *per se*. For the work and thought of some of its outstanding *figures*, interested readers are referred as follows.

(a) Hoskins: Joan Thirsk, `William George Hoskins 1908-1992', *Proceedings of the British Academy*, 87, 1994, 339-354; Roy Millward, `William George Hoskins, landscape historian 1908-1992', *Landscape History*, 14, 1993, 65-70; Charles Phythian-Adams, `Hoskins's England: a local historian of genius and the realisation of his theme', *Transactions of the Leicestershire Archaeological and Historical Society*, LXVI, 1992, 143-159; also published in *The Local Historian*, 22, 1992, 170-183.

(b) Finberg: M.W. Beresford, `Herbert Finberg: An appreciation', in Joan Thirsk, ed., *The Agricultural History Review*, 18, 1970, Supplement, *Land, Church, and People: Essays Presented to Professor H.P.R. Finberg*, vii-xii.

(c) Thirsk: A.M. Everitt, `Joan Thirsk: a personal appreciation' in J. Chartres and D. Hey, ed. *English Rural Society, 1500-1800: Essays in Honour of Joan Thirsk*, 1990, 17-26.

PART II
INTRODUCTION TO
The Bibliography of Writings

This new bibliography of published writings or unpublished theses and dissertations, by past and present members of the Department of English Local History, has been compiled in the main according to the same principles as those enunciated in 1981 by Alan Everitt in the case of *English Local History at Leicester 1948-1978*. In order to illustrate work or interests developed at Leicester, with few exceptions, publications are included only from the date at which staff or students joined the department. The earlier writings of W.G. Hoskins, H.P.R. Finberg and Peter Eden, however, have been incorporated because of their formative influence on the beginnings of the `Leicester approach' to the subject. Equally the first edition of such a work as Keith Snell's *Annals of the Labouring Poor*, for which there have been subsequent editions during membership of the department, has also been included. The writings of distinguished visitors from other institutions (often abroad) and of temporarily resident Honorary Fellows have not, however, been claimed for the department, nor has the work of historians in other departments of History at the University of Leicester.

The continuing expansion of thematic concerns in English Local History over the last 20 years has necessitated some mild adjustment to the method of categorising and ordering this new bibliography, though readers who wish to, may still make <u>broad</u> comparisons between the state of the art in 1978 and 1998 respectively. The introductory section on `The Discipline', for example, has been slightly re-arranged and re-ordered; `Landscape and Building' (enlarged by the transfer to it of cartography) has been given second pride of place because of its fundamental significance for the Leicester approach; the poor and social problems have been introduced to the section on `Society and Economy';  and new sections on `Population' and `Culture' (which include some subsections included under `Society and the Economy' in the earlier volume), give some indication of the directions in which the emphasis of the field is shifting. As previously, however, it is most noticeable that the steady focus of the subject remains on the reconstruction of local and regional societies and economies and, where possible, their comparison.

PART II

I   THE DISCIPLINE: SCOPE, METHODOLOGIES and PUBLISHING

A   Scope

1   Content

EVERITT, A.M.
The grass-roots of history, *T.L.S.*, 28 July 1972, 889-891.

New Avenues in English Local History: an Inaugural Lecture, Leicester University Press, 1970, 33pp.

The study of local history, *A.H.*, VI, 1964, 38-44.

FINBERG, H.P.R.
Editor, *Approaches to History*, Routledge and Kegan Paul, 1962, 222pp.

Local history, *ibid.*, 111-125.

The Catholic historian and his theme, *D.R.*, LXXVII, 1959, 254-265.

The Local Historian and his Theme, University College of Leicester, D.E.L.H. Occasional Papers, 1, 1952,18pp.

Local History in the University: an Inaugural Lecture, Leicester University Press, 1964, 20pp.

FINBERG, H.P.R. (with Everitt, A.M.)
Growing interest in local history, *The Times*, 1 Feb. 1964.

FINBERG, H.P.R. (with Skipp,V.H.T.)
Local History: Objective and Pursuit, David and Charles, 1967,130pp.

HOSKINS, W.G.
English Local History, the Past and the Future: an Inaugural Lecture, Leicester University Press, 1966, 22pp.

LORD, E.
The boundaries of local history: a discussion paper, *Journal of Regional and Local Studies*, 1991, 75-81.

PHYTHIAN-ADAMS, C.V.
Re-thinking English Local History, University of Leicester, D.E.L.H. Occasional Papers, 4th ser., 1, Leicester University Press, 1987, 58pp. 2nd edn, 1991.

Local history and national history: the quest for the peoples of England, *R.H.E.S.C.*, 2, 1991, 1-23.

Storia locale e storia nazionale: il caso Inglese, *Proposte e Ricerche Economia e Societe Storia dell'Italia Centrale,* 29, 1992, 28-43.

English local history, in J.Agirreazkuenaga, ed. *Perspectives on English Local History,* Universidad del Pais Vasco, Bilbao, 1993, 23-36.

Introduction: an agenda for English local history, *Societies, Cultures and Kinship, 1580-1850: Cultural Provinces and English Local History,* Leicester University Press, 1993, 1-23.

Editorial, *ibid.,* xi-xv.

Local history and societal history, *L.P.S.,* 51, 1993, 30-45.

Some futures for our local pasts, *D.H.,* 47, 1993, 4-5.

Time, society and nation: conceptualizing English local history, in L. Repina *et al.* ed. *Social History: a Problem of Synthesis,* Moscow, 1994, 22-23.

The Irish Sea Province: a plea for academic co-operation, *Newsletter* of the Group for the Study of Irish Historic Settlement, 3, 1994, 2-3.

RAVENSDALE, J.R.
History on your Doorstep, B.B.C. publications, 1982, 152pp.

REED, M.A.
International local history: paradox or prospect?, *L.,* XXVI, 1976, 231-242.

Local history at Loughborough, *J.E.L.,* XVI, 1975, 95-104.

Local history today: current themes and problems for the local history library, *J.L.,* VII, 1975, 161-181.

SNELL, K.D.M.
English local history at the University of Leicester, *The Harborough Historian,* December, 1994.

SPUFFORD, H.M.
The total history of village communities, *L.H.,* X, 1973, 398-400.

Chippenham to the World: Microcosm to Macrocosm, Inaugural Lecture, Roehampton Institute London, 1995, 12pp.

STEDMAN, J.O.
Publishing local history, *Newsletter,* Friends of D.E.L.H., 1, 1989.

TRANTER, E.M.
Local history or nostalgia? Nurturing local history groups, *Newsletter,* Friends of D.E.L.H., 7, 1994, 23-4.

THIRSK, J.
The present state of local history studies in England, *Chihoshi Kenkyu* [*Local History Studies*], 149, October 1977, 2-8.

WILLIAMS, M.I.
Local history in Wales, *L.H.,* IX, 1970, 16-22.

2 Historiography

DOREE, S.G.
Nathaniel Salmon [1674-1742]: Hertfordshire's neglected historian, in D.Jones-Baker, ed. *Hertfordshire in History* (Papers presented to Lionel Munby), 1991, 205-222.

EVERITT, A.M.
Introduction, E. Hasted, *The History and Topographical Survey of the County of Kent,* E.P. Publishing, 3rd edn, 1972, I, v-xlix.

Edward Hasted, in Jack Simmons ed. *English County Historians*, 1st ser., 1978, 189-221.

W.G.Hoskins and the real England, *Newsletter,* Friends of D.E.L.H., 5, 1992, 9-10.

Norman: editor and friend, in Jeremy Green, ed. *Norman Scarfe: for his 70th birthday*, 1993, 37-39.

Joan Thirsk: a personal appreciation, in J. Chartres and D.Hey, ed. *English Rural Society, 1500-1800: Essays in Honour of Joan Thirsk*, Cambridge University Press, 1990, 17-26.

FOX, H.S.A. (with Stoddart, D.R.)
The original 'Geographical Magazines', 1790 and 1874, *Geog.Mag.*, XLVII, 1975, 482-487.

GRAHAM, M.
The development of local history in Oxfordshire, *Oxfordshire Local History*, 2, 8, Spring 1988.

HART, Cyril R.
Proper studies: an amateur of English local history reminisces on the early days of the Department, *Newsletter,* Friends of D.E.L.H., 4, 1991, 21-22.

Editing the Anglo-Saxon Chronicle: a review article, *Med. Aev.*, 86, 1997.

HEY, D.G.
Louis Ambler: a West Riding architectural historian, *O.W.R.*, 4, 2, 1983, 26-60.

William Hoskins: an address at the memorial service in St Nicholas Church Leicester, *Newsletter*, Friends of D.E.L.H., 5, 1992, 10-12.

Entries on Celia Fiennes; Richard Gough, *Dictionary of National Biography, Supplementary Volume,* Oxford University Press, 1993.

Local and regional history, modern approaches, in D.G.Hey, ed. *The Oxford Companion to Local and Family History,* 1996, 280-284.

HOSKINS, W.G.
Introduction, Richard Gough [1634-1723], *Human Nature Displayed in a History of Myddle, also known as Antiquities and Memoirs of the Parish of Myddle, County of Salop,* Fontwell Centaur Press, 1968, 211pp.

MOIR, E.A.L.
The early English antiquaries, *H.T.*,VIII,1958, 781-786.

The historians of Gloucestershire: retrospect and prospect, in H.P.R. Finberg, ed. *Gloucestershire Studies,* Leicester University Press, 1957, 267-294.

The Discovery of Britain: the English Tourists, 1540-1840, Routledge and Kegan Paul, 1964, 183pp.

PAWLEY, S.J.
The author of Creasey's 'History of Sleaford', *Lincolnshire Past and Present,* 15, 1994, 20-21.

PETCHEY, W.J.
Ripon historians: William Collings Lukis, 1817-1892, *The Ripon Historian,* I, vi, 5-9.

PHYTHIAN-ADAMS, C.V.
Local history in England: some current approaches appraised, *Acadiensis: Journal of the History of the Atlantic Region,* 1976, 117-134.

Local history, English, in J.Cannon, R.H.C.Davis, W.Doyle, and J.P.Greene, ed. *The Blackwell Dictionary of Historians,* Blackwell, 1988, 250-252.

Hoskins's England: a local historian of genius and the realisation of his theme, *T.L.A.S.,* 67, 1992, 143-59.

Hoskins's England : a local historian of genius and the realization of his theme, *L.H.,* 22, 1992, 170-183.

Hoskins's England: a local historian of genius and the realisation of his theme, (transl. into Russian), in L.Repina, ed. *Dialogue with Time: Historians in the Changing World* (English version of Russian title), Moscow, 1996, 83-99.

Leicestershire and Rutland, in C.R.J.Currie and C.P.Lewis, ed. *English County Historians: a Guide. A Tribute to C.R.Elrington,* 1994, 228-45.

W.G.Hoskins and the local springs of English history, *The Historian,* 45, 1995, 9-12.

REED, M.A.
Introduzione: la situazione attuale della storia urbana inglese, being the editor's introduction to a special issue of *Storia Urbana,* 67-68, 1994.

SMITH, J.R.
Phillip Benton, 1815-1898, gentleman farmer and antiquarian, in the *Companion Volume* to reprint of Phillip Benton, *The History of Rochford Hundred,* Unicorn Press, 1991, 1-13.

The printing and reprinting of Benton's History, *ibid.,* 14-16.

SNELL, K.D.M.
Dr.George Fussell: following the plough without flapdoodle, *Guardian,* 31.1.90.

SNELL, L.S.
John Stow, *T.L.M.A.S.,* XXVIII, 1977, 305-309.

THIRSK, J.
Professor H.P.R. Finberg, *A.H.R.,* XXIII, 1975, 96.

Professor H.P.R. Finberg: a tribute, *L.H.,* XI, 1975, 306-307.

Women local and family historians, in D.G.Hey, ed. *The Oxford Companion to Local and Family History,* Oxford University Press, 1996, 498-504.

William George Hoskins, 1908-1992: a memoir, *Proceedings of the British Academy,* 87, 1994, 339-54.

William George Hoskins, 1908-1992, *Independent* reprinted in *Newsletter,* Friends of D.E.L.H., 5, 1992, 7-9.

Hasted as historian, *Arch. Cant.,* CXI, 1993, 1-15.

The tribute of an agricultural historian, in Hilary Diaper, ed. *A Favoured Land. Yorkshire in Text and Image. The work of Marie Hartley, Joan Ingilby, and Ella Pontefract,*1994, 64-70.

Scadbury and the Walsinghams, *Archives,* Orpington and District Archaeological Society, 17, 4, 1995, 59-69.

WILLIAMS, M.I.
Emeritus Professor A.H. Dodd, *Arch.Camb.,* CXXXIV, 1975, 137-138.

B Methodologies

1 Introductions and Approaches

BENNETT, C.I.
Local history and geographical information systems, in *Local History*, 62, July/August 1997, 19-23.

COURTNEY, P.
After Postan: English medieval archaeology and the growth of commerce before the Black Death, in G. de Boe and F. Verhaeghe ed. *Method and Theory in Historical Archaeology: Papers of the 'Medieval Europe Brugge 1997' Conference*, 10, Asse Zellik, 175-80.

The tyranny of concepts: some thoughts on periodisation and culture change, P.Stamper and D.Gaimster, ed. *The Age of Transition A.D.1400-1600*, Oxford, 1997, 9-23.

Ceramics and the history of consumption: pitfall and prospects, *Medieval Ceramics*, 21, 1998.

EVERITT, A.M.
Ways and Means in Local History, National Council of Social Service for the Standing Conference for Local History, 1971, 50pp.

FOX, H.S.A.
The study of field systems, *D.H.*, 4, 1972, 3-11.

HEY, D.G.
Family History & Local History in England, Longman, 1987, 160pp.

The Oxford Guide to Family History, Oxford University Press, 1993, 246pp. (Paperback 1998)

The Local History of Family Names, British Association for Local History, 1997, 20 pp.

Editor, *The Oxford Dictionary of Local and Family History*, Oxford University Press, 1997, 297pp.

HOSKINS, W.G.
Fieldwork in Local History, Faber, 1967, 192pp.

Fieldwork in local history, *A.H.,* III, 1956, 1-8.

Local History in England, Longman, 1959, 196pp; 2nd edn, Longman, 1972, 268pp.

The writing of local history, *H.T.,* II, 1952, 487-491.

IREDALE, D.A.
Discovering Local History, Shire Publications, 1973, 2nd edn 1998, 72 pp.

Discovering This Old House, Shire Publications, 1969, 2nd edn 1977, 64pp.

Enjoying Archives: What They Are, Where to Find Them, How to Use Them, David and Charles, 1973, 264pp. New edn Phillimore, 1985.

How can I trace the history of my house?, *A.H.*, VII, 1967, 182-189.

Local History Research and Writing: a Manual for Local History Writers, Elmfield Press, 1974, 225pp.

This old house, *Bucks Life*, 2, 9, 1967, 22-3.

KILBURN, T.
Marginalising local history, *Newsletter,* Friends of D.E.L.H., 3, 1990.

Methods and materials for local historians, *Local History,* 18, 1988.

LORD, E.
The anatomy of a small region: defining Longendale, *Journal of Regional and Local Studies*, 1993, 51-63.

POSTLES, D.
H-Albion (H-Net Humanities-On-Line, Michigan State University and National Endowment for the Humanities), 1996.

RAVENSDALE, J.R.
The Making of your Neighbourhood: a Course in Local History, Cambridge National Extension College, 1972, 45pp.

SNELL, K.D.M.
Oral history and the academic historian, *Common Voice*, 1, 1988.

TRANTER, E.M.
Early medieval settlement: problems, pitfalls and possibilities, *Derbyshire Miscellany*, XII, 6, Autumn 1991, 159-163.

Local history or nostalgia? Nurturing local history groups, *Newsletter,* Friends of D.E.L.H., 7, 1994, 23-4.

TRINDER, B.S.
Industrial archaeology: foundations for a discipline, *De kunst van bet bewaren Industrieel Erfgoed in Leiden*, Stichting Industrieel Erfgoed Leiden, 1992, 102-6.

The industrial heritage: training and education, *VIII Congreso Internacional para la Conserfacion del Patrimonio*, ed. Cehopu, Cehopu, 1994.

Archeologia industriale e formazione: un filo conduttore per vecchie e nuove professionalita, *Scuolaofficina*, 1994, 21-23.

2 Materials

ALEXANDER-MACQUIBAN, T.S.
Survey of the School Archives in the Doncaster Metropolitan Borough. Part 1: Doncaster County Borough Area, Doncaster Metropolitan Borough Council Library Service, 1978, 45pp.

BOURNE, J.M. (with Goode, A.)
The Rutland Hearth Tax 1665, Rutland Record Society, 1991, 49pp.

DOREE, S.G.
The Parish Register and Tithing Book of Thomas Hassall of Amwell, Hertfordshire Record Society, 5, 1989, 281pp.

The Early Churchwardens' Accounts of Bishops Stortford, 1431-1558, Hertfordshire Record Society, 10, 1994, 365pp.

EDWARDS, P.R.
Farming: Sources for Local Historians, Batsford, 1991, 226pp.

FINBERG, H.P.R.
The cartulary of Tavistock, *D.C.N.Q.,* XXII, 1942, 55-61.

Some early Tavistock charters, *E.H.R.,* LXII, 1947, 352-377.

The Tavistock scriptorium, *D.C.N.Q.,* XXVII, 1956, 27-28

Some early Gloucestershire estates, ed. H.P.R. Finberg, *Gloucestershire Studies,* Leicester University Press, 1957, 1-16.

The Early Charters of the West Midlands, Leicester University Press, 1961, 256pp.

The Early Charters of Devon and Cornwall, University College of Leicester D.E.L.H, Occasional Papers, 2, 1953, 31pp. Reprinted Leicester University Press, 1963, 32pp.

Supplement to *The Early Charters of Devon and Cornwall,* D.E.L.H., Occasional Papers,13, Leicester University Press, 1960, 23-44.

The Early Charters of Wessex, Leicester University Press, 1964, 282pp.

Some Crediton documents re-examined: with some observations on the criticism of Anglo-Saxon charters, *Ant.Jnl.,* XLVIII, 1968, 59-86. Reprinted in H.P.R. Finberg, *West-Country Historical Studies,* David and Charles, 1969.

GRAHAM, M.
Oxford city archives, *Oxfordshire Family History,* Summer 1982.

HAYDON, E.S.
Co-editor, *Widworthy Manorial Court Rolls 1453-1617*, Marwood, 1997, 72pp.

HEY, D.G.
The use of probate inventories for industrial archaeology, *I.A.*, X, 1973, 201-213.

Editor, W.G.Hoskins, *Local History in England*, 3rd edn, Longman, 1984.

Editor, *The Hearth Tax Returns for South Yorkshire, Ladyday 1672*, University of Sheffield, 1991, 123pp.

Editor, *The Oxford Dictionary of Local and Family History*, Oxford University Press, 1997, 297pp.

Editor, *The Militia Men of Burnley District, 1806: an analysis of the Staincross Militia Returns,* University of Sheffield, 1998, 135pp.

HART, Cyril R.
The Mersea charter of Edward the Confessor, *Essex Archaeology and History*, 12, 1980, 94-102.

The East Anglian Chronicle, *Journal of Medieval History*, 7, 1981, 249-82.

Byrhtferth's Northumbria Chronicle, *E.H.R.,* 97, 1982, 558-82.

The B text of the Anglo-Saxon Chronicle, *Journal of Medieval History*, 8, 1982, 241-99.

The Thorney Annals, *Peterborough's Past: Journal of the Peterborough Museum Society*, 1, 1982-3, 15-34. Revised and reprinted as *The Thorney Annals*, 1997, 80pp.

The early section of the Worcester Chronicle, *Journal of Medieval History*, 9, 1983, 251-315.

The charter of King Edgar for Brafield-on-the-Green, *N.P.P.,* 7, 1987-8, 301-4. Revised and reprinted in *The Danelaw*, 1992.

The Anglo-Saxon Chronicle at Ramsey, in J. Roberts *et al.*, ed. *Alfred the Wise*, Brewer, 1997, 65-88.

HART, Cyril R. (with Syme, A.)
The earliest Suffolk charter (Chelsworth), *P.S.I.A.*, 36, 1987, 165-71. Revised and reprinted in *The Danelaw*, 1992.

HOSKINS, W.G.
Courtenay Pole's account book, *D.C.N.Q.,* XXII, 1946, 239-240, 251-252.

Devon hearth tax returns, *D.C.N.Q.*, XXIV, 1950-51, 211-212.

Feodaries' surveys, *D.C.N.Q.*, XXIII, 1947-49, 54-55.

Historical sources for hedge dating, *Hedges and Local History,* Standing Conference for Local History, 1971, 14-19.

Editor, *Exeter Militia List, 1803*, Phillimore with Devon and Cornwall Record Society, 1972, 145pp.

IREDALE, D.A.
An opinion of Joseph Priestley and his latest book, 1775, *Lancashire Record Office Report for 1959,* 1960, 6-7.

Modern problems in olden days, *Lancashire Record Office Report for 1959,* 1960, 10-12.

Documents from Messrs. Pilgrim & Badgery, Colne solicitors, *Lancashire Record Office Report for 1960,* 1961, 20-3.

The sale of the manor of Winstanley in 1596, *Lancashire Record Office Report for 1961,* 1962, 15-18.

Organisation of biographical material for use in village histories, *A.H.*, 6, 5, 1964, 163-4.

Records of the Richmond Monthly Meeting of the Religious Society of Friends, *North Riding Record Office Report for 1966,* 1967, 25-38.

Ferreting out the Fox muniments, *Metropolitan Borough of Stockport, Department of Culture, Staff Bulletin,* 14, 1975, 2-3.

Organising archives, *Library Review*, XXVI, 1977, 110-113.

Some sources of railway and canal history in the North Riding Record Office: the Wyvill of Constable Burton family archive, *North Riding Record Office Report,* 1967, 28-34.

Discovering Old Handwriting, Shire Publications, 1995.

Introduction to C.T.Martin, *The Record Interpreter*, Phillimore, 1982.

KISSOCK, J.A.
Medieval feet of fines: a study of their uses with a catalogue of published sources, *L.H.*, 24, 1994, 66-82.

LORD, E.
Sources for the history of Cheshire in the John Rylands Library, *Cheshire History*, 1993, 20-23.

McDERMOTT, M.B.
Co-editor, *Churchwardens' Accounts*, Somerset Record Society, LXXXIV, 1996.

MIDGLEY, L.M.
Some Staffordshire poll tax returns, *Staffordshire Record Society*, 4th ser., VI, 1970, 1-25.

MITSON, A.
An introduction to sources for local history, *History Review,* 20, 1994, 54-57.

NEWTON, K.C.
Medieval Local Records, Help for Students of History, 83, Historical Association, 1971, 28pp.

A source for mediaeval population statistics, *J.Soc.Arch.*, III, 1969, 543-546.

PAGE, D.
Commercial directories and market towns, *L.H.*, XI, 1974, 85-88.

PARRY, D.
The Meadley Index to the Hull Advertiser, vol.1: 1826-1845, 323pp.; vol.2, 314pp., Humberside College of Further Education, 1987.

PHYTHIAN-ADAMS, C.V.
Records of the craft gilds, *L.H.*, IX, 1971, 267-274.

POSTLES, D.
The Garendon cartularies in BL. Lansdowne 415, *The British Library Journal,* 22, 1996, 161-71.

POTTS, R.A.J.
A calendar of Cornish glebe terriers and allied documents, 1679-1727, Leicester M.A. thesis, 1971.

Editor, *A Calendar of Cornish Glebe Terriers, 1673-1735,* Devon & Cornwall Record Society, n.s., XIX, 1974, 210pp.

POUND, J.F.
Subsidy returns: an exercise in interpretation, *Norfolk Research Committee Bulletin,* 19 March 1978, 12-14.

REED, M.A.
Archives, *British Librarianship and Information Science, 1971-1975,* 1976, 325-331.

Buckinghamshire Anglo-Saxon charter boundaries, in M.Gelling, ed. *The Early Charters of the Thames Valley,* Leicester University Press, 1979, 168-187.

Ipswich probate inventories, 1583-1631, *Suffolk Records Society,* 24, 1981, 122pp.

Archives, *British Library and Information Work, 1976-1980*, 1, 1982, 248-258.

Buckingham probate inventories, 1661-1714, *Buckinghamshire Records Society*, 24, 1987, xxiv and 330.

Buckinghamshire glebe terriers, 1578-1640, *Buckinghamshire Records Society*, 30, 1997, xxvi and 295.

SNELL, L.S.
Short guides to records: chantry certificates, *H*, XLVIII, 1963, 332-335.

Accessions to archives, 1969, *M.H.*, I, 1971, 48-54.

Accessions to archives, 1970, *M.H.*, I, 1971, 42-47.

Accessions to archives, 1971, Part I, *M.H.*, I, 1972, 47-54.

Accessions to archives, 1971, Part II, *M.H.*, II, 1973, 42-47.

Accessions to archives, 1972, *M.H.*, III, 1975, 42-58.

Editor, The Edwardian inventories of Middlesex, *T.L.M.A.S.*, XXV, 1974; XXVI, 1975; XXVII, 1976; XXIX, 1978.

SPUFFORD, H.M.
The scribes of villagers' wills in the sixteenth and seventeenth centuries and their influence, *L.P.S.*, VII, 1971, 28-43.

Will formularies: a note, *L.P.S.* XIX, 1977, 35-36.

The limitations of the probate inventory, in J.Chartres and D.Hey, ed. *English Rural History 1500-1800*, Cambridge University Press, 1990, 139-74.

THIRSK, J.
The content and sources of English agrarian history after 1500, *A.H.R.*, III, 1955, 66-79.

The content and sources of English agrarian history after 1500, with special reference to Lincolnshire, *Lincs. H.*, II, 1955, 31-44.

Sources of information on population, *A.H.*, IV, 1959, 129-132, 182-184.

List of books and articles on agrarian history issued since September 1961, *A.H.R.*, XI, 1963, 8-12.

Unexplored sources in local records, *Arch.*, VI, xxix, 1963, 8-12.

Sources of Information on Population, 1500-1760, and Unexplored Sources in Local Records, Phillimore, 1965, 24pp.

TRANTER, E.M.
Editor, *The Derbyshire Returns to the 1851 Religious Census,* Derbyshire Record Society, XXIII, 1995, 238pp.

TRINDER, B.S. (with Cox, J.)
Editor, *Yeomen and Colliers in Telford: Probate Inventories for Dawley, Lilleshall, Wellington and Wrockwardine 1660-1750,* Phillimore, 1980, 488pp.

WEST, F
The Protestation Returns of 1642, *E.M.L.H.B.,* VI, 1971, 50-54.

WARNER, P.
Doorstep Recovery: Working on a Local History Study, English Heritage Education Service Video, 1993.

WICKES, M.J.L.
The Marriage Registers of Clovelly, Welcombe and Landcross in Devon (pre 1938), H.Galloway Publishing, 1998.

WRIGHT, S.J.
Easter books and parish rate books: a new source for the urban historian, *U.H.Y.B.,* Leicester University Press, 1985, 30-45.

C Publishing

1 Bibliographies and Libraries

EVERITT, A.M.
Work in progress in agrarian history, *A.H.R.,* XIII, 1965, 116-125.

Work in progress in agrarian history, *A.H.R.,* XV, 1967, 113-126.

FOX, H.S.A.
Register of Research in Historical Geography, Historical Geography Research Group, Institute of British Geographers, 1976, 37pp.

HART, Cyril R.
H.P.R. Finberg: a bibliography, in J. Thirsk, ed. *Land, Church and People: Essays Presented to Professor H.P.R. Finberg, A.H.R.,* XVIII, Supplement, 1970, 1-6.

HEY, D.G.
Annual list and brief review of articles on agrarian history, *A.H.R.,* XXII, 1974, 75-81.

List of books and articles on agrarian history issued since June 1969, *A.H.R.,* XIX, 1971, 82-87.

List of books and articles on agrarian history issued since June 1970, *A.H.R.*, XX, 1972, 64-75.

List of books and articles on agrarian history issued since June 1971, *A.H.R.*, XXI, 1973, 57-65.

Work in progress, *A.H.R.*, XVIII, 1970, 161-172.

Work in progress, *A.H.R.*, XXII, 1974, 162-177.

Work in progress, *A.H.R.*, XXXVI, 1978, 115-126.

MORRIS, C.I.
Cheese-making Bibliography: Gloucestershire, general, Gloucester Folk Museum, 1981.

PAUL, E.D.
The bibliography of local history, in M.D.Dewe, ed. *Local Studies Collections. A Manual,* 2, 1991, 102-118.

SNELL, L.S.
Historical societies of the Midlands and their publications, Part I, *M.H.*, II, 1973, 110-117.

Historical societies of the Midlands and their publications, Part II, *M.H.*, II, 1974, 187-195.

Compiler, Sixteenth-century section, *Annual Bulletin of Historical Literature*, LIX, LX, LXI, LXII, LXIII, Historical Association, 1973-77.

THIRSK, J.
List of books and articles on agrarian history issued since September 1953, *A.H.R.*, III, 1955, 41-47.

List of books and articles on agrarian history issued since September 1954, *A.H.R.*, IV, 1956, 52-57.

List of books and articles on agrarian history issued since September 1955, *A.H.R.*, V, 1957, 52-57.

List of books and articles on agrarian history issued since September 1956, *A.H.R.*, VI, 1958, 42-51.

List of books and articles on agrarian history issued since September 1957, *A.H.R.*, VII, 1959, 38-47.

List of books and articles on agrarian history issued since September 1958, *A.H.R.*, VIII, 1960, 38-44.

List of books and articles on agrarian history issued since September 1959, *A.H.R.*, IX, 1961, 55-63.

List of books and articles on agrarian history issued since September 1960, *A.H.R.*, X, 1962, 46-55.

List of books and articles on agrarian history issued since September 1961, *A.H.R.*, XI, 1963, 8-12.

List of books and articles on agrarian history issued since September 1962, *A.H.R.*, XII, 1964, 47-56.

List of books and articles on agrarian history issued since September 1963, *A.H.R.*, XIII, 1965, 50-60.

Work in progress, *A.H.R.*, VI, 1958, 101-110.

Work in progress, *A.H.R.*, VII, 1959, 110-120.

Work in progress, *A.H.R.*, IX, 1961, 112-119.

THIRSK, J. (with Mingay, G.E.)
A list of publications on the economic history of Great Britain and Ireland, *Ec.H.R.*, 2nd ser., XII, 1960, 519-552.

THIRSK, J. (with Thompson, F.M.L.)
A list of publications on the economic history of Great Britain and Ireland published in 1960, *Ec.H.R.*, 2nd ser., XIV, 1962, 524-551.

A list of publications on the economic history of Great Britain and Ireland published in 1961, *Ec.H.R.*, 2nd ser., XV, 1963, 610-634.

A list of publications on the economic history of Great Britain and Ireland published in 1962, *Ec.H.R.*, 2nd ser., XVI, 1964, 539-559.

A list of publications on the economic history of Great Britain and Ireland published in 1963, *Ec.H.R.*, 2nd ser., XVII, 1965, 648-669.

TRANTER, E.M.
Joan Thirsk: a bibliography, in J.Chartres and D. Hey, ed. *English Rural History, 1500-1800; Essays in Honour of Joan Thirsk*, Cambridge University Press (Past and Present publications), 1990, 369-82.

Leicestershire studies in the Department of English Local History, University of Leicester, *Leics.H.*, II, 12, 1981-2, 30-4.

East Midland Studies in the Department of English Local History, University of Leicester, *E.M.L.H.B.*, XX, 1985, 25-8.

Richard McKinley: a bibliography, in D.Postles, ed. *Name, Place, Time*, Leopard's Head Press, forthcoming.

WILLIAMS, M.I.
Cardiganshire in periodical literature, *Cer.*, IV, 1962, 290-311.

2 General Editorships

CROMPTON, J.
Editor, *Five Arches - the Journal of the Radstock, Midsomer Norton and District Museum Society.*

EVERITT, A.M.
Editor, University of Leicester, Department of English Local History Occasional Papers, 2nd ser., 1968-74; 3rd ser., 1975.

FINBERG, H.P.R.
Editor, *Agricultural History Review*, 1953-64.

Editor, University of Leicester, Department of English Local History Occasional Papers, 1st Ser., 1952-65.

General Editor, *The Agrarian History of England and Wales*, 1956-74.

FOX, H.S.A.
Reviews Editor, *Journal of Historical Geography*, 1-28, 1975-81.

Co-editor (with C.V.Phythian-Adams), University of Leicester, Department of English Local History Occasional Papers, 4th ser., 1987-98.

Editor, *Newsletter*, Friends of D.E.L.H., 1989-95. (1993-5 with R.Keep)

GOODACRE, J.D.
Co-editor, *The Leicestershire Historian*, 1971-74; Editor, 1975-95.

HEY, D.G.
Editor, *The Oxford Companion to Local and Family History*, Oxford University Press, 1996, 517pp.

PHYTHIAN-ADAMS, C.V.
Reviews editor, *Urban History Yearbook*, 1973-75.

Co-editor (with H.S.A.Fox), University of Leicester, D.E.L.H. Occasional Papers, 4th ser., 1987-91.

General editor, *Communities, Contexts and Cultures: Leicester Studies in English Local History*, Leicester University Press, 1986-94.

General editor's foreword to A.Everitt, *Continuity and Colonization*, Communities, Contexts and Cultures: Leicester Studies in English Local History, Leicester University Press, 1986, xiii-xv.

General editor's foreword to D.Hey, *The Fiery Blades of Hallamshire,* Communities, Contexts and Cultures: Leicester Studies in English Local History, Leicester University Press, 1991, xiii-xvi.

General editor's foreword to J. Goodacre, *The Transformation of a Peasant Economy: Townspeople and Villagers in the Lutterworth area, 1500-1700,* Leicester University Press, 1994, v-xvi.

POSTLES, D.
Co-editor, *Nomina,* Journal of the Society for Name Studies in Britain and Ireland, 1991 onwards.

POTTS, R.A.J.
Editor, *The Leicestershire Historian,* 1967-68; Co-editor, 1971-74.

Editor, *Tyne and Tweed*, Bulletin of the Association of Northumberland Local History Societies, 1978 onwards.

SAUNDERS, A.L.
Editor, *Costume: the Journal of the Costume Society*, 1967 onwards.

Editor, *The London Topographical Society*, 1975 onwards.

Assistant editor, *Journal of the British Archaeological Association,* 1963-1975

SNELL, K.D.M. (with Bellamy, L. and Williamson, T.)
Editor, *Rural History: Economy, Society, Culture*, 1990 onwards.

SNELL, L.S.
Editor, *Bulletin of the Middlesex Local History Council,* 1961-64.

Editor, *The London and Middlesex Historian,* 1965-68.

Editor, *Newsletter, London and Middlesex Archaeological Society*, 1968 onwards.

Editor, *Transactions of the London and Middlesex Archaeological Society*, 1968 onwards.

SNELLING, J.
Co-editor, *The Harborough Historian*, from 1997.

STEDMAN, J.O.
Co-editor, *Portsmouth Paper Series,* City of Portsmouth.

Editor, N.J.Grundy, W.L.Wyllie, RA: the Portsmouth years, *Portsmouth Paper*, 68, 1996, 28pp.

THIRSK, J.
Editor, *Agricultural History Review,* 1964-72.

General editor, *The Agrarian History of England and Wales,* 1975 onwards.

THOMPSON, M.G.
Editor, *Newsletter*, Friends of D.E.L.H., 1997 onwards.

TRANTER, E.M.
Editor, *A History of Weston on Trent, Derbyshire.* Weston on Trent Local History Society, Weston on Trent, Derbyshire. 1988-
> *1. Weston on Trent - an illustrated guide,* 1988, 12pp.
>
> *2. Weston on Trent Old and New,* 1990, 40pp.
>
> *3. By Water, Road and Rail: a history of transport in Weston on Trent,* 1993, 37pp.
>
> *4. Houses and everyday life in Weston on Trent,* 1994, 40pp.
>
> *5. Change in a Derbyshire Village: Weston on Trent 1900-1950,* 1996, 59pp.

3 Occasional Papers

FINBERG, H.P.R.
The Local Historian and his Theme, University College of Leicester, D.E.L.H. Occasional Papers, 1, 1952, 18pp.

The Early Charters of Devon and Cornwall, University College of Leicester, D.E.L.H. Occasional Papers, 2, 1953, 31pp.

THIRSK, J.
Fenland Farming in the Sixteenth Century, University College of Leicester, D.E.L.H. Occasional Papers, 3, 1953, 45pp.

CROSS, M.C.
The Free Grammar School of Leicester, University College of Leicester, D.E.L.H. Occasional Papers, 4, 1953, 51pp.

HALLAM, H.E.
The New Lands of Elloe, University College of Leicester, D.E.L.H. Occasional Papers, 6, 1954, 42pp.

MARTIN, G.H.
The Early Court Rolls of the Borough of Ipswich, University College of Leicester, D.E.L.H. Occasional Papers, 5, 1954, 45pp.

FINBERG, H.P.R.
Roman and Saxon Withington: a Study in Continuity, University College of
Leicester, D.E.L.H. Occasional Papers, 8, 1955, 40pp.

SLADE, C.F.
The Leicestershire Survey, c.A.D.1130, University College of Leicester, D.E.L.H.
Occasional Papers, 7, 1956, 98pp.

EVERITT, A.M.
The County Committee of Kent in the Civil War, University College of Leicester,
D.E.L.H. Occasional Papers, 9, 1957, 54pp.

HART, Cyril R.
The Early Charters of Essex: the Saxon Period, D.E.L.H. Occasional Papers, 10,
Leicester University Press, 1957, 31pp; revised edn 1971, 55pp.

The Early Charters of Essex: the Norman Period, D.E.L.H. Occasional Papers, 11,
Leicester University Press, 1957, 48pp.

CRACKNELL, B.E.
Canvey Island: the History of a Marshland Community, D.E.L.H. Occasional Papers,
12, Leicester University Press, 1959, 47pp.

HOSKINS, W.G.
The Westward Expansion of Wessex, D.E.L.H. Occasional Papers, 13, Leicester
University Press 1960, 44pp.

BARNES, T.G.
The Clerk of the Peace in Caroline Somerset, D.E.L.H. Occasional Papers, 14,
Leicester University Press, 1961, 48pp.

SMITH, R.B.
Blackburnshire: a Study in Early Lancashire History, D.E.L.H. Occasional Papers,
15, Leicester University Press, 1961, 44pp.

BURGESS, L.A.
The Origins of Southampton, D.E.L.H. Occasional Papers, 16, Leicester University
Press, 1964. 31pp.

ALLISON, K.J. (with Beresford, M.W. and Hurst, J.G.).
The Deserted Villages of Oxfordshire, D.E.L.H. Occasional Papers, 17, Leicester
University Press 1965, 47pp.

The Deserted Villages of Northamptonshire, D.E.L.H. Occasional Papers, 18,
Leicester University Press, 1966, 48pp.

MOORE, J.S.
Laughton: a Study in the Evolution of the Wealden Landscape, D.E.L.H. Occasional
Papers, 19, Leicester University Press, 1965, 55pp.

SPUFFORD, H.M.
A Cambridgeshire Community: Chippenham from Settlement to Enclosure,
D.E.L.H. Occasional Papers, 20, Leicester University Press, 1965, 55pp.

EVERITT, A.M.
Change in the Provinces: the Seventeenth Century, D.E.L.H. Occasional Papers, 2nd
ser.,1, Leicester University Press, 1969, 56pp.

McKINLEY, R.A.
Norfolk Surnames in the Sixteenth Century, D.E.L.H. Occasional Papers, 2nd ser., 2,
Leicester University Press, 1969, 60pp.

HART, Cyril R.
The Hidation of Northamptonshire, D.E.L.H. Occasional Papers, 2nd ser., 3, Leicester
University Press, 1970, 78pp.

EVERITT, A.M.
The Pattern of Rural Dissent: the Nineteenth Century, D.E.L.H. Occasional Papers,
2nd ser., 4, Leicester University Press, 1972, 90pp.

HEY, D.G.
*The Rural Metalworkers of the Sheffield Region: a Study of Rural Industry
before the Industrial Revolution*, D.E.L.H. Occasional Papers, 2nd ser., 5, Leicester
University Press, 1972, 60pp.

HART, Cyril R.
The Hidation of Cambridgeshire, D.E.L.H. Occasional Papers, 2nd ser., 6, Leicester
University Press, 1974, 67pp.

MORRILL, J.S.
The Cheshire Grand Jury, 1625-1659, D.E.L.H. Occasional Papers, 3rd ser., 1,
Leicester University Press, 1976, 60pp.

NAUGHTON, K.S.
The Gentry of Bedfordshire in the Thirteenth and Fourteenth Centuries, D.E.L.H.
Occasional Papers, 3rd ser., 2, Leicester University Press, 1976, 92pp.

MOYLAN, P.A.
The Form and Reform of County Government: Kent 1889-1914, D.E.L.H Occasional
Papers, 3rd ser., 3, Leicester University Press, 1978, 97pp.

PHYTHIAN-ADAMS, C.V.
Continuity, Fields and Fission: the Making of a Midland Parish, D.E.L.H. Occasional
Papers, 3rd ser., 4, Leicester University Press, 1978, 53pp.

DAVEY, B.J.
Ashwell 1830-1914: the Decline of a Village Community, D.E.L.H.Occasional Papers,
3rd ser., 5, Leicester University Press, 1980, 64pp.

SCHUMER, B

The Evolution of Wychwood to 1400: Pioneers, Frontiers and Forests, D.E.L.H.
Occasional Papers, 3rd ser., 6, Leicester University Press, 1984, 72pp.

PHYTHIAN-ADAMS, C.V.

Re-thinking English Local History, D.E.L.H. Occasional Papers, 4th ser., 1, 1987, 2nd
edn, Leicester University Press, 1991, 58pp.

WARNER, P.

*Greens, Commons and Clayland Colonization: the Origins and the Development of
Green-side Settlement in East Suffolk*, D.E.L.H. Occasional Papers, 4th ser., 2,
Leicester University Press, 1987, 66pp.

SNELL, K.D.M.

*Church and Chapel in the North Midlands: Religious Observance in the Nineteenth
Century*, D.E.L.H. Occasional Papers, 4th ser., 3, Leicester University Press, 1991,
77pp.

DYER, C.

Hanbury: Settlement and Society in a Woodland Landscape, D.E.L.H. Occasional
Papers, 4th ser., 4, Leicester University Press, 1991, 73pp.

4 Communities, Contexts and Cultures: Leicester Studies in English Local History

EVERITT, A.M.

Continuity and Colonization: The Evolution of Kentish Settlement, Communities,
Contexts and Cultures: Leicester Studies in English Local History, Leicester
University Press, 1986, xxi and 426pp.

HEY, D.G.

The Fiery Blades of Hallamshire: Sheffield and its Neighbours, 1660-1740,
Communities, Contexts and Cultures: Leicester Studies in English Local History,
Leicester University Press, 1991, xx and 365pp.

GOODACRE, J.D.

*The Transformation of a Peasant Economy: Townspeople and Villagers in the
Lutterworth Area, 1500-1700*, Communities, Contexts and Cultures: Leicester Studies
in English Local History, Scolar Press, 1994, xvi and 322pp.

II   LANDSCAPE AND BUILDINGS

A   The Making of the Landscape

AUSTIN, J.P.

The trees and woodlands of the Cecils, Leicester M.A. dissertation, 1993.

Sherrards Park: an ancient wood, *Hertfordshire Countryside*, 47, 1992, 17-18.

Birchall: a lost wood, *Hertfordshire Countryside*, 48, 1993, 21.

Hatfield Great Wood and its inclosure, *Hertfordshire Past*, 38, 1995, 2-7.

Early Anglo-Saxon settlement in Leicestershire and Rutland - the place-name evidence, *T.L.A.S.*, LIII, 1977-8.

BARKER, A.

Insular farms and muddy lanes: pre-conquest and medieval settlement on the Culm Measures of Devon, Leicester M.A. dissertation, 1986.

BOURNE, J.M.

Editor, *Anglo-Saxon Landscapes in the East Midlands,* Leicestershire Museums, Arts and Records Service, 1996, 196pp.

BOWMAN, P.

Settlement, territory and land use in the East Midlands: the Langton hundred *c.*150 BC- *c.*AD 1350, Leicester Ph.D. thesis, 1995.

Contrasting *pays*; Anglo-Saxon settlement and landscape in Langton Hundred, in J. Bourne, ed. *Anglo-Saxon Landscapes in the East Midlands*, Leicestershire Museums, Arts and Records Service, 1996, 121-146.

BURT, J.

Northamptonshire gardens and parks, 1660-1825, Leicester M.A. dissertation, 1986.

The Garden History Society, *Newsletter,* Friends of the D.E.L.H., 3, 1990.

CLIFFORD, M.C.S.

Fifteen Leicestershire villages: a study of their morphology and location, Leicester M.A. dissertation, 1987.

COURTNEY, P.

The origins of Leicester's market-place: archaeology in perspective, *Leics.H.*, 4, 4, 1995, 5-15.

Leicester: the archaeology of space in an industrial city, ed. G. de Boe and F.Verhaeghe, *Method and Theory in Historical Archaeology: Papers of the 'Medieval Europe Brugge 1997' Conference*, 1, Asse Zellik, 89-96.

Saxon and medieval Leicester: the making of an urban landscape, *T.L.A.S.*, 72, 1998, 110-45

DOWNER, S.
Place names and the reconstruction of woodland in North Worcestershire, Part I, *The Recorder*, Worcestershire Archaeological Society, Autumn 1996, 12-13.

Place names and the reconstruction of woodland in North Worcestershire, Part II, *The Recorder*, Worcestershire Archaeological Society, Spring 1997, 10-11.

EDEN, P.
Waterways of the Fens: an Essay on the Commercial Archaeology of the Cambridge Region with drawings by Warwick Hutton, The University Printer, Cambridge, 1972, 69pp.

EVELEIGH, N.G.
Landscape and environment: their contribution to the evolution of settlement in early medieval Kesteven, Leicester M.A. dissertation, 1992.

EVERITT, A.M.
The making of the agrarian landscape of Kent, *Arch.Cant.*, XCII, 1976, 1-32.

FINBERG, H.P.R.
Pirate Gore in Scilly, *D.C.N.Q.,* XXII, 1945, 250-251.

Gloucestershire: an Illustrated Essay on the History of the Landscape, Hodder and Stoughton, 1955, 128pp. Revised and reprinted as *The Gloucestershire Landscape*, Hodder and Stoughton, 1975, 141pp.

FLETCHER, S.M. (with Hunter, E.)
Moated sites in Odsey hundred, *Hertfordshire's Past*, 30, Spring 1991, 13-23.

Hitchin 1898, Old Ordnance Survey maps, Hertfordshire sheet 12.01, Alan Godfrey Maps, 1990.

FOX, H.S.A.
Editor and contributor, Dispersed settlement, *Medieval Village Research Group Annual Report,* 31, 1983, 39-45.

Southwestern borderlands: the land; prehistory and early history; rural settlements; farming landscapes; industries and towns; coastal settlements, in *The Domesday Project*, BBC Publications, 1986, 133 frames.

Cellar settlements along the South Devon coastline, in H.S.A.Fox, ed. *Seasonal Settlement*, University of Leicester, Vaughan Papers in Adult Education, 39, 1996, 61-9.

Landscape history; the countryside, in D.Hey, ed. *The Oxford Companion to Family and Local History*, Oxford University Press, 1996, 266-73.

From seasonal use to permanent settlement: fishing sites along the South Devon coast from the fourteenth century to the sixteenth, *Northern Seas Yearbook*, Esbjerg, 1998, 7-19.

Foreword: woodland history, in B. Schumer, *The Evolution of Wychwood to 1400: Pioneers, Frontiers and Forests*, Wychwood Press, 1998, vi-xi.

Wolds, in J. Thirsk, ed. *The English Rural Landscape: an Illustrated History*, Oxford University Press (in press).

GLASSON, M.O.J. (with Mullins, S.)
Hidden Harborough: the Making of the Townscape of Market Harborough, with S.Mullins, Leicestershire Museums, 1985.

HALL, T.
Minster churches in the Dorset landscape, Leicester M.Phil thesis, 1997.

HART, Clive R.
Searches for the early Neolithic: a study of Peakland long cairns, in T.G.Manby & P.Turnbull, ed. *Archaeology in the Pennines*, British Archaeological Record, 158, 1986.

Recent surface finds from a barrow on Wetton Low, Wetton, Staffs. *Derbyshire Archaeological Journal*, CVII, 1987.

Two late Anglo Saxon strap-ends from South Yorkshire, *Yorkshire Historical Journal*, 61, 1989.

Brunaburgh: the Don Valley, Sheffield, Sheffield Museums, 1989.

The Medieval Borough and Castle of Sheffield, Sheffield Museums, 1989.

The North Derbyshire Archaeological Survey to A.D. 1500, 4th edn., North Derbyshire Archaeological Survey, 1990.

The archaeological potential of Sheffield's medieval Angel Street and High Street, *South Yorkshire Archaeological Unit*, 1990.

The ancient woodland of Ecclesall Woods, Sheffield, *Sorby Scientific Society*, 27, 1992.

Cockfield Fell, Co. Durham: archaeological assessment, *Tyne & Wear Museums*, 1994.

Co-editor with J.Horsley, *The Golden Age of Northumbria*, 1996.

East Street, Tynemouth, *Arbeia Journal*, IV, 1996.

Mickley Farm, Morton, Derbyshire: archaeological assessment, *Tyne & Wear Museums*, 1996.

AES Walbottle Power Station, Newburn, Tyne & Wear: archaeological assessment, *Tyne & Wear Museums*, 1996.

Bishopwearmouth, Sunderland: archaeological assessment, *Tyne & Wear Museums,* 1996.

Houghton-le-Spring: conservation initiative, *Tyne & Wear Museums,* 1997.

HART, Clive R. (with Coulston, J.C.N.)
An altar from Chipchase, Northumberland, *Archaeologica Aeliana,* 5, XXI, 1993.

HART, Clive R. (with Makepeace, G.A.)
Crane's Fort, Conksbury, Youlgreave, Derbyshire: a newly discovered hillfort, *Derbyshire Archaeological Journal*, CXII, 1992.

HART, Clive R. (with Robinson, F.)
Recent fieldwork on Beeley Warren, Beeley, Derbyshire, *T.H.A.S.,* 1993.

HART, Clive R. (with Rotherham, I.D.)
Ecclesall Woods: an 'ancient' woodland in Sheffield, in P. Beswick and I.D. Rotherham eds. *Ancient Woodlands: Their Archaeology and Ecology*, 1993.

HART, Clive R. (with Speak, S.)
The Kirk Lee, Houghton-le-Spring: archaeological assessment, *Tyne & Wear Museums*, 1993.

South Shields riverside, South Tyneside: archaeological assessment, *Tyne & Wear Museums*, 1994.

Wylam Wharf, Sunderland: archaeological assessment, *Tyne & Wear Museums,* 1994.

The Croxdale estate, Co. Durham: archaeological assessment, *Tyne & Wear Museums*, 1995.

HART, Clive R. (with Speak, S. and Snape, M.)
Bishopmiddleham: archaeological assessment, *Tyne & Wear Museums,* 1996.

HEATH, J.
Settlement and land-use in North Wiltshire with special reference to the 1st to 11th centuries A.D., Leicester M.Phil. thesis, 1989.

HEY, D.G.
Fresh light on the South Yorkshire saltways, *T.H.A.S.*, IX, 1967, 151-157.

The parks at Tankersley and Wortley, *Y.A.J.*, XLVII, 1975, 109-119.

HOSKINS, W.G.

The anatomy of the English countryside: 1. The anatomy of the English countryside; 2. A hand-made world; 3. The road between; 4. The 'rash assault'; 5. The house through the trees, *The Listener*, LI, 1954, 732-734, 772-774, 819-820, 864-866, 917-918.

Introduction, *Mirror of Britain or the History of British Topography,* catalogue of the National Book League exhibition, 1957, 6-10.

The English Landscape, in A.L.Poole, ed. *Medieval England*, Oxford University Press, 1958, 1-36.

English Landscapes: How to Read the Man-Made Scenery of England, B.B.C. Publications, 1973, 120pp.

An exploration of England: 1. Devon farms without a village; 2. Evolving townscapes, *The Listener,* LXXIV, 1965, 82-85, 122-125.

The landscape of towns: 1. The planned town; 2. The open field town; 3. The market town, *The Listener*, XLVIII, 1952, 457-458, 499-500, 539-540, 555.

Landscapes of England, *The Listener*, XCV, 1976, 71-72, 105-106, 136-137, 172-173, 210-211, 242-243.

Leicestershire: an Illustrated Essay on the History of the Landscape, Hodder and Stoughton, 1957, 13pp.

The Making of the English Landscape, Hodder and Stoughton, 1955, 240pp. Revised edition, Hodder and Stoughton, 1977, 326pp. Re-published with an introduction and commentary by C. Taylor, Hodder and Stoughton, 1988, 256pp.

The Making of the Landscape, *The West in English History*, ed. A.L. Rowse, Hodder and Stoughton, 1949, 57-66.

Midland England: a Survey of the Country between the Chilterns and the Trent, B.T. Batsford, 1949, 120pp.

One Man's England, B.B.C. Publications, 1978, 144pp.

The threatened countryside, VI, beautiful Devon, *The Listener*, LXVII, 1962, 988-989.

KISSOCK, J.A.

The open fields of Gower: a case study and a reconsideration, *Journal of the Gower Society*, 37, 1986, 41-49.

Gower field systems, *Archaeology in Wales*, 27, 1987, 69.

The origins of the village in South Wales: a study in landscape archaeology, Leicester Ph.D. thesis, 1990.

A morphogenetic approach to village origins in South Wales, *Archaeology in Wales*, 28, 1988, 40.

The origins of the village in South Wales: a study in landscape archaeology, *M.S.R.G. Annual Report*, 5, 1990, 6-7.

The origins of the medieval nucleated rural settlement in Glamorgan: a conjectural model, *Morgannwg*, 35, 1991, 31-49.

Farms, fields and hedges: aspects of the rural economy of north-west Gower, *c*.1300 to *c*.1650, *Arch. Camb.*, 140, 1991, 130-147.

The origins of the Midland village (a discussion session at the Economic History Society conference), *M.S.R.G. Annual Report*, 6, 1991, 16.

Planned villages in Wales, *Medieval World*, 6, 1992, 39-43.

Recent research into the medieval landscape of South West Wales: the Dyfed Archaeological Trust's historic settlement project, *M.S.R.G. Annual Report*, 7, 1992, 10-12.

Medieval Britain in 1992: South Pembrokeshire and Dinefwr, *Med. Arch.*, 37, 1993, 307-308.

The Dyfed Archaeological Trust's historic settlement project, *Society for Landscape Studies Newsletter*, Autumn 1992, 3-4.

The historical settlements of South Pembrokeshire, *Ruralia I, Pamatky Archeologicke - Supplementum*, 5, 1996, 115-118.

Cefn Drum research project, interim report in *M.S.R.G. Annual Report*, 11, 1996, 53.

Cefn Drum research project, interim report in *Archaeology in Wales*, 36, 1996, 88.

'God made nature and men made towns': post-conquest and pre-conquest villages in Pembrokeshire, in N.Edwards, ed. *Landscape and Settlement in Medieval Settlement in Wales*, 123-137, Oxbow (Monograph 81), 1997.

Cefn Drum research project, interim reports in 'Medieval Britain in 1996', *Med.Arch.* and *Archaeometry*, forthcoming.

Cefn Drum project, interim reports in *Archaeology in Wales, M.S.R.G Annual Report* and Medieval Britain in 1998 in *Med. Arch.*, forthcoming.

KISSOCK, J.A. (with Cooper, R.N.)
Gower field systems, *Archaeology in Wales*, 28, 1988, 36-7.

Gower farms and field systems, *Archaeology in Wales*, 29, 1989, 34-5.

JENKINS, S.C.
Some thoughts on the topography of Saxon Witney, *R.W.*, 12, 1981, 6.

LYND-EVANS, P.
Morphology of villages in the central region of Lincolnshire from the early Saxon period, Leicester M.A. dissertation, 1997.

MOORE, J.S.
Laughton: a Study in the Evolution of the Wealden Landscape, D.E.L.H. Occasional Papers, 19, Leicester University Press, 1965, 55pp.

MULLINS, S (with Glasson, M.)
Hidden Harborough: the Making of the Townscape of Market Harborough, with S.Mullins, Leicestershire Museums, 1985.

PAWLEY, S.J.
Medieval old Sleaford, old Sleaford revealed, in. S.M. Elsdon, ed. *A Lincolnshire Settlement in Iron Age, Roman, Saxon and Medieval Times: Excavations 1882-1995,* Oxbow, 1997, 68-73.

Grist to the mill: A new approach to the early history of Sleaford, *Lincs. H.A.,* 23, 1988, 37-41.

PETCHEY, W.J.
The topography of paradise, *The Ripon Historian*, 2, 2, 34-37

PETFORD, A.J.
The process of enclosure in Saddleworth 1625-1834, *Transactions of the Lancashire and Cheshire Antiquarian Society*, 84, 1987, 78-117.

PHYTHIAN-ADAMS, C.V.
Frontier valleys, in J. Thirsk, ed. *The English Rural Landscape: an Illustrated History*, Oxford University Press (in press)

PHYTHIAN-ADAMS, H.V.
The planning of Aberaeron - some new evidence, *Cer.*, 8, 4, 1979, 404-407

RAVENSDALE, J.R.
The historical evolution of the landscape of three north Cambridgeshire villages: Landbeach, Cottenham, and Waterbeach, A.D. 450-1850, Leicester Ph.D. thesis, 1971.

Liable to Floods: Village Landscape on the Edge of the Fens A.D.450-1850, Cambridge University Press, 1974, 206pp.

Co-editor with C.Hall, *The West Fields of Cambridge*, Cambs Record Society, 1988, 168pp.

REDMONDS, G.
Old Huddersfield, 1500-1800, GR Books, 1981, 58pp.

Almondbury: Places and Place-names, GR Books, 1982, 64pp.

Changing Huddersfield, Kirklees Libraries, 1985, 79pp.

Slaithwaite: Places and Place-names, GR Books, 1988, 52pp.

Holmfirth: Place-names and Settlement, GR Books, 1994, 70pp.

Tong Street, *O.W.R.,* 1/2, 1981, 4pp.

Spring woods, *O.W.R.,* 3/2, 1983, 6pp.

Steaners and weirs, *O.W.R.,* 1/1, 1981, 5pp.

Dog pits, *O.W.R.,* 2/2, 1982, 1p.

Colne or Holme?, *O.W.R.,* 2pp.

Surnames and settlement, *O.W.R.,* 4/2, 1984, 4pp.

Turf pits, *O.W.R.,* 7/1, 1987, 2pp.

A view of the moors, *O.W.R.,* 9, 1989, 1p.

Hedges and walls in West Yorkshire, *O.W.R.,* 10, 1990, 7pp.

Stubbin, *O.W.R.,* 13, 1993, 1p.

Personal names and surnames in some West Yorkshire 'royds', *Nomina,* 9, 1985.

REED, M.A.
The Buckinghamshire Landscape, Hodder and Stoughton, 1979, 288pp.

The Georgian Triumph, Routledge and Kegan Paul, 1983, 230pp. Paperback edn, 1987

Editor and introduction to, *Discovering Past Landscapes,* Croom Helm, 1984, 320pp.

Anglo-Saxon charter boundaries, *Discovering Past Landscapes,* 261-306.

The Age of Exuberance, Routledge and Kegan Paul, 1986, 306pp. Paperback edn, 1987.

The Landscape of Britain, Routledge, 1990, 387pp. Paperback edn, 1997.

A History of Buckinghamshire, Phillimore, 1993, 136pp.

SAUNDERS, A.L.
The manor of Tyburn and the Regent's Park, 1086-1965, Leicester Ph.D. thesis, 1965.

Regent's Park: a Study of the Development of the Area from 1086 to the Present Day, David and Charles, 1969, 244pp. Revised edn, 1981.

Regent's Park, Bedford College, 1981.

SCHUMER, B.
The Evolution of Wychwood to 1400: Pioneers, Frontiers and Forests, D.E.L.H. Occasional Papers, 3rd ser., 6, Leicester University Press, 1984.

Wychwood, the Evolution of a Wooded Landscape, Wychwood Press, 1998.

SHEPPARD, D.
In search of the Forest of Arden, Leicester M.A. dissertation, 1997.

SPARLING, T.
An enquiry into the effect of drainage and watersheds on settlement from the end of the Roman period to the Norman period, Leicester M.A. dissertation, 1992.

SPUFFORD, H.M.
The Street and ditchways in S.E. Cambridgeshire, *P.Camb.A.S.,* LIX, 1966, 129-131.

Eccleshall, Staffordshire, in J. Thirsk, ed. *Oxford Illustrated History of the English Rural Landscape,* Oxford University Press, forthcoming.

STOKES, P.A.
The organisation of landscape and territory on the estates of Glastonbury Abbey: a case study of the manors of Ditcheat and Pennard, Leicester M.A. dissertation, 1997.

TERRY, C.
The church in the landscape: two case studies from Norfolk, Leicester M.A. dissertation, 1983.

THORNTON, C.
Common lands, in *The Victoria History of the County of Essex Volume IX, The Borough of Colchester,* ed. J.Cooper, Oxford University Press, 1994, 255-59.

TRANTER, E.M.
A view from across the border, in J.Bourne, ed. *Anglo-Saxon Landscapes of the East Midlands,* Leicestershire Museums and Art Galleries and Education Service, 1996, 181-90.

Name, race, terrain: the making of a Leicestershire boundary, in D.Postles, ed. *Name, Place, Time,* Leopard's Head Press, forthcoming.

TRINDER, B.S.
The Making of the Industrial Landscape, Dent; 2nd edn, Alan Sutton, 1987, 308pp; 3rd edn, Orion, 1997, 272pp.

UPTON, P.
Place-names of Warwickshire revisited, Leicester M.A. dissertation, 1997.

WARNER, P.
Greens, Commons and Clayland Colonization: the Origins and Development of Green-side Settlements in East Suffolk, D.E.L.H. Occasional Papers, 4th ser., 2, Leicester University Press, 1987.

Shared church-yards, freemen church-builders and the development of parishes in eleventh-century East Anglia, *Landscape History*, 8, 1986, 39-52.

The documentary survey, *Bulletin of the Sutton Hoo Research Committee*, 3, July 1985, 14-21.

Documentary sources: interim report, 1st April 1984, *Bulletin of the Sutton Hoo Research Committee*, 2, April 1984, 6-9.

Origins: the example of green-side settlement in East Suffolk, *Medieval Village Research Group Report*, 31, 1983, 42-4.

The Origins of Suffolk, Manchester University Press, 1996, 200pp.

WILLIAMS, M.I.
The Making of the South Wales Landscape, Hodder and Stoughton, 1975, 271pp.

B Cartography

BENDALL, S.
Editor, *Dictionary of Land Surveyors and Local Map-makers of Great Britain & Ireland 1530-1850*, vol. I, 2nd edn., 1997, 312pp.

Editor, *Dictionary of Land Surveyors and Local Map-makers of Great Britain & Ireland 1530-1850*, vol. II, 2nd edn., 1997, 578pp.

CHRISTMAS, E.
Longlevens - the place and its name, *Glevensis*, 30, 1997, 35.

EDEN, P.
Dictionary of Land Surveyors and Local Cartographers of Great Britain and Ireland, 1550-1850: Part I, A-F, 1-108, Dawson, 1975; Part II, G-R, 109-221, Dawson, 1976; Part III, S-Z, Appendix and Indices, 222-377, Dawson, 1976. Bound edn., Dawson, 1979. 2nd edn, 2 vols, British Library, 1997.

Land surveyors in Norfolk, 1550-1850: Part I, The estate surveyors, *N.A.*, XXXIV, 1973, 474-482.

Land surveyors in Norfolk, 1550-1850: Part II, The surveyors of inclosure and index of surveyors, *N.A.*, XXXVI, 1975, 119-148.

Three Elizabethan estate surveyors: Peter Kempe, Thomas Clerke and Thomas Langdon, in S. Tyacke, ed. *English Map-Making 1500-1650*, The British Library, 1983, 68-84.

FOX, H.S.A.
Exeter, Devonshire, *c.*1420, in R.A.Skelton and P.D.A.Harvey, ed. *Local Maps and Plans from Medieval England*, Clarendon Press, 1986, 163-9.

Exeter, Devonshire, *c.*1499, in R.A.Skelton and P.D.A.Harvey, ed. *Local Maps and Plans from Medieval England*, Clarendon Press, 1986, 329-36.

Local History through Maps (catalogue of an exhibition. Leicester University Jubilee Open Day), 1982, 8pp.

IREDALE, D.A.
Places of power, *Scots Magazine*, Sept. 1998.

MORRIS, C.I.
Surveyors and commissioners of enclosure in Bedfordshire, 1760-1820: the growth of professionalism, Leicester M.A. dissertation, 1975.

NICHOLS, H.
Local maps of Derbyshire to 1770: an inventory and introduction, Leicester M.A. thesis, 1973.

Map Librarianship, C. Bingley, 1976, 298pp.

PETFORD, A.J. (with Barnes, B., Buckley, P.M., & Hunt, J.M.)
Saddleworth Surveyed, Selected Maps of the Township, 1625-1851, Saddleworth Historical Society and Festival of the Arts, 1983, 127pp.

C Buildings and Historical Monuments

ALDRED, D.H.
Contributions to: R.Leech, ed. *Historic Towns in Gloucestershire,* Committee for Rescue Archaeology in Avon, Gloucestershire and Somerset, 1981, 72, 90, 96.

COURTNEY, P.
Excavations on the outer precinct of Tintern Abbey, *Med. Arch.*, 33, 1989, 99-143.

The historical background, in K.Blockley, Landstone Castle motte: excavations by L.Alcock in 1964, *Archaeology in Wales*, 34, 1994, 22-4.

The historical background, in K.Blockley, Excavations at Oxwich Castle, Gower, *P.-Med.Arch.*, 31, 1997, 32-3.

DOREE, S.G.
T*rent Park, a Short History to 1939,* Middlesex Polytechnic, 1990, 36pp. (mostly incorporated in P.Campbell, *Trent Park, a History*, Middlesex University Press, 1997)

EDEN, P.
Anglo-Saxon churches, Norman churches, Early English churches, Decorated churches, Perpendicular churches, *O.D.& C.*, XIV, xii - xv, v, 1954.

An architectural description of St Mary's church, Wirksworth, Derbyshire, *Arch.Jnl.*, CXVIII, 1961, 228-230.

Introduction to *Bridges on the Backs*: a Series of Drawings by David Gentleman, The University Printer, Cambridge, 1961.

Contributions to *The City of Cambridge*, I and II, H.M.S.O., for the R.C.H.M., 1959.

Contributions to *The County of Cambridge*, II, *North-East Cambridgeshire*, H.M.S.O., for the R.C.H.M., 1972.

Contributions to *An Inventory of the Historical Monuments in Dorset*, I, *West Dorset*, H.M.S.O., for the R.C.H.M., 1952.

Lanercost Priory, *Arch.Jnl.*, CXV, 1958, 220-225.

Ottery St Mary church, *Arch.Jnl.*, CXIV, 1957, 163-165.

Paignton church, *Arch.Jnl.*, CXIV, 1957, 171-172.

Smaller post-medieval houses in eastern England, L.M. Munby, ed. *East Anglian Studies*, Heffer, 1968, 71-93.

Small Houses in England, 1520-1820: Towards a Classification, The Historical Association, Pamphlet H.75, 1969, 35pp.

Sompting: church of St Mary, *Arch.Jnl.*, CXVI, 1959, 245-246.

Studying your parish church - from the building, *A.H.*, VII, 1965, 53-59.

Totnes church, *Arch.Jnl.*, CXIV, 1957, 177.

Vernacular architecture, in N. Pye, ed. *Leicester and its Region*, Leicester University Press, 1972, 578-589.

Worth: church of St Nicholas, *Arch.Jnl.*, CXVI, 1959, 240-241.

EDEN, P. (with Spittle, S.D.T.)
Editors, *An Inventory of the Historical Monuments in the County of Cambridge*: I. *West Cambridgeshire*, H.M.S.O., for the R.C.H.M., 1968, 256pp .

ELLIOTT, B.S.
Hamnett Pinheys's English house: Rose Cottage at Merton, Surrey, in *Horaceville Herald*, 11, 1987, 12, 1988.

FINBERG, H.P.R.
The Castle of Cornwall, *D.C.N.Q.*, XXIII, 1947, 123.

Lydford Castle, *D.C.N.Q.*, XXIII, 1949, 386-387.

GILES, C.
Domestic architecture in the north Staffordshire moorlands: the vernacular buildings of Grindon and Waterfall, Leicester M.A. dissertation, 1976.

Rural Houses of West Yorkshire 1400-1830, West Yorkshire Metropolitan County Council, R.C.H.M., Supplementary series: 8, 19, 260pp.

GOODACRE, J.D.
Observations on a mill: Lutterworth subscription windmill, *Leics.H.*, II, iv, 1973, 9-16.

GRAHAM, M.
Folly Bridge (City of Oxford Local History Teaching Unit, 1), Oxford City Council, 1972.

On foot in Oxford (12 booklets), Oxford City Council & Oxfordshire County Council, 1973-87.

The building of new St Clement's Church, Oxford, *Top Oxon*, 20, 1975.

Oxford Old and New, EP Publishing, 1976.

St. Frideswide's Church, Osney, Oxford, Robert Dugdale, 1978.

The Building of Oxford Covered Market, *Ox.*, 44, 1979.

St. Frideswide's Church, Osney, Oxford, St.Frideswide's Church, 1997.

GRAHAM, M. (with Waters, L)
Oxfordshire Yesterday and Today, Sutton Publishing, 1997.

HART, Cyril R.
The Aldewerke and Minster at Shelford, Cambridgeshire, *Anglo-Saxon Studies in Archaeology and History*, 8, 1995, 43-68.

HEY, D.G.
Wentworth Castle: a Short History, Northern College, 1991, 16pp.

Extensive notes on field visits to Tickhill, Bawtry, Rotherham, Eccleshall and Midhope, *Arch. Jnl.*, 137, 1981, 418-22, 430-1, 452, 459-60, 472-3.

Yorkshire: the Buildings of Britain, 1500-1750, Morland, 1981, 165pp.

Saxon churches in South Yorkshire: the historical background, in P.Ryder, ed. *Saxon Churches in South Yorkshire*, South Yorkshire County Council Archaeological Monograph, 2, 1982, 12-15.

St Peter's church, Warmsworth, *Y. A. J.*, 11, 1983, 27-60.

HILLIER, K.A.
The Castle of Ashby-de-la-Zouch, K & M Hampson, 1988, 40pp.

Country Houses Around Ashby-de-la-Zouch, K & M Hampson, 1989, 72pp.

HOSKINS, W.G.
Burrow Farm in Stoke Canon, *D.C.N.Q.*, XX, 1939, 27-28.

Butcher Row, Exeter, *D.C.N.Q.*, XXVI, 1955, 109.

The development of the small house, *T.D.A.*, CX, 1978, 1-8.

The Englishman's house: 1. The house in the town; 2. Farmhouses and cottages; 3. The interior of the house, *The Listener*, LVII, 1957, 953-955, 995-997, 1035-1036.

Farmhouses and history, *H.T.*, X, 1960, 333-341.

The Great Rebuilding, *H.T.*, V, 1955, 104-111.

The rebuilding of rural England, 1570-1640, *P.& P.*, IV, 1953, 44-59. Reprinted in W.G. Hoskins, *Provincial England*, Macmillan, 1963.

Stone Farm, Thorverton, *D.C.N.Q.*, XXIV, 1950-51, 145-147.

IREDALE, D.A.
How can I trace the history of my house, *A.H.*, 7, 6, 1967, 182-9.

Houses and genealogy, *Gen.Mag.*, 21, 4-6, 1983-4.
Discovering Your Old House, Shire Publications, 1991.

JENKINS, S.C.
The industrial archaeology of Witney, *R. W.*, 3, 1978, 18-22.

Some thoughts on Witney church tower, *R.W.*, 5, 1978, 13-15.

JENKINS, S.C. (with Cooper, T.J.)
Builders in stone, *R.W.*, 8, 1980, 3-9.

(with Gott, C.) Mill and chapel, *R.W.*, 8, 1980, 17-24.

The great fires of Witney, *R.W.*, 9, 1980, 8-12.

George Wilkinson of Witney, *R.W.*, 17, 1984, 3-8.

The effect of the Witney railway on the vernacular architecture of Witney, *R.W.*, 18, 1984, 19-22.

Some old Witney houses, *R.W.*, 20, 1988, 16-18.

Witney Court, Worcestershire, *Transactions of the Worcestershire Archaeological Society,* 15, 1996, 283-303.

Minster Lovell Hall, *R.W.*, n.s., 2., 8, 1997, 137-159.

Early Great Western architecture, *R.M.*, XXV, 1974, 134-136.

Great Western architecture: the East Gloucestershire Railway, *R.M.*, XXVIII, 1977, 306-308.

Brunel stations on the OW & WR, *Model Railway Constructor*, July 1983, 419-423.

Brunel stations - a postscript, *Model Railway Constructor*, August 1983, 487-489.

Another Brunel chalet, *Model Railway Constructor*, August 1984.

Great Western architecture, *R. M.*, October 1977, 306-308.

Pendennis Castle, Cornwall: some notes on its history, architecture and ordnance, *Fort*, 25, 1997.

JENKINS, S.C. (with Steane, J., Carroll, N. and Cooper, T.)
Walk Round Witney, Witney and District Hist. & Arch. Society, 1979, 20pp.

KISSOCK, J.A. (with Schlesinger, A., Walls, C. Lovegrove, C., Pollard, K. and Wright, N.) An early church and medieval farmstead site: excavations at Llanelen, Llanrhidian, *Journal of the Gower Society*, 46, 1994, 58-79.

An early church and medieval farmstead site: excavations at Llanelen, Gower, *Arch. Jnl.,* 153, 1996, 104-147.

LAITHWAITE, J.M.W.
Survey of pre-1700 houses in Banbury, *C. & C.*, II, 1962, 34.

The Reindeer Inn, Banbury, *C.& C.*, II, 1964, 159-163.

A Ship-Master's house at Faversham, Kent, *P.-Med.Arch.*, II, 1968, 150-162.

Two medieval houses in Ashburton, *P.D.A.S.*, XXIX, 1971, 181-194.

Middle Moor, Sowton: a re-assessment, *T.D.A.*, CIII, 1971, 77-83.

The buildings of Banbury, pre-1700, and other contributions, in A. Crossley, ed. *The Victoria History of the County of Oxford*, X, 1972, Oxford University Press, 28-33, 45, 82, 100.

Contribution to 'Post-Medieval Britain in 1971', *P.-Med. Arch.*, VI, 1972, 215-216. [Burford.]

Contribution to 'Medieval Britain in 1972, *Med. Arch.*, XVII, 1973, 178.

The buildings of Burford: a Cotswold town in the fourteenth to nineteenth centuries, A. Everitt, ed. *Perspectives in English Urban History*, Macmillan, 1973, 60-90, 244-245, 254-256.

Contributions to 'Post-Medieval Britain in 1973', *P.-Med.Arch.*, VIII, 1974, 128, 130. [Bovey Tracey, Banbury.]

Contributions to 'Post-Medieval Britain in 1975', *P.-Med.Arch.*, X, 1976, 170. [Bishopsteignton, Branscombe, Brentor.]

Sanders, Lettaford, *P.D.A.S.*, 35, 1977, 84.

Contribution to 'Post-Medieval Britain' in 1976', *P.-Med. Arch.*, XI, 1977, 97. [Boycombe, Farway.]

Town houses up to 1700, *Devon's Traditional Buildings*, Devon County Council Planning Department, 1978, 30-42.

A comparison with standing long-houses in Devon, in D.Austin, ed. Excavations in Okehampton Deer Park, Devon, 1976-1978, *P.D.A.S.*, 36, 1978, 218-220.

Documentary evidence for the occupation of 39 Fore Street Totnes, in D.M.& F.M. Griffiths, ed. An Excavation at 39 Fore Street, Totnes, *P.D.A.S.*, 42, 1984, 78-79.

Early owners and occupiers of 61-65 Fore Street, Totnes, in A.Davison & C.G.Henderson, Excavations at Fore Street, Totnes, 1984-5, *Exeter Archaeology*, 1985, 66-68.

Totnes houses 1500-1800, in P. Clark, ed. *The Transformation of English Provincial Towns*, Hutchinson, 1984, 62-98. Paperback 1989.

Town houses: medieval to mid seventeenth-century, P.Cherry and N. Pevsner, ed. *The Buildings of England: Devon*, 2nd edn, 1989, 78-82.

Victorian Ilfracombe, Devon Books, 1992.

Town houses up to 1660, in P. Beacham, ed. *Devon Building*, Devon Books, 1990, 95-115. Paperback 1995.

Frank Chesher (1916-1996), *Devon Buildings Group Newsletter*, 15, Easter 1997, 23-24.

LAITHWAITE, J.M.W. (with Alcock, N.W.)
Medieval houses in Devon and their modernization, *Med. Arch.*, XVII, 1973, 100-125.

LAITHWAITE, J.M.W. (with Alcock, N.W. and Child, P.) .
Sanders, Lettaford: a Devon long-house, *P.D.A.S.*, 30, 1972, 227-233.

LAITHWAITE, J.M.W. (with Child, P.)
Little Rull: a late-medieval farmhouse near Cullompton, *P.D.A.S.*, 33, 1975, 303-310.

LAITHWAITE, J.M.W. (with Brown, S.)
Northwood Farm, Christow: an abandoned farmstead on the eastern fringe of Dartmoor, *P.D.A.S.*, 51, 1993, 161-184.

LAUGHTON, J.
The Rows research project - Chester, *Newsletter,* Friends of D.E.L.H., 2, 1989.

'The house that John built': a study of the building of a seventeenth-century house in Chester, *Journal of the Chester Archaeological Society*, LXX, 1987-88, 99-132.

McDERMOTT, M.B.
Church house at Spaxton, *S.A.N.H.,* 119, 1975, 62-64.

Little Poundisford farmhouse, *S.A.N.H.,* 120, 1976, 104-105.

Two examples of vernacular architecture in the parishes of Llansantffraid and Aberarth, *Cer.*, 1978, 323-328.

Single-storeyed medieval houses: two examples from West Somerset, *S.A.N.H.,* 126, 1981-82, 93-101.

Early bench-ends in All Saints' church, *S.A.N.H.,* 138, 1994, 117-130.

The restoration of Stocklinch Magdalen church, *S.A.N.H.,* 139, 1995, 135-147.

Garnival's Week farmhouse, Milverton, Somerset, *Vernacular Architecture*, 28, 1997, 99-101.

Peter Greenwood: a plasterer's apprentice, *Somerset and Dorset Notes and Queries*, XXXIV, 343, March 1996, 18-19.

West gallery at All Saints' church, Trull, *Somerset and Dorset Notes and Queries*, XXXIV, 345, March 1997, 89-92.

MITSON, A. (with Cox, B.)
Victorian estate housing on the Yarborough estate, Lincolnshire, *R.H.E.S.C.*, 6, 1, 1995, 29-46.

OLIVER, D.P.
First duties, truest pleasures: an examination of cottage building on the Russell estates in Bedfordshire, Buckinghamshire and Cambridgeshire between 1802-1914, Leicester M.A. dissertation, 1997.

REED, M.A.
Seventeenth-century Stowe, *Huntingdon Library Quarterly*, 44, 1981, 189-203.

Osterley Park in 1669: the probate inventory of Sir William Waller, *T.L.M.A.S.*, 42, 1991, 1994, 115-120.

ROLES, J. (with Beevers, D. and Marks, R.)
Sussex Churches and Chapels, Brighton Royal Pavilion, Art Gallery and Museums, 1989.

SAUNDERS, A.L.
Regent's Park Villas, Bedford College, 1981, 43pp.

The Royal Exchange, 1991, 44pp.

Editor, *The Royal Exchange*, London Topographical Society, 1997, 444pp.

Gresham's Intentions, in *Sir Thomas Gresham and the Royal Exchange*, Gresham College, 1997.

The Shops about the pawn, in *Sir Thomas Gresham and the Royal Exchange*, Gresham College, 1997.

Reconstructing London: Sir Thomas Gresham in Bishopsgate, F.Ames-Lewis ed. *Sir Thomas Gresham and Gresham College*, forthcoming.

SELL, M.R.
Farmsteads in the parishes of Holmesfield, Barlow and Brampton in N.E. Derbyshire, Leicester M.A. dissertation, 1969.

SHERRINGTON, M.
Beech House, Esprick, *L.A.B.*, III, 1977, 41.

SKEMPTON, K.G.B.
Gypsum plaster panels in timber-framed buildings: a study of a local building material in part of the Trent valley, Leicester M.A. dissertation, 1970.

SMITH, J.R.
Robert Darcy's chantry priests' house, Maldon, Essex, *Med. Arch.*, 19, 1975, 213-219.

THOMPSON, M.G.
The building of a barn, byre and carthouse on Glastonbury Abbey's manor of Street between 1340 and 1343, *S.A.N.H.*, forthcoming.

TRANTER, E.M.
General editor's preface to B. Hutton, *Houses and Everyday Life in Weston on Trent*, 1994, 40pp.

TRINDER, B.S.
The first iron bridges, *I.A.R.*, III, 1979, 112-21.

Coalport Bridge: a study in historical interpretation, *I.A.R.*, III, 1979, 153-57.

TRINDER, B.S. (with Cossons.N)
The Iron Bridge: Symbol of the Industrial Revolution, Moonraker, 1979, 140pp.

WILLIAMS, M.I.
Glamorgan houses and their interiors in the seventeenth and eighteenth centuries, *Glam.H.*, X, 1974, 157-176.

D Guidebooks

ALDRED, D.H.
Chipping Campden and its Buildings: an Urban Trail for Schools, Chipping Campden School, 1976, 12pp.

CARTER, M.P.
'Hemingford Grey is famous for its enormous gooseberries' - History through Road Names, 1998, 48 pp.

CARTER, R.A.
A Visitor's Guide to Yorkshire Churches, Watmoughs 1976, 124pp.

COURTNEY, P.
Castle Park Souvenir Guide, Leics. County Council, 1995.

Castle Park Site Guides, Leics. County Council, 1995.

CROMPTON, J.
Radstock, Midsomer Norton and District Museum Guide, The Museum Society, 1993, 12pp.

ENGLISH, S.
About Burford, Private Publication, 1976, 23pp.

Discovering Burford, Shire Publications, 1971, 23pp.

GLASSON, M.O.J.
Walsall Leather Museum: Guidebook, Walsall M.B.C., 1991

Willenhall Town Trail, Walsall M.B.C., 1987

HEY, D.G.
Historical Guide to the Parish Church of St Mary, Ecclesfield, published by the Church, 1969, 20pp.

HOSKINS, W.G.
Chilterns to the Black Country, About Britain Series, 5, Collins, 1951, 60pp.

Dartmoor from Roman times to the present day, and places of special interest in the National Park, W.G. Hoskins, ed. *Dartmoor National Park*, H.M.S.O., 1957, 67pp.

East Midlands and the Peak, About Britain Series, 8, Collins, 1951, 62pp.

Introduction to Devon, *Devon and Cornwall in Pictures*, Odhams Press, 1950, 127pp.

Leicestershire, Faber, Shell Guide, 1970, 123pp.

Old Exeter: a Description of its Growth and Old Buildings, Illustrated with Photographs, Plans, and a Map, Compton-Dando, 1952, 22pp.

Rutland, City of Leicester Publicity and Development Department, Information Bureau, 1949.

Rutland, Faber, Shell Guide, 1963, 52pp.

Touring Leicester, City of Leicester Publicity and Development Department, Information Bureau, 1948, 50pp.

Introduction, *The Shell Book of English Villages.*

JENKINS, S.C. (with Steane, J., Carroll, N. and Cooper, T.)
A Walk round Witney, Witney and District Historical and Archaeological Society, 1978, 20pp.

KAYE, D.
Editor, *Louth Industrial Trail,* Louth Teachers' Centre, 1977, 24pp.

The Louth Industrial Trail, *T.E.S.*, 13 Jan. 1978.

McDERMOTT, M.B.
A History of St Peter's Church, Langford Budville, private publication, 1972, revised 1977, 19pp.

St.Giles' Church, Bradford on Tone, Somerset: A Short History and Guide, Bradford on Tone Parochial Church Council, 1980, 26pp.

St.Mary's Church, Stocklinch Ottersey, Somerset, Redundant Churches Fund, 1993, 8pp.

St.Mary's Church, Seavington, Somerset, C.C.T., 1994, 4pp.

All Saints Church, Otterhampton, Somerset, C.C.T., 1995, 4pp.

Sutton Mallet Church, Somerset, C.C.T., 1995, 4pp.

St.Andrew's Church, Northover, Somerset, C.C.T., 1995, 4pp.

West Ogwell Church, Devon, C.C.T., 1996, 8pp.

St.Michael's Church, Clapton-in-Gordano, Somerset, C.C.T., 1996, 9pp.

All Saints' Church, Langport, Somerset, C.C.T., 1998, 12pp.

St.Mary the Virgin's Church, Emborough, Somerset, C.C.T., 1998, 8pp.

MORRIS, C.I.
St Ives in Cambridgeshire: Official Guide, J. Burrow, 1978, 52pp.

PHYTHIAN-ADAMS, H.V.
The Market Hall, and St John's House, Warwick, *Guide to the Borough of Warwick,* 1971, 55, 59, 65.

RAVENSDALE, J.R.
The Domesday Inheritance (Landbeach), Souvenir, 1986.

Cornwall, National Trust Histories, Collins, 1984, 95pp.

SAUNDERS, A.L.
London: the City and Westminster, Revision of Arthur Mee, Hodder and Stoughton, 1975, 436pp.

London North of the Thames except the City and Westminster, Revision of Arthur Mee, Hodder and Stoughton, 1972, 432pp.

The Art and Architecture of London: an Illustrated Guide, Phaidon, 1984, 480pp.

St. Martin-in-theFields: a Short History and Guide, 1989, 24pp.

STARR, C.
St Mary the Virgin, Little Bromley, Essex, 1991, 5pp.

THIRSK, J.
Hadlow Castle: a Short History, Hadlow Historical Society, 1985, 20pp.

Hadlow Castle. A Short History, 2nd edn., revised, Hadlow Historical Society, 1997, 24pp.

TRANTER, E.M.
Weston on Trent: an Illustrated Guide, Weston on Trent Local History Society, 1987, 12pp.

TRINDER, B.S.
Editor, *The Most Extraordinary District in the World: Ironbridge and Coalbrookdale,* Phillimore, 1977, 126pp.

Corvedale: a Motor Trail, Shropshire County Museum Service, 1976, 16pp.

The district and its past, *Bridgnorth District Official Guide,* Burrow, 1977, 15-35.

WICKES, M.J.L.
A History of the Parish of Great, Steeple and Little Gidding, Great Gidding Church Publications, 1979, 43pp.

WATSON, A.F. *et al.*
Find Out about the Past (a series of local history trails relating to Cromford Village, Cromford Canal and the Cromford and High Peak Railway), Tawney House, Matlock.

III SOCIETY AND ECONOMY

A General

ALDRED, D.H.
Cleeve Hill: the History of the Common and its People, 1990, 174pp.

BRADY, R.L.
A comparison of attitudes towards domestic service in England during the Victorian period and the early to mid-twentieth century, Leicester M.A. dissertation, 1997.

EDWARDS, J.
Brewham Lodge, Somerset: from receivership to sale - highlighting legal matters of the period 1799-1816, Leicester MA dissertation, 1996.

EVERITT, A.M.
Change in the Provinces: the Seventeenth Century, D.E.L.H, Occasional Papers, 2nd ser., 1, Leicester University Press, 1969, 56pp.

The peers and the provinces, *A.H.R.,* XVI, 1968, 60-67.

A royal welcome in 1660, *The Village,* XV, 1960, 69-70, 74.

Social mobility in early modern England, *P.& P.,* XXXIII, 1966, 56-73.

Landscape and Community in England, 1985, 362pp.

Country, county and town: patterns of regional evolution in England, *T.R.H.S.,* 5th ser., 29, 1979, 79-108.

FAITH, R.J.
The class struggle in fourteenth-century England, in R. Samuel, ed. *People's History and Socialist Theory,* 1981.

FINBERG, H.P.R.
Editor, *Gloucestershire Studies,* Leicester University Press, 1957, 304pp.

A sheaf of documents; A Cotswold boundary dispute; A disobedient loyalist; The canons of Cirencester and their physician; Sir Robert Morton's Will, in H.P.R. Finberg, ed. *Gloucestershire Studies,* Leicester University Press, 1957, 114-122.

A second sheaf of documents: John Chamberlayne and the Civil War; Social history in advertisements; Dramatic entertainment at Berkeley, in H.P.R.Finberg, ed. *Gloucestershire Studies,* Leicester University Press, 1957, 184-194.

West-Country Historical Studies, David and Charles, 1969, 232pp.

FINBERG, H.P.R. (with Hoskins, W.G.)
Devonshire Studies, Jonathan Cape, 1952, 470pp.

HEY, D.G.
Yorkshire from A.D.1000, Longman 1986, 343pp.*The Making of South Yorkshire*, Morland, 1979, 160pp.

HOSKINS, W.G.
The Age of Plunder: the England of Henry VIII, 1500-1547, Longmans, 1976, 262pp.

Devon, A New Survey of England, 2, Collins, 1954, 600pp.

Devon and its People, A. Wheaton, 1959. Reprinted, David and Charles, 1968, 175pp.

Essays in Leicestershire History, Liverpool University Press, 1950, 196pp.

The Human Geography of the South West, The George Johnstone Lecture, Seale-Hayne Agricultural College, Newton Abbot, 1968, 14pp.

Old Devon, David and Charles, 1966, 208pp.

Provincial England: Essays in Social and Economic History, Macmillan, 1963, 263pp.

HOSKINS, W.G. (with Finberg, H.P.R.)
Devonshire Studies, Jonathan Cape, 1952, 470pp.

HOSKINS, W.G. (with McKinley, R.A.)
Editors, *The Victoria History of the County of Leicester*, II, Clarendon Press, 1954, 270pp.

Editors, *The Victoria History of the County of Leicester*, III, Oxford University Press, 1955, 338pp.

IREDALE, D.A.
A haughty grocer, *East Anglian Magazine*, 28, 4, 1969, 156-8.

JENKINS, S.C.
West Oxfordshire in the first Civil War 1642-46, *R.W.*, 17, 1984, 11-21.

KAYE, D.
A History of Nottinghamshire, Phillimore, 1987, 128pp.

KISSOCK, J.A.
Village size, shape and the process of desertion in south-east Wales, *Siluria*, 6, 1990, 6-8.

The evidence for the consumption of wine at Llanelen, Gower, *Journal of Wine Research*, 2, 1991, 16.

MALTON, P.N.
The functions and importance of a chartered sanctuary: Beverley minster 1478-1539, Leicester M.A. dissertation, 1985.

McKINLEY, R.A. (with Lee, J.M.)
Editor, *The Victoria History of the County of Leicester*, V, Oxford University Press, 1964, 367pp.

MIDGLEY, L.M.
Editor, *The Victoria History of the County of Stafford*, IV, Oxford University Press, 1958, xxiii + 197pp.

Editor, *The Victoria History of the County of Stafford*, V, Oxford University Press, 1959, xxiii + 199pp.

PAWLEY, S.J.
Sleaford and the Slea, Griffin, 1990.

The Book of Sleaford, Baron Birch, 1996.

PETCHEY, W.J.
Armorial Bearings of the Sovereigns of England, Bedford Square Press, National Council of Social Service, 2nd edn, 1977, 32pp.

THIRSK, J.
Economic Policy and Projects: the Development of a Consumer Society in Early Modern England, Clarendon Press, 1978, 199pp.

Editor, *Land, Church, and People: Essays Presented to Professor H.P.R. Finberg*, A.H.R., XVIII, Supplement, 1970, 204pp.

The Restoration, Longmans, 1976, 205pp.

The Restoration land settlement, *J.Mod.H.*, XXVI, 1954, 315-328.

The sales of royalist land during the Interregnum, *Ec.H.R.*, 2nd ser., V, 1952, 188-207.

Editor, *Seventeenth Century Economic Documents*, Clarendon Press, 1972, 849pp.

L'Inghilterra dalla Restaurazione alla Gloriosa Rivoluzione, in N. Tranfaglia and M. Firbo, ed. *La Storia: I grandi problemi dal Medioevo all'Età Contemoranea*, V, *L'Età Moderna*, 3, *Stati e società* (Utet), 1986, 481-500.

TRINDER, B.S.
A History of Shropshire, Phillimore, 1983, 128pp, 2nd edn., 1998, 160pp.

WARNER, P.
The Basil Brown Papers, *Saxon: Journal of the Sutton Hoo Society*, 50th Anniversary Special Issue, 10, 1989, 1-2.

WICKES, M.J.L.
A History of Huntingdonshire, Phillimore, 1985, 128pp.

A History of Huntingdonshire, Phillimore, 1995, 144pp.

B The Origins of Local Societies

ALDRED, D.H.
Holm Castle, Tewkesbury: the documentary evidence, *Holm Castle Excavations at Windmill Hill, Glos: an Interim Note,* Tewkesbury Borough Council, 1974, 1-2.

Tewkesbury district: a preliminary archaeological survey, Section 2(3), 22-28, Section 4(5), 9-19, *Tewkesbury Archaeological & Architectural Committee,* 1973.

BARROW, V.
The *regio* of the Sunningas: an early Saxon tribal area in the mid-Thames valley, Leicester M.A. dissertation, 1977.

BOURNE, J.M.
Kingstons and *cyninges tuns,* Leicester M.A. dissertation, 1981.

Place-Names of Leicestershire and Rutland, 1st edn., Leicester Libraries and Information Service, 1977, 30pp.

Place-Names of Leicestershire and Rutland, 2nd edn., Leicester Libraries and Information Service, 1981, 80pp.

Some Anglo-Saxon multiple estates, C.V.Phythian-Adams, ed. *The Norman Conquest of Leicestershire and Rutland: a Regional Introduction to Domesday Book,* 1986, 13-16.

Kingston place-naming: an interim report, *J.E.P.N.S.,* 20, 1988, 13-37.

BENNETT, J.
The ecclesiastical topography of the Fenland : the Anglo-Saxon period, Leicester M.A. dissertation, 1994.

CAHILL, N.J.
Conquest and colonisation on the Isle of Wight - the effects of the island's strategic importance on early medieval organisation and settlement, Leicester M.A.dissertation, 1980.

CORCOS, N.J.
Early estates on the Poldens and the origin of settlement at Shapwick, *S.A.N.H.,* 127, 1983, 47-54.

The Shapwick Project, *Newsletter,* Friends of D.E.L.H. 3, 1990.

CHRISTMAS, E.
Longlevens. Parish and Place, Gloucester, 1996.

COURTNEY, P.
The early Saxon fenland: a reconsideration, in *Anglo-Saxon Studies in Archaeology and History*, B.A.R., British ser., 92, 1982, 89-102.The Norman invasion of Gwent: a reassessment, *Journal of Medieval History*, 12, 4, 1986, 297-314.

DOREE, S.G.
Domesday Book and the Origins of Edmonton Hundred, Edmonton Hundred Historical.

DOWNER, S.
Settlement, rank, status and territory in North Worcestershire 8th-11th centuries, Leicester M.A. dissertation, 1996.

DRAYCOTT, C.
The Soke of Peterborough: a study of the early history of Peterborough Abbey and its dependent local settlements, up to the time of the Domesday Survey with special emphasis on the Anglo-Saxon period, Leicester M.A. dissertation, 1991.

EVERITT, A.M.
River and wold: reflections on the historical origin of regions and *pays*, *J.Hist.Geog.*, III, 1977, 1-19.

Place-names and *pays*: the Kentish evidence, *Nomina*, 3, 1979, 95-112.

The wolds once more, *J.Hist.Geog.*, 5, 1979, 67-71.

Continuity and Colonization: the Evolution of Kentish Settlement, Communities, Contexts and Cultures: Leicester studies in English Local History, 1, 1986, 426pp.

FAITH, R.J.
Tidenham, Gloucestershire, and the origins of the manor in England, *Landscape History*, 16, 1994, 39-51.

Hides and Hyde farms, *M.S.R.G. Annual Report*, forthcoming.

FINBERG, H.P.R.
Ancient demesne in Devonshire, *D.C.N.Q.*, XXII, 1943, 178-179.

Anglo-Saxon England to 1042, in H.P.R. Finberg, ed. *The Agrarian History of England and Wales, I, Part II, A.D.43-1042*, Cambridge University Press, 1972, 383-532.

Ayshford and Boehill, *T.D.A.*, CIII, 1971, 19-24.

The bounds of Abbotsham, *D.C.N.Q.*, XXII, 1944, 201-202.

Bounds of the Devon stannaries, *D.C.N.Q.*, XXII, 1942, 121-123.

Childe's tomb, *T.D.A.*, LXXVIII, 1946, 265-280. Reprinted in W.G. Hoskins and H.P.R. Finberg, *Devonshire Studies*. 1952.

Church dedications in Devon, *D.C.N.Q.*, XXIV, 1951, 225-226.

The Devon-Cornwall boundary, *D.C.N.Q.*, XXIII, 1947, 104-107.

A Domesday identification, *D.C.N.Q.*, XXII, 1942, 95.

The Domesday plough-team, *E.H.R*, LXV, 1951, 67-71. Reprinted in H.P.R. Finberg, *Lucerna*, Macmillan, 1964.

The early history of Werrington, *E.H.R.*, LIX, 1944, 237-251. Rewritten as The making of a boundary, in W.G. Hoskins and H.P.R. Finberg, *Devonshire Studies*, 1952; reprinted in H.P.R. Finberg, *Lucerna, 1964.*

The Formation of England, 550-1042, Hart-Davis MacGibbon, 1974, 253pp.

The House of Ordgar and the foundation of Tavistock Abbey, *E.H.R.*, LVIII, 1943, 190-201.

Lucerna: Studies of some Problems in the Early History of England, Macmillan, 1964, 230pp.

Manumissions by Ordgar, *D.C.N.Q.*, XXII, 1942, 135-136.

The place-names of Devon, *D.C.N.Q.*, XXV, 1952, 34-38.

Roman and Saxon Withington: a Study in Continuity, University College of Leiceater D.E.L.H., Occasional Paper, 8, 1955, 40pp. Reprinted Leicester University Press, 1959.

St Patrick at Glastonbury (The O'Donnell Lecture delivered at the University of Oxford, 10 May 1966), *The Irish Ecclesiastical Record*, CVII, 1967, 345-361 (attributed by a printer's error to A.N.E.D. Schofield). Reprinted with corrections and additions in H.P.R. Finberg, *West-Country Historical Studies*, David and Charles, 1969.

St Rumon, *D.C.N.Q.*, XXII, 1946, 331-332.

Editor, *Scandinavian England. Collected Papers by F.T. Wainwright*, Phillimore, 1975, 387pp.

Sherborne, Glastonbury, and the expansion of Wessex, *T.R.H.S.*, 5th ser., III, 1953, 101-124.

Three Anglo-Saxon boundaries, *T.S.A.S.*, LVI, 1957-8, 28-33.

Two Cornish boundaries, *D.C.N.Q.*, XXIX, 1962, 27.

FORD, W.J.
The pattern of settlement in the central region of the Warwickshire Avon, Leicester M.A. thesis, 1973.

Some settlement patterns in the central region of the Warwickshire Avon, *Medieval Settlement,* ed. P.H. Sawyer, 1976, 274-294.

FOX, H.S.A.
The boundary of Uplyme, *T.D.A.*, CII, 1970, 35-47.

The people of the wolds, in English settlement history, in M.Aston, D.Austin and C.Dyer, ed. *The Rural Settlements of Medieval England: Studies Dedicated to Maurice Beresford and John Hurst,* Blackwell, 1989, 77-101.

Editor and introduction, *The Origins of the Midland Village, Papers Prepared for a Discussion Session at the Economic History Society's Annual Conference,* Leicester, April 1992, 106pp.

The agrarian context, in H.S.A.Fox, ed. *The Origins of the Midland Village,* papers prepared for a discussion session at the Economic History Society's annual conference, Leicester, April 1992, 36-72.

Editor, *Seasonal Settlement: Papers Presented to a Meeting of Medieval Settlement Research Group,* Leicester: Vaughan Papers in Adult Education, 39, 1996, 69pp.

Introduction: transhumance and seasonal settlement, in H.S.A.Fox, ed. *Seasonal Settlement: Papers Presented to a Meeting of Medieval Settlement Research Group,* Leicester: Vaughan Papers in Adult Education, 39, 1996, 1-23.

FOX, H.S.A. (with Kissock, J.)
The Leicester A.G.M. and conference, *Medieval Settlement Research Group Annual Report,* 8, 1993, 5-6.

FRIEL, I.
The *regio* of the Hicce: a tribal unit of the Hitchin Area, Leicester M.A. Dissertation, 1978.

HADLEY A.
Hill-tops, *cyninges-tuns* and *wics*: central places and trade in the south-west from Roman to Saxon times, Leicester M.A. Dissertation, 1998.

HAIGH, D.
The evolution of settlement in eastern Cambridgeshire, Leicester M.A. dissertation, 1978.

HAIGH, D. (with Savage, M. and Molyneux, N.A.D.)
A Roman villa at Radford Semele, Warwickshire, *T.B.W.A.S.*, LXXXVIII, 1976-77,
113-117.

HALL, T.
Witchampton: village origins, *P.D.N.H.A.S.*, 115, 1993, pp.121-132.

HART, C.E.
Archaeology in Dean, John Bellows, 1967, 68pp.

HART, Cyril R.
The Early Charters of Essex: the Saxon Period, D.E.L.H. Occasional Papers, 10,
Leicester University Press, 1957, 31pp; revised edn 1971, 55pp.

The Early Charters of Essex: the Norman Period, D.E.L.H. Occasional Papers, 11,
Leicester University Press, 1957, 48pp.

Eadnoth, first abbot of Ramsey, and the foundation of Chatteris and St Ives,
P.Camb.A.S., 56, 7, 1964, 61-7. Revised and reprinted, *ibid.* 77.

Some Dorset charter boundaries, *P.D.N.H.A.S.,* 86, 1965, 159-163.

The Early Charters of Eastern England, Leicester University Press, 1966, 280pp.

The site of *Assandun, H.S.,* 1, 1968, 1-12. Revised and reprinted *ibid.* no. 77.

The hidation of Huntingdonshire, *P.Camb.A.S.*, 61, 1968, 55-66.

Notes on Essex place-names, *J.E.P.N.S.*, 2, 1970, 39-48.

The Ramsey computus, *E.H.R.*, 85, 1970, 29-44.

The Hidation of Northamptonshire, D.E.L.H. Occasional Papers, 2nd ser., 3,
Leicester University Press, 1970, 78pp.

The *Codex Wintoniensis* and the king's *haligdom, A.H.R.* supplement to 18,, 1970,
7-38.

The Early Charters of Essex: the Saxon Period, D.E.L.H. Occasional Papers, 10,
Leicester University Press, 1957, 31pp; revised edn 1971, 55pp.

The Early Charters of Essex: the Norman Period, D.E.L.H. Occasional Papers, 11,
Leicester University Press, 1957, 48pp.

The Tribal Hidage, *T.R.H.S.,* 5th ser., 21, 1971, 133-157.

Shoelands, *J.E.P.N.S.*, 4, 1971-2, 133-157.

Byrhtferth and his manual, *Med.Aev.*, 61, 1972, 95-109.

Danelaw charters and the Glastonbury scriptorium, *D.R.*, 90, 1972, 125-132.

Athelstan 'Half-King' and his family, A-*S.Eng.*, 2, 1973, 115-144.

Hereward 'the Wake', *P.Camb.A.S.*, 65, 1974, 9-15.

The Hidation of Cambridgeshire, D.E.L.H. Occasional Papers, 2nd ser., 6, Leicester University Press, 1974, 67pp.

The Early Charters of Northern England and the North Midlands, Leicester University Press, 1975, 422 pp.

The kingdom of Mercia, in A. Dornier, ed. *Mercian Studies*, Leicester University Press, 1977, 43-61.

The Peterborough region in the tenth century, *N.P.P.*, 6, 1981, 243-45.

The ealdordom of Essex, in K. Neale, ed. *An Essex Tribute: Studies Presented to Frederick Emmison*, Leopard's Head Press, 1987, 57-84.

Oundle: its province and the eight hundreds, *N.P.P.*, 8, 1989-90, 2-23. Revised and reissued in *The Danelaw*.

The Danelaw, Hambledon Press, 1992, 702pp.

Essex in the late tenth century, in J. Cooper, ed. *The Battle of Maldon: Fiction and Fact*, Hambledon Press, 1993, 171-204.

England forever Danish, *British Archaeological News*, n.s. 13, May 1994, 4.

Land tenure in Cambridgeshire on the eve of the Norman Conquest, *P. Camb. A. S.*, 84, 1995, 59-90.

HORTON, M.
An investigation into the 'manor' of Auckland, County Durham. The evolution and structure of a medieval estate, Leicester M.A. dissertation, 1978.

HOSKINS, W.G.
The Anglian and Scandinavian settlements of Leicestershire, *T.L.A.S.*, XVIII, 1935, 110-147.

'Cross' place-names near Silverton, *D.C.N.Q.*, XX, 1939, 184-185.

A Domesday identification (Leigh Barton, Silverton), *D.C.N.Q.*, XXIV, 1950-51, 111-112.

Earthwork in Cruwys Morchard, *D.C.N.Q.*, XXI, 1941, 164-166.

Formation of parishes in Devon, *D.C.N.Q.*, XVII, 1933, 212-214.

Further Notes on the Anglian and Scandinavian settlements of Leicestershire, *T.L.A.S.*, XIX, 1937, 93-111.

The Westward Expansion of Wessex, D.E.L.H. Occasional Papers, 13, Leicester University Press 1960, 44pp.

JENKINS, S.C.
The 969 charter of Witney, *R.W.*, 9, 1980, 13.

KEEP, R.I.
Settlement and territory in east Herefordshire: a study of the complex and dynamic patterns of settlement and territory in east Herefordshire in the Anglo-Saxon and medieval periods, Leicester M.A. dissertation, 1990.

LEWITT, S.M.
Aspects of the evolution of the distribution and pattern of settlement up to the Norman Conquest in the southern part of the rape of Pevensey, Sussex, Leicester M.A. dissertation, 1980.

PAWLEY, S.J.
Lincolnshire coastal villages and the sea, Leicester Ph.D. thesis, 1984.

PHYTHIAN-ADAMS, C.V.
Rutland reconsidered, Ann Dornier, ed. *Mercian Studies*, Leicester University Press, 1977, 63-84.

Continuity, Fields, and Fission: the Making of a Midland Parish, D.E.L.H. Occasional Papers, 3rd ser., 4, Leicester University Press, 1978, 53pp.

The emergence of Rutland and the making of the realm, *Rutland Record*, I, 1980, 5-12.

Editor, *The Norman Conquest of Leicestershire and Rutland: A Regional Introduction to Domesday Book*, Leicestershire Museums, Art Galleries and Records Service, 1986,
51pp, including: Introduction, vii-viii;
Leicestershire and Rutland: Contexts, origins and the Domesday record, 7-11;
Lordship and the patterns of estate fragmentation, 16-18;
Landed Influence on the eve of the Conquest, 18-23;
The House of Leofric, 20;
Who was Hugh de Grandmesnil? a summary of his life, 27;
The sorts and conditions of people, 29-30;
Leicestershire and Rutland in the eleventh century, 1, Introduction: The wealth of the region, 2, Population, settlement and rural economy, 31-38;
Conclusion, 48.

Genesi e primo sviluppa del territorio locali in Inghilterra, *Proposte e Richerche: Economia a Società nella Storia dell' Italia Centrale,* 30, 1993, 19-34.

Genesi e primo sviluppa del territorio locali in Inghilterra, *Alle Originè dei Territorio Locali,* Studi Storici Sammmarinesi Università degli Studi San Marino, 1993, 19-34.

Land of the Cumbrians: a Study in British Provincial Origins, AD 400 - 1120, Scolar Press, 1996, xiv + 207pp.

RAVENSDALE, J.R.
What's in a Name?, *L.H.,* XI, 1975, 357-359.

ROLLINGS, A.
Aspects of Anglo-Saxon history in the East Midlands with special reference to the lower Soar valley, Leicester Ph.D. thesis, 1998.

SHORT, C.D.
Braughing: a possible Saxon estate?, *Hertfordshire's Past,* 23, 1981 8-14.

SLADE, C.F.
The Leicestershire Survey, c. A.D. 1130, University College of Leicester, D.E.L.H. Occasional Papers, 7, 1956, 98pp.

SMITH, R.B.
Blackburnshire: a Study in Early Lancashire History, D.E.L.H. Occasional Papers, 15, Leicester University Press, 1961, 44pp.

THIRSK, J.
The beginning of the village, *A.H.,* VI, 1964, 166-168.

TURNOCK, B.M.
Land use in parts of Leicestershire as revealed in Domesday Book, Leicester M.A. dissertation, 1992.

WAINWRIGHT, J.A.
The evolution of parish and township boundaries on the Yorkshire wolds, Leicester M.A. dissertation, 1993.

WARNER, P.
The Origins of Suffolk, Manchester University Press, 1996.

Seven Wonders From Westhall: the Hidden Past of a Suffolk Parish, Black Bear Press, 1996.

Pre-conquest territorial and administrative organisation in East Suffolk, in D.Hooke, ed. *Anglo-Saxon Settlement,* Basil Blackwell, 1988.

WATSON, A.F.
The manors of Bakewell and Ashford and Domesday Book, *Bakewell Miscellany* (Journal of Bakewell and District Historical Society), Jan. 1976, 6-17.

WEEDON, R.
Howdenshire: early territorial organisation in the East Riding of Yorkshire, Leicester M.A. dissertation, 1987.

C County Society and Government

BARNES, T.G.
The Clerk of the Peace in Caroline Somerset, D.E.L.H. Occasional Papers, 14, Leicester University Press, 1961, 48pp.

BRINDLE, P.
Politics and society in Northamptonshire, 1649-1714, Leicester Ph.D. thesis, 1985.

CHRISTMAS, E.
The affairs of a country gentleman 1780-1790. The Parsons correspondence, *Gloucestershire in the Eighteenth Century*, University of Bristol Dept of Extra Mural Studies, 1966.

COURTNEY, P. (with Courtney, Y.C.)
The Changing Face of Leicester, Alan Sutton, 1995.

EVERITT, A.M.
An account book of the Committee of Kent for 1647-1648, *Kent Records: a Seventeenth-Century Miscellany*, Kent Archaeological Society Records Publication Committee, XVII, 1960, 115-152.

The Community of Kent and the Great Rebellion, 1640-60, Leicester University Press, 1966, 356pp.

The Community of Kent in 1640, *Gen.Mag.*, XIV, 1963, 229-258.

The County Committee of Kent in the Civil War, University College of Leicester, D.E.L.H. Occasional Papers, 9, 1957, 54pp.

The County Community, E.W. Ives, ed. *The English Revolution, 1600-1660*, Edward Arnold, 1968, 48-63.

The Local Community and the Great Rebellion, Historical Association, general ser., 70, 1969, 32pp. Reprinted in K.H.D. Haley, ed. *The Historical Association Book of the Stuarts*, Sidgwick and Jackson, 1973.

Suffolk and the Great Rebellion, 1640-1660, Suffolk Records Society, III, 1960, 144pp.

The Local Community and the Great Rebellion, R.C.Richardson, ed. *The English Civil Wars: Local Aspects*, 1997, 15-36.

FLEMING, D.
Some aspects of the gentry in Jacobean and Caroline Leicestershire, Leicester M.A. dissertation, 1977.

Faction and Civil War in Leicestershire, *T.L.A.S.*, LVII, 1981-2, 26-36.

A country life: the gentry in Stuart Leicestershire, *Leics.H*, 2, 9, 1978-9.

HOSKINS, W.G.
Devonshire gentry in Carolean times, *D.C.N.Q.*, XXII, 1946, 317-327, 353-362; XXIII, 1947-49, 1-10.

JACKSON, A.J.H.
The country house estate economy in decline: East Devon 1870-1939, Leicester M.A. dissertation, 1992.

JOYCE, R.
Intellectual, cultural and religious life in late eighteenth-century Derby, Leicester M.A. dissertation, 1997.

KILBURN, T. (with Milton, A.)
The public context of the trial and execution of Strafford, in J.F.Merritt ed. *The Political World of Thomas Wentworth, Earl of Strafford, 1621-1641*, 230-251.

LORD, E.
The voter's own will: voting patterns in south Derbyshire, 1868-1869, *The East Midland Historian*, Autumn 1995, 19-25.

McKINLEY, R.A.
Political history, 1885-1950, in W.G. Hoskins and R.A. McKinley, ed. *Victoria History of the County of Leicester*, II, Clarendon Press, 1954, 135-145.

MITSON, A.
The Earls of Yarborough - interests and influences, in S.Bennett and N. Bennett, ed. *An Historical Atlas of Lincolnshire,* 62-63.

MOIR, E.A.L.
Sir George Onesiphorus Paul, in H.P.R. Finberg, ed. *Gloucestershire Studies*, Leicester University Press, 1957, 195-225.

The Gloucestershire Association for Parliamentary Reform, 1780, *T.B.G.A.S.*, LXXV, 1956, 171-192.

Local Government in Gloucestershire, 1775-1800, Bristol & Gloucestershire Archaeological Society Records Section, VIII, 1969, 192pp.

The Justices of the Peace, Penguin, 1969, 206pp.

MORRILL, J.S.
The Cheshire Grand Jury, 1625-1659, D.E.L.H. Occasional Papers, 3rd ser., 1, Leicester University Press, 1976, 60pp.

MORTON-THORPE, A.M.
The Gentry of Derbyshire, 1640-1660, Leicester M.A. thesis, 1971.

MOYLAN, P.A.
The Form and Reform of County Government: Kent 1889-1914, D.E.L.H. Occasional Papers, 3rd ser., 3, Leicester University Press, 1978, 97pp.

NAUGHTON, K.S.
The Gentry of Bedfordshire in the Thirteenth and Fourteenth Centuries, D.E.L.H. Occasional Papers, 3rd ser., 2, Leicester University Press, 1976, 92pp.

PETCHEY, W.J.
Country gentry and estates, *Ripon: Some Aspects of its History,* Ripon Civic Society, 1972, 74-86.

POUND, J.F.
Biographies of Suffolk M.P.s, in S.T. Bindoff, ed. *The House of Commons 1509-1558,* 3 vols., Secker and Warburg, 1982.

The emergency services, in C.Wilkins-Jones, ed. *Centenary: A Hundred Years of County Government in Norfolk, 1889-1989*, 1989, 97-121.

REDPATH, C.R.
The Ishams of Lamport and their rôle as Justices of the Peace (1660-1737), Leicester M.A. dissertation, 1998.

REDPATH, F.M.
A Northamptonshire gentry family in the age of watering places, Leicester M.A. dissertation, 1998.

SLATER, D.
Summary justice in Northamptonshire - eighteenth and nineteenth centuries, Leicester M.A. dissertation, 1997.

WOLFE, G.
Keeping the peace: Warwickshire 1630-1700, Leicester M.A. dissertation, 1997.

D Rural Society and Agriculture

1 General

ALLISON, K.J., (with Beresford, M.W., Hurst, J.G., *et al.*)
The Deserted Villages of Oxfordshire, D.E.L.H. Occasional Papers, 17, Leicester
University Press, 1965, 47pp.

The Deserted Villages of Northamptonshire, D.E.L.H. Occasional Papers, 18,
Leicester University Press, 1966, 48pp.

COX, R.C.W.
From Sutton to Epsom: an outline history of five Surrey settlements, *C.N.H.S.S.*, XIII,
Part 5, 1967.

CRACKNELL, B.E.
Canvey Island: the History of a Marshland Community, D.E.L.H. Occasional Papers,
12, Leicester University Press, 1959, 47pp.

EDWARDS, P.R.
Farming in a north Worcestershire parish: Rushock, 1572-1972, Leicester M.A.
dissertation, 1974.

The Horse Trade of Tudor and Stuart England, Phillimore, 1988.

ENGLISH, S.
What is Wychwood?, Private publication, 1973 & 1974, 28pp.

EVERITT, A.M.
Fields, farms, and families: agrarian history in Kent, *A.H.R.,* XXIV, 1976, 149-152.

FINBERG, H.P.R.
Tavistock Abbey: a Study in the Social and Economic History of Devon, Cambridge
University Press, 1951, 320pp.

An Agrarian History of England, *A.H.R.,* IV, 1956, 54-55.

Editorial, *A.H.R.,* I, 1953, 1-3.

Morwell, *T.D.A.*, LXXVIII, 1945, 157-171. Reprinted in W.G. Hoskins and H.P.R.
Finberg, *Devonshire Studies,* Jonathan Cape, 1952, and in H.P.R. Finberg, *West-
Country Historical Studies*, David and Charles, 1969.

Pillas, an extinct grain, *D.C.N.Q.,* XXII, 1944, 226.

Preface, J. Thirsk, ed. *The Agrarian History of England and Wales, IV, 1500-1640*,
Cambridge University Press, 1967, v-vii.

Preface, V.H.T. Skipp and R.P. Hastings, *Discovering Bickenhill,* University of Birmingham Department of Extra-Mural Studies, 1963.

Recent progress in English Agrarian History, *Geografiska Annaler*, XLIII, 1961, 75-79.

Editor, *The Agrarian History of England and Wales, I, Part II, A.D. 43-1042,* Cambridge University Press, 1972, 566pp.

FOX, D.E.
Families, farming and faith: a study of two parishes in North Yorkshire, *c.*1300-1750, Leicester M.Phil. thesis, 1998.

FREEBODY, N.K.
A history of Scraptoft, Leicestershire, Leicester M.A. thesis, 1967.

HART, C.E.
The history of the Forest of Dean as a timber-producing Forest, Leicester Ph.D. thesis, 1964.

Royal Forest: a History of Dean's Woods as Producers of Timber, Clarendon Press, 1966, 367pp.

The Verderers and Forest Laws of Dean, David and Charles, 1973, 208pp.

HAYDON, E.S.
Secular and Divine - A History of Widworthy Parish in East Devon, Marwood, 1997, 154pp.

HEY, D.G.
The parish of Ecclesfield in an era of change, 1672-1851, Leicester M.A. thesis, 1967.

Co-editor, *English Rural Society, 1500-1800: Essays in Honour of Joan Thirsk*, Cambridge University Press, 1990, 384pp.

The Village of Ecclesfield, The Advertiser Press, 1968, 133pp.

Editor, Richard Gough, *The History of Myddle*, Penguin, 1981, 1988, 334pp.

HOSKINS, W.G.
Annals of the parish, *The Listener*, L, 1953, 496-498.

Galby and Frisby, *T.L.A.S.*, XXII, 1945, 173-211. Reprinted in W.G. Hoskins, ed. *Essays in Leicestershire History*, Liverpool University Press, 1950.

The Human Geography of the South-West, Seale-Hayne Agricultural College, 1968.

Editor, *History from the Farm*, Faber, 1970, 141pp.

History of Common Land and Common Rights, App. II, *Royal Commission on Common Lands, Report*, H.M.S.O., 1958, 149-166.

Introduction, W. G. Hoskins, ed. *Studies in Leicestershire Agrarian History, T.L.A.S.*, XXIV, 1949, 11-15.

The Midland Peasant: an Economic and Social History of a Leicestershire Village, Macmillan, 1957, 332pp.

No man's land, *D.C.N.Q.*, XX, 1939, 87.

Regional farming in England, *A.H.R.*, II, 1954, 3-11.

Seven deserted village sites in Leicestershire, *T.L.A.S.*, XXXII, 1956, 38-53. Reprinted in W.G. Hoskins, *Provincial England*, Macmillan, 1963.

Editor, *Studies in Leicestershire Agrarian History, T.L.A.S.*, XXIV, 1949, 186pp.

Wigston Magna lay subsidies, 1327-1599, *T.L.A.S.*, XX, 1939, 55-65.

HOSKINS, W.G. (with Stamp, L.D.)
The Common Lands of England and Wales, Collins, 1963, 366pp.

HOWELL, C.A.H.
Peasant inheritance customs in the Midlands, 1280-1700, J. Goody, J. Thirsk and E.P. Thompson, ed. *Family and Inheritance in Rural Western Europe, 1200-1700*, Cambridge University Press, 1976, 112-155.

Stability and change, 1300-1700: the socio-economic context of the self-perpetuating family farm in England, *J.P.S.* II, iv, 1975, 468-482.

MITSON, A.
Select documentary evidence for the parish of Aylesby, in K. Steedman and M. Foreman, Excavations at Aylesby, South Humbershire, 1994, in *Lincs.H.A.*, 30, 1995, 13-15.

NIX, M.
The Royal William Victualling Yard: an Illustrated History of Naval Victualling in Plymouth, Plymouth City Museums and Plymouth Development Corporation, 1997.

PINKHAM, L.
Starcross, Devon: 'a small creek...noted only for a small fishery of oysters and cockles', Leicester M.A. dissertation, 1986.

REDMONDS, G.
Huddersfield and District under the Stuarts, GR Books, 1985, 54pp.

RIDGARD, J.M.
The social and economic history of Flixton in South Elmham, Suffolk, 1300-1600, Leicester M.A. thesis, 1970.

SMITH, J.R.
Foulness: the History of an Essex Island Parish, Essex Record Office, 1970.

SNELL, K.D.M.
Rural history: towards a new disciplinary incorporation, *Scottish Economic and Social History*, 10, 1990, 127-8.

SNELL, K.D.M. (with Williamson, T. and Bellamy, L.)
Rural History: the prospect before us, *R.H.E.S.C.*, 1, 1, 1990, 1-4.

Defining the rural, *R.H.E.S.C.*, 1, 2, 1990, 143-145.

SPUFFORD, H.M.
A Cambridgeshire Community: Chippenham from Settlement to Enclosure, D.E.L.H. Occasional Papers, 20, Leicester University Press, 1965, 55pp.

SPUFFORD, H.M. (as Clark, H.M.)
Selion size and soil type, *A.H.R.,* VIII, 1960, 91-98.

STANIFORTH, L.
Rural and urban cotton plantations: some reasons for their establishment and the resultant effects upon the Macclesfield hundred of Cheshire (1780-1869), Leicester M.A. dissertation, 1993.

THIRSK, J.
The Agrarian History of Leicestershire, 1540-1950, W.G. Hoskins and R.A. McKinley, ed. *The Victoria History of the County of Leicester*, II, Clarendon Press, 1954, 99-264.

Die Agrargeschichtliche Forschung in England seit 1945: Ein überblick über das Agrarhistorische Schrifttum, *Zeitschrift für Agrargeschichte*, III, i, 1955, 54-65.

English Peasant Farming: the Agrarian History of Lincolnshire from Tudor to Recent Times, Routledge and Kegan Paul, 1957, 350pp.

The common fields, *P.& P.*, XXIX, 1964, 3-25.

The origin of the common fields, *P.& P.*, XXXIII, 1966, 142-147.

Foreword, G.C. Cowling, *The History of Easingwold and the Forest of Galtres*, Huddersfield Advertiser Press, 1967, 13-14.

Enclosure, *The Encyclopaedia Britannica*, 1967, VIII, 361-363.

Field systems of the East Midlands, A.R.H. Baker and R.A. Butlin, ed. *Studies of Field Systems in the British Isles*, Cambridge University Press, 1973, 232-280.

Albrecht Daniel Thaers Stellung unter der zeitgenössischen Agrarschriftstellern Europas, *Albrecht-Daniel-Thaer-Tagung*, Band 5: *Landwirtschaftliche Produktion und Agrarwissenschaften im 19 Jahrhundert*, D.D.R. Akademieder Landwirtschaftswissenschaften, 1978, 35-9.

Saving the medieval farms of Laxton village, *Popular Archaeology*, Feb. 1980, 21.

Foreword and bibliography in W. Abel, *Agricultural Fluctuations in Europe from the 13th to 20th Century*, 1980, ix-x; 351-56.

The rural economy, in *Our Forgotten Past: Seven Centuries of Life on the Land*, Jerome Blum, 1982, 81-108.

Large estates and small holdings in England, P. Gunst and T. Hoffman ed. *Large Estates and Small Holdings in Europe in the Middle Ages and Modern Times*, Budapest, 1982.

Ausländische Wahrnehmungen des englischen Landlebens im 16 und 17 Jahrhundert, *Wolfenbütteler Forschungen*, Band 21, A. Maçzak and H.J. Teuteberg, ed. *Reiseberichte als Quellen europäischer Kulturgeschichte*, 1982, 115-29.

The horticultural revolution: a cautionary note on prices, *Journal of Interdisciplinary History*, XIV, II, 1983, 299-302.

Editor (with Aston, T.H., Cross, P.R. and Dyer, C.), *Social Relations and Ideas: Essays in Honour of R.H. Hilton*, 1983, xiii+337pp.

Plough and pen: agricultural writers in the seventeenth century, in T.H. Aston, *et al. Social Relations and Ideas: Essays in Honour of R.H. Hilton*, 295-318, 1983.

The agrarian landscape: fads and fashions, in S.R.J. Woodell, ed. *The English Landscape, Past, Present and Future*, Wolfson College lectures,1983, Oxford University Press, 1985, 129-47.

The Rural Economy of England, collected essays, 1984, iv+420pp.

Agricultural policy: public debate and legislation, in *The Agrarian History of England and Wales, V, II, 1640-1750, Agrarian Change*, 1985, 298-388

England's Agricultural Regions and Agrarian History, 1500-1750, Studies in Economic and Social History, ed. for the Economic History Society (Macmillan Education), 1987, 77pp.

L'agriculture et les plantes nouvelles en Angleterre aux XVIe
et XVIIe siècles, *Plantes-et-Cultures Nouvelles en Europe occidentale
au Moyen Age et à l'Epoque Moderne,* Flaran, 12, Centre Culturel de
l'Abbaye de Flaran, Auch, 1990, 69-80

Plants of the future. Can past history teach any lessons? P.C.Struik *et al., Plant
Production on the Threshold of a New-Century*, Wageningen, 1994, 57-70.

Alternative Agriculture: a History from the Black Death to the Present Day, Oxford
University Press, 1997, 365pp.

From farming to food: forty years in Lincolnshire history, *Lincs.H.A.,* 32, 1997, 9-11.

WEEDON, R.
Agriculture in the Harborough area, *The Harborough Historian,* Market Harborough
Historical Society, 7, 1988, 19.

Agriculture and farming life in the Harborough area, *ibid.,* 8, 1989, 22-23.

Agriculture and farming life in the farming area, *Common Voice,* 4, 1989, 5.

WILLIAMS, M.I.
The Vale of Glamorgan: an introduction, *Glam.C.M.,* V, 1950, 18-21.

WRIGHT, S.
Kingsthorpe, village or suburb: a study of a Northamptonshire parish 1700-1931,
Leicester M.A. dissertation, 1998.

2   Medieval

COURTNEY, P.
The monastic granges of Leicestershire, *T.L.A.S.,* 56, 1980, 33-45.

A native Welsh medieval settlement: excavations at Beli Bedw, *Bulletin Board of
Celtic Studies*, 38, 1991, 233-56.

DAVIS, D.K.
The Glastonbury manor of Sowy, 1086-1308, Leicester M.A. dissertation, 1993.

DYER, C.
Hanbury: Settlement and Society in a Woodland Landscape, D.E.L.H. Occasional
Papers, 4th ser., 4, Leicester University Press, 1991.

FAITH, R.J.
The peasant land market in Berkshire during the later Middle Ages, Leicester Ph.D.
thesis, 1962. Published as Berkshire:fourteenth and fifteenth centuries, in P.D.A.
Harvey, ed. *The Peasant Land Market in Medieval England*, 1984,

The 'Great Rumour' of 1377 and peasant ideology, in T.H. Aston and R.H. Hilton, ed. *The English Rising of 1381*, 1984, 43-73.

Demesne resources and labour rent on the manors of St Paul's Cathedral 1066-1222, *Ec.H.R.*, 47, 4, 1994, 657-678.

The topography and social structure of a small soke in the middle ages: The Sokens, Essex, *Essex Archaeology and History*, 1997.

The English Peasantry and the Growth of Lordship, Leicester University Press, 1997, 304pp.

FINBERG, H.P.R.
The customs of Stokenham, *D.C.N.Q.*, XXIV, 1950, 69-70. Reprinted in W.G. Hoskins and H.P.R. Finberg, *Devonshire Studies*, Jonathan Cape, 1952, and H.P.R. Finberg, *West-Country Historical Studies*, David and Charles, 1969.

An early reference to the Welsh cattle trade, *A.H.R.*, II, 1954, 12-14.

Illegal fairs, *D.C.N.Q.*, XXII, 1945, 280-281.

The manor of Roborough, *D.C.N.Q.*, XXIII, 1948, 241.

The meaning of Barton, *D.C.N.Q.*, XXIII, 1949, 326-327, 363.

What is a farleu? *D.C.N.Q.*, XXIII, 1948, 133-135. Reprinted in W. G. Hoskins and H.P.R. Finberg, *Devonshire Studies*, Jonathan Cape, 1952, and H.P.R. Finberg, *West-Country Historical Studies*, David and Charles, 1969.

The open field in Devonshire, *Ant.*, XXIII, 1949, 180-187. Enlarged and reprinted in W.G. Hoskins and H.P.R. Finberg, *Devonshire Studies*, Jonathan Cape, 1952, and in H.P.R. Finberg, *West-Country Historical Studies*, David and Charles, 1969.

FOX, H.S.A.
Subdivided fields in South and East Devon, *Transactions and Proceedings of the Torquay Natural History Society*, 16, 1971, 12-17.

Field systems of East and South Devon: Part I, East Devon, *T.D.A.*, CIV, 1972, 81-135.

The study of field systems, *D.H.*, IV, 1972, 3-11.

Outfield cultivation in Devon and Cornwall: re-interpretation, in M. Havinden, ed. *Husbandry and Marketing in the South-West, 1500-1800*, University of Exeter, Papers in Economic History, 8, 1973, 19-38.

The chronology of enclosure and economic development in medieval Devon, *Ec.H.R.* 28, 1975, 181-202.

The origins of the two- and three-field system in England: past conjectures and future research, in M. Kielczewska-Zaleska, ed. *Rural Landscape and Settlement Evolution in Europe*, Polish Academy of Sciences, 1978, 109-118.

Approaches to the adoption of the Midland system, in T.Rowley, ed. *The Origins of Open-Field Agriculture*, Croom Helm, 1981, 64-111.

Some ecological dimensions of medieval field systems, in K. Biddick, ed. *Archaeological Approaches to Medieval Europe*, Kalamazoo: Western Michigan University, Studies in Medieval Culture, 18, 1984, 119-58.

The alleged transformation from two-field to three-field systems in medieval England, *Ec.H.R.*, 39, 1986, 526-48.

Social relations and ecological relationships in agrarian change: an example from medieval and early modern England, *Geografiska Annaler,* 70B, 1988, 105-15.

Peasant families, patterns of settlement and *pays*: transformations in the landscapes of Devon and Cornwall during the later Middle Ages, in N. Higham, ed. *Landscape and Townscape in the South-West*, University of Exeter Press, Exeter Studies in History, 22, 1989, 41-73.

Agriculture and the village (conference report) *A.H.R.*, 37, 1989, 111-2.

The occupation of the land: Devon and Cornwall, in E. Miller, ed. *The Agrarian History of England and Wales, III, 1348-1500,* Cambridge University Press, 1991, 152-74.

Farming practice and techniques: Devon and Cornwall, in E. Miller, ed. *The Agrarian History of England and Wales, III, 1348-1500,* Cambridge University Press, 1991, 303-23.

Tenant farming and tenant farmers: Devon and Cornwall, in E. Miller, ed. *The Agrarian History of England and Wales, III, 1348-1500*, Cambridge University Press,, 1991, 722-43.

Land, labour and people, 1042-1350, *J. Hist.*, 17, 1991, 457-64.

Medieval Dartmoor as seen through its account rolls, in D. Griffiths, ed. *The Archaeology of Dartmoor: Perspectives from the 1990s*, being *Devon Archaeological Society Proceedings*, 52, 1994, 149-71.

The people of Woodbury in the fifteenth century, *D.H.*, 56, 1998, 3-8.

Agriculture and field systems, in P.E. Szarmuch, T. Tuvormina and J.T. Rosenthal, ed. *Medieval England: an Encyclopedia*, Connecticut: Garland Press, 1998, 11-12.

Co-operation between rural communities in medieval England, in P. Sereno, ed. *Proceedings of the Sixteenth Meeting of the Permanent European Conference for the Study of Rural Landscape,* Alessandra: Edizioni dell Orso, forthcoming

Medieval farming and rural settlement, in R.J.P. Kain and W.L.D. Ravenhill, ed. *An Historical Atlas of South-West England,* Exeter University Press, forthcoming.

GARVEN, M.
Change or continuity? An evaluation of the economy and society of Suffolk through nominal and fiscal evidence within the lay subsidy rolls of 1327 and 1524, Leicester M.A. dissertation, 1993.

HALLAM, H.E.
The New Lands of Elloe, University College of Leicester, D.E.L.H. Occasional Papers, 6, 1954, 42pp.

HARRISON, J.D.
The composite manor of Brent, 1189-1307, Leicester M.A. dissertation, 1987.

The composite manor of Brent: a study of a large wetland-edge estate up to 1350, Leicester Ph.D. thesis, 1998.

HART, C.E.
The regard of the forest of Dene in 1282, *De Archaeologische Pers, Netherland,* 1987, 70.

HART, Cyril R.
The early history of Water Newton, Huntingdonshire, *P.Camb.A.S.,* 56-7, 1964, 86-87.

HAYDON, E.S.
Castle Hill at Widworthy, *D.H.,* 50, 1995, 18-23.

HOSKINS, W.G.
The meaning of Barton, *D.C.N.Q.,* XXIII, 1947-9, 273-277.

Murder and sudden death in medieval Wigston, *T.L.A.S.,* XXI, 1940, 175-187.

Cadbury and Thorverton subsidies, *D.C.N.Q.,* XX, 1939, 74-76.

Croft Hill, *T.L.A.S.,* XXVI, 1950, 83-92.

The deserted villages of Leicestershire, *T.L.A.S.,* XXII, 1945, 241-265. Revised and reprinted in W.G. Hoskins, ed. *Essays in Leicestershire History,* Liverpool University Press, 1950.

Devon parish notes, *D.C.N.Q.,* XXVI, 1955, 101-102, 132-134.

Devon parish notes, *D.C.N.Q.,* XXVII, 1958, 37-38, 144-149.

Farway subsidies, *D.C.N.Q.*, XX, 1939, 32-34.

The fields of Wigston Magna, *T.L.A.S.*, XIX, 1937, 163-169.

Sheep Farming in Saxon and Medieval England: a Lecture to the Royal Society of Arts, London, 3 Nov. 1955, Department of Education of the International Wool Secretariat, 1955, 16pp.

The lost villages, *A.A. Book of British Villages,* Drive Publications Ltd, 1980, 298-301.

KISSOCK, J.A.
Some recent examples of co-axial field systems in Pembrokeshire, *Bulletin of the Board of Celtic Studies*, 40, 1993, 190-197.

KISSOCK, J.A (with Fox, H.S.A.)
The Leicester AGM and conference on seasonal settlement, *M.S.R.G. Annual Report*, 8, 1993, 5-6.

McHARG, G.
Cell by the sea. The study of the priory of Saint Bees in its religious, economic and cultural setting within the barony of Coupland and Cumbria as a whole, Leicester M.A. dissertation, 1997.

LANGWORTH, P.J.
Glebeland and field systems in Cambridgeshire, Leicester M.A. dissertation, 1992.

McKINLEY, R.A.
The forests of Leicestershire, W.G. Hoskins and R.A. McKinley, ed. *The Victoria History of the County of Leicester*, II, Clarendon Press, 1954, 265-270.

NEWTON, K.C.
The manor of Writtle, Essex, *c.*1086-*c.*1500, Leicester M.A. thesis, 1967.

The Manor of Writtle: the Development of a Royal Manor in Essex, 1086-1500, Phillimore, 1970, 131pp.

Foreword, P.H.Reaney, *Essex,* S.R.Publishers, 1970, v-vii.

PALMER, B.
Landscape, economy and peasant society: the Ramsey manor of Elton 1275-1347, Leicester M.A. dissertation, 1997.

PARKIN, K.
The commercialization of the Cambridgeshire economy, *c.*1300, Leicester M.A. dissertation, 1993.

PARSONS, B.
Status, occupations and land-holding: the emergence of an independent peasantry in the High Weald of East Sussex in the late thirteenth century - the evidence of Ashdown Forest and its region, Leicester M.A. dissertation, 1996.

PAWLEY, S.J.
Lincolnshire coastal villages and the sea, Leicester Ph.D. thesis, 1984.

PITT, J.
Land and people in a late-medieval forest: an investigation of woodland society, Leicester M.A. dissertation, 1994.

POSTLES, D.
The perception of profit before the leasing of demesnes, reprinted from *A.H.R.* in R.H.Parker and B.S.Yamey, ed. *Accounting History, Some British Contributions*, Oxford, 1994, 116-38.

Cleaning the medieval arable, *A.H.R.*, 37, 1989, 130-43.

Brewing and the peasant economy: some manors in late medieval Devon, *R.H.E.S.C.*, 3, 1992, 133-44.

RAVENSDALE, J.R. (with Hall, C.P.)
Editors, *The West Fields of Cambridge*, Cambridge Antiquarian Records Society, III, 1976, 168pp.

THIRSK, J.
General Editor, *The Agrarian History of England and Wales, II, 1042-1350*, Cambridge University Press, 1987, 1086pp.

General Editor, *The Agrarian History of England and Wales, III, 1348-1500*, Cambridge University Press, 1991, 982pp.

THOMPSON, M.G.
The Polden Hill manors of Glastonbury Abbey: land and people *c.*1260 to 1352, Leicester Ph.D. thesis, 1997.

THORNTON, C.
The demesne of Rimpton 938 to 1412: a study in economic development, Leicester Ph.D. thesis, 1989.

The determinants of land productivity on the Bishop of Winchester's demesne of Rimpton, 1208-1403, in B.M.S. Campbell and M. Overton, ed. *Land, Labour and Livestock: Historical Studies in European Agricultural Productivity*, Manchester University Press, 1991, 183-210.

Efficiency in medieval livestock farming: the fertility and mortality of herds and flocks at Rimpton, Somerset, 1208-1349, in P.R.Coss and S.D.Lloyd, ed. *Thirteenth Century England IV: Proceedings of the Newcastle upon Tyne Conference 1991*, The Boydell Press, 1992, 25-46.

3 Early Modern

AUSTIN, J.P.
The leasing of Lord Burghley's Hoddesdon woodlands in 1595, *Hertfordshire's Past*, 41, 1996, 11-21.

CROSSMAN, A.B.
The Buckinghamshire *posse comitatus*, 1798, Leicester M.A. dissertation, 1972.

DAVIES, R.
Community, parish and poverty: Old Swinford, 1660-1730, Leicester Ph.D. thesis, 1987.

EVERITT, A.M.
Farm labourers, in J. Thirsk , ed. *The Agrarian History of England and Wales, IV, 1500-1640,* Cambridge University Press, 1967, 396-465. Reprinted in C. Clay, ed. *Rural Society: Landowners, peasants and labourers 1500-1750*, 1990, 161-245.

The marketing of agricultural produce, in J. Thirsk, ed. *The Agrarian History of England and Wales, IV, 1500-1640,* Cambridge University Press, 1967, 466-592. Reprinted in J. Chartres, ed. *Agricultural Markets and Trade, 1500-1750*, 1990, 15-156.

FARRELL, S.
The chaining of the countryside: an evaluation of parliamentary enclosure with reference to three Northamptonshire parishes, Leicester M.A. dissertation, 1998.

FLEMING, D.
A local market system: Melton Mowbray and the Wreake valley, 1549-1720, Leicester Ph.D. thesis, 1981.

FOX, A.W.
The agrarian economy of six parishes in the Wreake Valley from 1540-1680, Leicester M.A. dissertation, 1997.

FOX, H.S.A.
Outfield cultivation in Devon and Cornwall: a reinterpretation, M. Havinden, ed. *Husbandry and Marketing in the South-West, 1500-1800,* Exeter Papers in Economic History, VIII, University of Exeter, 1973, 19-38.

Editor (with Butlin, R.A.) and introduction to: *Change in the Countryside: Essays on Rural England 1500-1900*, Blackwell and Institute of British Geographers, 1979, 187pp.

The functions of bocage landscapes in Devon and Cornwall between 1500 and 1800, in M.J. Missioner, ed. *Les Bocages: Histoire, Ecologie, Economie*, Institute National de la Recherche Agronomique, 1977, 55-61.

Bocage landscapes in Devon and Cornwall: practices and preferences, 1500-1850, in P.Flatrès, ed. *Paysages Ruraux Européens*, Université de Haut Bretagne, 1979, 297-313.

GOODACRE, J.D.
Lutterworth in the sixteenth and seventeenth centuries: a market town and its area, Leicester Ph.D. thesis, 1978.

The Transformation of a Peasant Economy: Townspeople and Villagers in the Lutterworth Area, 1500-1700, Scolar Press, 1994, 322pp.

HART, Clive R.
Bolsover and its manor, A.D. 1600-1700, Leicester M.A. dissertation, 1985.

HAYDON, E.S.
The parish registers of Widworthy and Offwell, *D.H.*, 1996, 16-21.

HAIGH, B.
A West Riding clothing community: Kirkburton, 1664-1816, Leicester M.A. dissertation, 1973.

HEY, D.G.
An English Rural Community: Myddle under the Tudors and Stuarts, Leicester University Press, 1974, 260pp.

A Shropshire woodland community: Myddle 1524-1701, Leicester Ph.D. thesis, 1971.

Yorkshire and Lancashire; the North-West Midlands, in J. Thirsk, ed. *The Agrarian History of England and Wales, V, I, Regional Farming Systems, 1640-1750*, Cambridge University Press, 59-88, 129-58.

HOSKINS, W.G.
The occupation of land in Devonshire, 1650-1800, *D.C.N.Q.* XXI, 1941, 2-12.

East Devon yeoman, *D.C.N.Q.*, XXI, 1941, 241-248.

The reclamation of waste in Devon, 1550-1800, *Ec.H.R.*, 1st ser., XIII, 1943, 80-92.

The Leicestershire farmer in the seventeenth century, *T.L.A.S.*, XXII, 1945, 33-95. Revised and reprinted in W.G. Hoskins, ed. *Essays in Leicestershire History,* , Liverpool University Press, 1950.

A Devon yeoman in 1648, *D.C.N.Q.*, XXII, 1946, 162-164.

The Leicestershire farmer in the seventeenth century, *Ag.H.*, XXV, 1951, 9-20

English agriculture in the seventeenth and eighteenth centuries, *Relazioni del X Congresso Internazionale di Scienze Storiche, Roma*, V, 1955, 205-226.

Harvest and hunger, *The Listener*, LXXII, 1964, 931-932.

Harvest fluctuations in English economic history, 1480-1619, *A.H.R.*, XII, 1964, 28-47. Reprinted in W.E. Minchinton, ed. *Essays in Agrarian History*, I, David and Charles, 1968, 93-115.

Harvest fluctuations and English economic history, 1620-1759, *A.H.R.* XVI, 1968, 15-31.

IREDALE, D.A.
Canal settlement: a study of the canal settlement at Barnton in Cheshire between 1775 and 1845, Leicester Ph.D. thesis, 1967.

IRONFIELD, C.
The parish of Chipping during the seventeenth century, Leicester M.A. dissertation, 1975.

The parish of Chipping during the seventeenth century, *T.H.L.C.*, CXXVII, 1978, 25-46.

KING, W.
The economic and demographic development of Rossendale *c.*1650-1800, Leicester Ph.D. thesis, 1980.

LAUGHTON, J.
Seventeenth-Century Rainow: the Story of a Cheshire Hill Village, privately printed, 1990.

NEILL, T.M.
Minchinhampton, 1550-1700: a study of a clothing parish, Leicester M.A. dissertation, 1973.

PAUL, E.D. (with Barber, B.J.)
Catherine Chichester and Cardiganshire, 1705-1735, *Cer.*, XI, 1992, 371-384.

PAWLEY, S.J.
Land, labour and the locality: Braunstone and the typology of the closed village, Leicester M.A. dissertation, 1982.

PETFORD, A.J.
Saddleworth: the enclosure of an upland parish, Leicester M.A. dissertation, 1978.

PHYTHIAN-ADAMS, H.V.
Domestic life in Wingham: a study of the probate inventories of a Kentish parish, 1631-1750, Leicester M.A. thesis, 1969.

POSTLES, S.
Barkby: the anatomy of a closed township, 1535-1780, Leicester M.A. thesis, 1980.

POUND, J.F.
Editor, *The Military Survey of 1522 for Babergh Hundred*, Suffolk Records Society, XXVIII, 1986.

Arms and armour in early sixteenth century Suffolk: the military return for Babergh hundred in 1522, *P.S.I.A.*, 36, 1988, 305-8.

The military survey of 1522 for the hundred of West Flegg, in A. Longcroft and K.Joby, ed. *East Anglian Studies: Essays presented to J.C.Barringer on his Retirement*, Centre for East Anglian Studies, 1995, 223-27.

RAVENSDALE, J.R.
Landbeach in 1549: Ket's rebellion in miniature, in L.M. Munby, ed. *East Anglian Studies*, Heffers, 1968, 94-116.

RAYBOULD, W.
Around the gap: an investigation into the character of a group of parishes and the relationship between them in the Northamptonshire uplands at the end of the eighteenth century and the beginning of the nineteenth century, Leicester M.A. dissertation, 1994.

REED, M.A.
Pre-parliamentary enclosure in the East Midlands, *Landscape Studies*, 3, 1982, 59-68.

Pre-parliamentary enclosure in North Buckinghamshire, 1550-1750, *A.H.R.*, 1984, 133-144.

SCHUMER, B.
An Elizabethan survey of North Leigh, Oxfordshire, *Ox.*, XL, 1975, 309-324.

SPUFFORD, H.M.
Rural Cambridgeshire, 1520-1680, Leicester M.A.thesis, 1962.

The significance of the Cambridgeshire hearth tax, *P.Camb. A.S.*, LV, 1962, 53-64.

People, land, and literacy in Cambridgeshire in the sixteenth and seventeenth centuries, Leicester Ph.D. thesis, 1970.

Contrasting Communities: English Villagers in the Sixteenth and Seventeenth Centuries, Cambridge University Press, 1974, 374pp.

Peasant inheritance customs and land distribution in Cambridgeshire from the sixteenth to the eighteenth centuries, in J. Goody, J. Thirsk and E.P. Thompson, ed. *Family and Inheritance: Rural Society in Western Europe, 1200-1800*, Cambridge University Press, 1976, 156-176.

Poverty Portrayed: Gregory King and Eccleshall in Staffordshire in the 1690s, Staffordshire Studies, VII, Keele, 1995, 78pp.

TENNANT, A.J.
Brailes: a feldon community, 1550-1800, Leicester M.Phil. thesis, 1978.

TESTER, C.E.
Halberton 1751-1851: the community of an east Devon parish, Leicester M.A. dissertation, 1975.

THIRSK, J.
The Isle of Axholme before Vermuyden, *A.H.R.*, I, 1953, 16-28.

Fenland Farming in the Sixteenth Century, University College of Leicester, D.E.L.H. Occasional Papers, 3, 1953, 45pp.

Farming in Kesteven, 1540-1640, *Lincolnshire Architectural and Archaeological Society Reports and Papers*, n.s., VI, 1955, 37-53.

Corn Laws down to 1791, *Encyclopaedia Britannica*, 1955, VI, 458-460.

Tudor Enclosures, Historical Association, 1959, 22pp. (Revised edn, 1988.)

Tudor enclosures, *Tochiseidoshigaku* (Tokyo), 2, 2, 1960, 35-43.

Introduction, A.H. Johnson, *The Disappearance of the Small Landowner*, Merlin Press, 1963, v-xiii.

Editor, *The Agrarian History of England and Wales, IV, 1500-1640,* Cambridge University Press, 1967, xl + 919pp, including:
The farming regions of England, 1-112;
Farming techniques, 161-199;
Enclosing and engrossing, 200-255.

Horn and thorn in Staffordshire: the economy of a pastoral county, *N.S.J.F.S.*, IX, 1969, 1-16.

Younger sons in the seventeenth century, *H.*, LIV, 1969, 358-377.

Seventeenth-century agriculture and social change, in J. Thirsk, ed. *Land, Church, and People: Essays Presented to Professor H.P.R. Finberg, A.H.R.,* XVIII, Supplement, 1970, 148-177.

The peasant economy of England in the seventeenth century, *International Colloquium on Peasant Economy before and during the Early Period of the Industrial Revolution,* Biatowieza, 1973, 47-59.

New crops and their diffusion: tobacco-growing in seventeenth-century England, in C.W. Chalklin and M.A. Havinden, ed. *Rural Change and Urban Growth, 1500-1800: Essays in English Regional History in Honour of W.G. Hoskins,* Longman, 1974, 76-103.

Seventeenth-century agriculture and social change, in P.S. Seaver, ed. *Seventeenth-Century England: Society in an Age of Revolution,* New Viewpoints, 1976, 71-110.

Projects for gentlemen, jobs for the poor: mutual aid in the Vale of Tewkesbury, 1600-1630, in P. McGrath and J. Cannon, ed. *Essays in Bristol and Gloucestershire History,* Bristol and Gloucestershire Archaeological Society, 1976, 147-169.

Horses in Early Modern England: for Service, for Pleasure, for Power, University of Reading, Department of History, 1978, 28pp.

Editor *The Agrarian History of England and Wales, V, I, 1640-1750, Regional Farming Systems,* Cambridge University Press, 1984, 480pp, including:
Introduction, xix-xxxi;
The south-west midlands: Warwickshire, Worcestershire, Gloucestershire,and Herefordshire, 159-193.

Editor *The Agrarian History of England and Wales, V, II, 1640-1750, Agrarian Change* Cambridge University Press, 1985, 952pp, including:
Preface, xxvii-viii;
Agricultural policy: public debate and legislation, 298-388;
Agricultural innovations and their diffusion, 533-589.

Patterns of agriculture in seventeenth-century England, *Seventeenth-Century New England: a Conference held by the Colonial Society of Massachusetts,* The Colonial Society of Massachusetts, 1984, 39-54.

English Agrarian History before 1700: Some Current Themes of Research, St Paul's University, Tokyo. Translated into Japanese by Prof. K.Ugawa, 1985, 115pp.

The Englishman's food in the seventeenth century, *Rikkyo Keizaigaki Kenkyu (St Paul's Economic Review),* XXXIX, 2, 1985, 1-18. Translated into Japanese by Prof. K. Ugawa.

Forest, field and garden, in J.F. Andrews, ed. *William Shakespeare: his World, his Work, his Influence,* 1, Charles Scribner and Sons, 1985, 257-67.

Raleigh's England, *Raleigh and Quinn: the Explorer and his Boswell,* paper presented to the International Sir Walter Raleigh Conference, North Carolina Society inc., 1987, 35-49.

Tudor Enclosures, 2nd revised edn, Historical Association, general series, 41, 1988, 24pp.

English rural communities: structures, regularities, and change in the sixteenth and seventeenth centuries, in Brian Short, ed. *The English Rural Community: Image and Analysis*, Cambridge University Press, 1992, 44-61.

Making a fresh start: sixteenth-century agriculture and the classical inspiration, in M. Leslie and T. Raylor, ed. *Culture and Cultivation in Early Modern England,* Leicester University Press, 1992, 15-34.

Agrarian problems and the English revolution, in R.C. Richardson, ed. *Town and Countryside, The English Revolution,* Manchester University Press, 1992, 169-97.

WARREN, P.
The agrarian economy of South Walsham, *c.*1566-1774, Leicester M.A dissertation, 1982.

WATKINSON, M.A.
Population change and agrarian development, the parishes of Bradley, Scartho and Humberston, South Humberside, c.1520-1730, Leicester M.Phil. thesis, 1985.

WATKINSON, M.A. (with Ambler, R.W.)
The agrarian problem in sixteenth-century Lincolnshire: two cases from the Court of Star Chamber, *Lincs.H.A.*, XI, 1976, 13-19.

WEST, F.
The social and economic history of the east fen village of Wrangle, 1603-1837, Leicester Ph.D. thesis, 1967.

WICKES, M.J.L.
Oliver Cromwell and the Drainage of the Fens, Cambridgeshire County Council, 1981, 9pp.

WILCOX, P.
Enclosure in Leicestershire: the case of three villages enclosed between 1652 and 1780, Leicester M.A. dissertation, 1998.

WILLIAMS, M.I.
Agriculture and society in Glamorgan, 1660-1760, Leicester Ph.D. thesis, 1967.

A Cardiganshire will: a mirror of life in the parish of Henfynyw, *c.*1656, *Cer.*, IV, 1961, 202-204.

The economic and social history of Glamorgan, 1660-1760, in Glanmor Williams, ed. *Glamorgan County History, IV, Early Modern Glamorgan*, 1974, 311-373.

A general view of agriculture and life in Glamorgan, 1660-1670, *Journal of the Royal Welsh Agricultural Society,* XXX, 1961, 67-78.

Life in seventeenth-century Carmarthenshire, *Carm.H.*, XIV, 1977, 5-19.

Some aspects of the economic and social life of the southern region of Glamorgan, 1600-1800, *Morgannwg*, III, 1959, 21-40.

Some aspects of Glamorgan farming in pre-industrial days, *Glam.H.*, II, 1965, 174-185.

WILLIAMS, N.K.
The levies of the constables - the account for Wymeswold, Leicestershire 1602-1668, Leicester M.A. dissertation, 1986.

4 Modern

ALDERSON, J.
A study of the landscape and population of the parish of Coleorton in North-West Leicestershire, Leicester M.A. dissertation, 1998.

ALDRED, D.H.
Lifeblood of the villages, *G.A.L.*, Oct., 1978, 26-28.

When Cleeve ceased to be common, *G.A.L.*, Oct. 1977, 66-69.

ALI, L.S.
The social and economic history of the Hope valley from the mid- to the late-nineteenth century, Leicester M.A. dissertation, 1991.

BONSALL, M.
The land tax evidence for South Derbyshire in 1793-1830, Leicester M.A. dissertation, 1981.

BROWN, M.
Aspects of parliamentary enclosure in Nottinghamshire, Leicester Ph.D. thesis, 1994.

BUTLER, S.P.
Contrasting rural communities in mid-nineteenth century Leicestershire, Leicester M.A. dissertation, 1977.

CAFFYN, S.
Social structure in mid-nineteenth century Newick, *Sussex Archaeological Collections*, 125, 1987, 155-174.

CARPENTER, R.
Peasants and stockingers - socio-economic change in Guthlaxton Hundred, Leicestershire 1700-1851, Leicester Ph.D. thesis, 1993.

CARTER, R.A.
Aspects of the economic history of Kirkburton (Yorkshire) in the nineteenth century, Leicester M.A. dissertation, 1975.

COOPER, T.D.C.
Enclosure and the creation of isolated farmsteads in Rutland 1781-1887, Leicester M.A. dissertation, 1983.

CORDLE, C.
The culture of the hop: Wealden Kent, 1830-1996, Leicester M.A. dissertation, 1997.

CUMMINS, H.A.
Higher Walton: an industrial community, 1851-1871, Leicester M.A. dissertation, 1985.

DAVEY, B.J.
Ashwell 1830-1914: the Decline of a Village Community, D.E.L.H. Occasional Papers, 3rd ser., 5, Leicester University Press, 1980.

DEBNEY, C.
A village community, Greetham, *c.*1840-1871, Leicester M.A. dissertation, 1981.

DE CLERCQ, P.
A Leicestershire framework knitters' community: Earl Shilton 1845-1871, Leicester M.A. dissertation, 1979.

DEXTER, J.
Custom, protest and self-help in mining communities of North-East Somerset, 1750-1930, Leicester, M.Phil thesis, 1998.

DOREE, S.G.
Amwell and Stanstead's Past in Pictures, 1997, 184pp.

EDWARDS, E.J.M.
The agricultural societies of the upper Eden valley, 1840-1900, Leicester M.A. dissertation, 1975.

EVERITT, A.M.
Transformation and Tradition: Aspects of the Victorian Countryside (The Second Helen Sutermeister Memorial Lecture, University of East Anglia, 1982), 1984, 33pp.

Past and present in the Victorian countryside, *A.H.R.,* 31, 1983, 156-169.

FOX, H.S.A.
Editor (with R.A. Butlin) and introduction to, *Change in the Countryside: Essays on Rural England 1500-1900*, Blackwell and Institute of British Geographers, 1979, 187pp.

Local farmers' associations and the circulation of agricultural information in nineteenth-century England, *ibid.*, 43-63.

GOODWIN, D.
The relationship between landlord and tenant in nineteenth-century North Wales, Leicester M.A. dissertation, 1993.

HALL, J.L.
'Let agriculture flourish': the diffusion of new ideas among agricultural improvers in Richmondshire 1815-1870, Leicester M.A. dissertation, 1979.

HAYDON, E.S.
Recording history for the future: Widworthy occupations in 1992, *D.C.N.Q.*, XXXVII, Pt. III, 1993, 87-90.

Observations on the reconstitution of farms in Widworthy, *c.*1840, *D.H.*, 48, 1994, 3-8.

Aspects of the house repopulation of the village of Wilmington, *circa* 1840, *D.H.*, 49, 1994, 11-18.

Employment patterns in East Devon parishes in the nineteenth century, *T.D.A.*, 126, 1994, 167-180.

HEY, D.G.
The 1801 crop returns for South Yorkshire, *Y.A.J.*, XLII, 1971, 455-464.

HOSKINS, W.G.
The Leicestershire crop returns of 1801, W.G. Hoskins, ed. *Studies in Leicestershire Agrarian History, T.L.A.S.*, XXIV, 1949, 127-153.

HUNT, I.D.J.
A change of direction: for the rural economy of North-West Leicestershire, 1791-1841, Leicester M.A. dissertation, 1997.

JENKINS, S.C.
West Oxfordshire at war, *R.W.*, V, 1978, 8-13.

LEWITT, G.
'The last bastion'. Agriculture and landownership in Medbourne in the eighteenth and nineteenth centuries, Leicester M.A. dissertation, 1985.

LORD, E.
In love and war: episodes in the life of a country gentleman, *Arch.*, 89, 1993, 42-47.

The Friendly Society movement and the respectability of the rural working class, *R.H.E.S.C.*, 8, 1997, 165-173.

MOIR, J.
'A world unto themselves'?: squatter settlements in Herefordshire, 1780-1880, Leicester Ph.D. thesis, 1991.

PHELAN, L.
Commoning in the New Forest in the nineteenth century, Leicester M.A. dissertation, 1993.

SNELL, K.D.M.
Editor, Alexander Somerville, *The Whistler at the Plough: Containing Travels, Statistics and Descriptions of Scenery and Agricultural Customs in Most Parts of England*, Merlin Press, 1989, 438 pp.

Agrarian histories and our rural past, *J.Hist.Geog.*, 1991, 195-203.

Deferential bitterness: the social outlook of the rural proletariat in eighteenth- and nineteenth-century England and Wales, in Michael Bush, ed. *Social Orders and Social Classes in Europe since 1500: Studies in Social Stratification*, London, 1992, 158-184.

Annals of the Labouring Poor: Social Change and Agrarian England, 1660-1900, Cambridge University Press, 1985, i-x and 464 pp. 2nd edn, 1987. 3rd edn, 1993. 4th edn, 1995.

The standard of living and agrarian social change in northern England, *c.*1660-1870, *Industry, the Economy and the Environment Research Development Group Inheritance Paper,* E.S.R.C., London, 1988.

STEDMAN, J.O.
Tangmere Village Day & D-Day Commemoration, 1944-1994, Souvenir Program, Tangmere, 1994, 16pp.

THIRSK, J.
Agricultural conditions in England, *c.*1680, in R.S. Dunn and M.M. Dunn, ed. *The World of William Penn*, University of Pennsylvania Press, 1986, 87-97.

General Editor, *The Agrarian History of England and Wales, VI, 1750-1850*, Cambridge University Press 1989, 1214pp.

Preface to Adrian Hall, *Fenland Worker-Peasants. The Economy of Smallholders at Rippingale, Lincolnshire, 1791-1871,* A.H.R. Supplement, I, 1992.

THIRSK, J. (with Imray, J.)
Suffolk Farming in the Nineteenth Century, Suffolk Records Society, I, 1958, 17pp.

TRANTER, E.M. (with Smalley, Y.)
Change in a Derbyshire Village: Weston on Trent, 1900-1950, Weston on Trent Local History Society, 1996, 60pp.

Editor, Barbara Hutton, *Houses and Everyday Life in Weston on Trent,* Weston on Trent Local History Society, 1994, 40pp.

E Industry and Trade

AUSTIN, J.P.
The return of the charcoal burners: an old craft revived, *Hertfordshire Countryside,* 1991, 46, 29.

BABINGTON, I.
The hand-made nail industry of the Black Country: a study of an occupational culture,. Leicester M.A. dissertation, 1994.

BATES, D.
Northampton's first steam engine: an early case of industrial pollution, *N.P.P.,* VIII, 4, 1992-3, 297-298

Cotton-spinning in Northampton: Edward Cave's mill, 1742-1761, *N.P.P., IX,* 3, 1996-7, 237-251.

Cotton-spinning in Northampton: the Gibson & Forbes mill, 1785-1806, *N.P.P.,* 51, 1998.

BROOKER, J.
Prosperity and decline in fourteenth-century Hertfordshire: an evaluation of commerce, mobility and wealth distribution, Leicester M.A. dissertation, 1992.

COOPER, A.W.
Hawton Bleachworks & Linen Manufactory, 1841-1851, *N.A.L.H.S.N.,* XL, 1972, 2.
Newark, 1830-1901, Leicester M.A. dissertation, 1969.

COURTNEY, P.
Documentary evidence for post-medieval potters in Gwent, *Medieval and Later Pottery in Wales,* 4, 1981, 89-91.

A non-ferrous industrial complex at Tintern Abbey, *Historical Metallurgy,* 1982, 22-24.

The windmills of Gwent, *Monmouthshire Antiquary,* 1982, 37-39.

The medieval pottery in excavations at Pen-y-coed, *Carm. Ant.,* 1983, 104.

Two early-modern pottery groups from Tintern, *Medieval and Later Pottery in Wales,* 8, 1984, 70-78.

An Elizabethan potter in Haverfordwest?, 78-80; Exotic imports and other ceramic finds from the Gwent Levels, 23-30; Documentary evidence for the Gwehelog pottery industry, 71-3; Modelled Cistercian ware from Tintern Abbey, 68-9; Medieval pottery from the National Provincial Bank, Newport, 16-22; Imported ceramics and glass in 16th century Beaumaris, 31-3; Documentary evidence for the use of vessel glass and ceramics in two great houses: Tredegar Court, Gwent and Chirk Castle, Clwyd, 7-15, *Medieval and Later Pottery in Wales*, 9, 1986-7.

The medieval pottery of the border counties: an overview, *Newsletter,* West Midlands Medieval Pottery Research Group, 1986, 6-10.

Documentary evidence for the use of ceramics and glass in the Wynn of Gwydir Papers, *Medieval and Later Pottery in Wales*, 10, 1988, 65-8.

The pottery, small finds, coins and industrial debris, in J. Manley, Excavations at Clydemutha (Rhuddlan), in *Med. Arch.*, 32, 1988, 27-37.

Small-arms accessories of the seventeenth century, in *Small Finds Research Group Datasheet*, 1988.

The medieval pottery; The medieval and post-medieval metalwork and worked bone; The weapons, in P. Ellis, ed. *Excavations at Beeston Castle, Cheshire 1969-85*, English Heritage Monograph, 1993, 134-60 and 180-1.

The medieval pottery; The small finds and industrial debris, in J. Manley, Excavations at Caergwrle Castle, *Med. Arch.*, 38, 1994, 110-8.

The pottery, in K. Blockley, Langstone Castle motte: excavations by L. Alcock in 1964, *Archaeology in Wales*, 34, 1994, 21-2.

A twelfth century candlestick foot and other finds, in W. Britnell, Excavations and recording at Penant Melangell church, *Montgomeryshire Collections*, 82, 1994, 86-9.

The medieval and post-medieval pottery, in Excavations at Belmont Rd., Hay-on-Wye, *Brycheiniog*, 27, 1994-5, 35-7.

The ironwork, in R.Newman and P.Wilkinson, ed. Excavations at Llamnaes: a deserted Glamorgan farmstead, *P.- Med. Arch.*, 30, 1996, 211-5.

Evidence for glass manufacturing, in C.Cumberpatch, ed. *Excavations in Bawtry, South Yorkshire: an Inland Port*, Oxford, 1996, 64-6.

Medieval and post-medieval finds from field-walking, in A.G. Gibson, Survey in the Walton Basin (Radnor Valley), Powys, *Transactions of the Radnor Society*, 67, 1997, 30-33.

COURTNEY, P. (with Jones, N.)
The pottery, in Excavations in Orchard St., Montgomery by J. Britnell, *Montgomeryshire Collections*, 77, 1989. 64-71.

Some new light on the Gwent iron industry in the seventeenth century, *Monmouthshire Antiquary*, 7, 1991, 65-70.

COURTNEY, P. (with Locock, M. and Sell, S.)
The finds, in M. Locock, Excavations behind Bank St., Chepstow 1994, *Monmouthshire Antiquary*, 11, 1995, 67-70.

COURTNEY, P. (with Sell, S. and Compton, J.)
The finds, in M. Locock, Bethel Square, Brecon: excavations in the medieval town, *Brycheiniog*, 28, 1995-6, 57-65.

CROMPTON, J.
The 1893 lock-out, *Five Arches*, 16, 17-20.

The mines rescue service, *Five Arches*, 17, 1993, 8-9.

125 years of the Radstock Co-operative Society, *Five Arches*, 18, 8-9.

Smoking can seriously damage your health (Mackintosh Pit explosion, 1869), *Five Arches*, 19, 1994, 12.

CROUCH, P.J.
Cheese-making in East Leicestershire 1610-1911: the genesis of Stilton cheese, Leicester M.A. dissertation, 1988.

DAVENPORT, C.
Daventry's craft companies 1590-1675, Leicester M.A. dissertation, 1998.

EDWARDS, H.
Follow the Banner: an Illustrated Catalogue of the Northumberland Miners' Banners, Mid Northumberland Arts Group and Carcanet Press, 1998, 49pp.

EDWARDS, P.R.
The horse trade of the Midlands in the seventeenth century, *A.H.R.*, 27, 1979, 90-109.

ELLIOTT, B.
John Foster of Woolley: an early eighteenth-century coalmaster, *S.Y.H.*, III, 1976, 18-21.

FOX, H.S.A.
Medieval rural industry, in R.J.P.Kain and W.L.D.Ravenhill, ed. *An Historical Atlas of South-West England*, University of Exeter Press, 1998.

The millstone makers of medieval Dartmoor, *D.C.N.Q.*, 37, 1994, 153-7.

Fishing in Cockington documents, in T.Gray, ed. *Devon Documents in Honour of Mrs Margery Rowe*, *D.C.N.Q.*, 1996, 76-82.

FINBERG, H.P.R.
The stannary of Tavistock, *T.D.A.*, LXXXI, 1949, 154-184.

An unrecorded stannary parliament, *T.D.A.*, LXXXII, 1950, 295-310.

FLETCHER, S.M. (with Goodwin, D.)
Watercress growing in Hampshire: a forgotten industry?, *Southampton University Archaeology Group Journal*, 1, Nov. 1992, 15-21.

GLASSON, M.O.J.
Stitching and Skiving: a History of Walsall's Women Leather-workers, Walsall M.B.C., 1991.

Leather Bibliography: Sources for the History of Leatherworking and Leather Crafts, Walsall M.B.C., 1993.

The Origins and Early History of the Walsall Leather Trades, Walsall M.B.C., 1997.

GOODACRE, J.D.
Swannington coal-master seeks capital: Gabriel Holland in 1760, *Leics.H.*, III, i, 1983, 5-12.

GRAHAM, M.
Oxfordshire at Work in Old Photographs, Alan Sutton Publishing, 1991.

GREENFIELD, E.M.
The social and economic effects of the decline of lead mining on villages in North Derbyshire, 1851-1891, Leicester M.A. dissertation, 1996.

HAMMOND, C.
Aspects of the occupational structures of four villages in South Nottinghamshire 1851-1871, Leicester M.A. dissertation, 1998.

HART, C.E.
Charcoal-burning in the Royal Forest of Dean, *History of Metallurgy Bulletin*, II, 1968, 7-15.

The Industrial History of Dean: with an Introduction to its Industrial Archaeology, David and Charles, 1971, 466pp.

A résumé of the history of the Forest of Dean's ironworking industries, *History of Metallurgy*, II, 1968, 33-39.

HAWKER, K.
'Instructed in the art and mystery', Leicestershire apprentices in Hanoverian and early Victorian times, Leicester M.A. dissertation, 1998.

HEY, D.G.
A dual economy in South Yorkshire, *A.H.R.*, XVII, 1969, 108-119.

The chronology of the onset of industrialisation: the Sheffield region, in M. Palmer, ed. *The Onset of Industrialisation*, Department of Adult Education, University of Nottingham, 1978, 24-27.

The ironworks at Chapeltown, *T.H.A.S.*, X, 1977, 252-259.

The nailmaking background of the Walkers and Booths, *T.H.A.S.*, X, 1971, 31-36.

The Rural Metalworkers of the Sheffield Region: a Study of Rural Industry before the Industrial Revolution, D.E.L.H. Occasional Papers, 2nd ser., 5, Leicester University Press, 1972, 60pp.

Industrial villages, in G.E.Mingay, ed. *The Victorian Countryside*, Routledge & Kegan Paul, 1981, 353-63.

The development of the English toolmaking industry during the seventeenth and eighteenth centuries, in J.M.Gaynor, ed. Eighteenth-century woodworking tools, *Colonial Williamsburg Historical Trades*, III, 1997, 9-22.

HEY, D.G. (with Binfield, C.)
Editor, *Misters to Masters: a History of the Company of Cutlers in Hallamshire*, Oxford University Press, 1997, 341pp.

HOSKINS, W.G.
Devonshire trade in the early eighteenth century, *D.C.N.Q.*, XX, 1939, 151-154.

Woollen industry, *D.C.N.Q.*, XV, 1929, 154.

INGLESANT, D.
Retailing furniture 1850-1950, Leicester M.A. dissertation, 1996.

IREDALE, D.A.
A haughty grocer, *East Anglian Magazine*, 1969, 156-158.

John & Thomas Marshall and the Society for Improving the British Salt Trade: an example of trade regulation, *Ec.H.R.*, 2nd ser., XX, 1967, 79-83.

The rise and fall of the Marshalls of Northwich, salt proprietors: a saga of the industrial era in Cheshire, 1720-1917, *T.H.L.C.*, CXVII, 1965, 59-82.

Industry, trade and people since 1700, W.B. Stephens, ed. *A History of Congleton*, Manchester University Press, 1970, 121-200.

Herman Eugen Falk (1820-1898), salt manufacturer, in *Dictionary of Business Biography*, London, 1985-7.

H.E.Falk, salt manufacturer, in *New Dictionary of National Bibliography*, Oxford, forthcoming.

JAMES, T.M.
The walnut trade in Croydon, *S.A.C.*, 67, 1970, 132-3.

The English provincial inn, *Clio*, 2, 1970, 33-36.

The Surrey walnut trade, *C.N.H.S.S. Proceedings*, 17, 9, 1979, 348-52.

JENKINS, S.C.
Clinch's brewery & Witney inns & taverns, *R.W.*, 7, 1980, 13.

The gentry and industrial development in Witney: a reappraisal, *R.W.*, 19, 1985, 3-8.

KELLEY, J.W.
The medieval markets and fairs of Leicestershire, Leicester M.A. dissertation, 1986.

KISSOCK, J.A.
A roulette-decorated Monnow Valley ware jug from Llanelen, Gower, *Medieval and Later Pottery in Wales*, 14, 1993-4, 9-13.

McKINLEY, R.A.
Industries of Leicestershire: mining, quarrying, banking, W.G. Hoskins and R.A. McKinley, ed. *The Victoria History of the County of Leicester*, III, Oxford University Press, 1955, 30-46, 50-56.

McKINLEY, R.A. (with Fagg, J.J.)
The extractive industries, N. Pye, ed. *Leicester and its Region*, Leicester University Press, 1972, 340-362.

MITCHELL, J.W.
Ruddle's Langham brewery, *Rutland Record*, 5, 1985, 172-180.

MOIR, E.A.L.
Benedict Webb, clothier, *Ec.H.R.*, 2nd ser., X, 1957, 256-264.

Cloth mills of the Stroud valley, *H.T.*, IX, 1959, 319-325.

The gentlemen clothiers: a study of the organization of the Gloucestershire cloth industry, 1750-1835, H.P.R. Finberg, ed. *Gloucestershire Studies*, Leicester University Press, 1957, 225-266.

The Industrial Revolution: a romantic view, *H.T.*, IX, 1959, 589-597.

Marling and Evans, King's Stanley and Ebley mills, Gloucestershire, *T.H.*, II, 1971, 28-56.

MOORE, M.
Stone quarrying in the Isle of Purbeck: an oral history, Leicester M.A. dissertation, 1992.

MORRIS, S.G.
An investigation into an early industrial neighbourhood - its status and its nature [Sheffield], Leicester M.A. dissertation, 1987.

NIX, M.
The maritime history of Bideford and Barnstaple, 1786-1841, Leicester Ph.D. thesis, 1991.

The timber crisis of 1809 and the North Devon shipbuilding industry, *D.H.*, 49, October 1994, 28-31.

Aspects of North Devon's timber trade, 1780-1830, *D.H.*, 51, October 1995, 3-9.

North Devon's Irish wool trade, *North Devon Heritage*, 8, 1996, 16-19.

The export trade in North Devon earthenware, 1780-1840, *D.H.*, 53, October 1996, 4-10.

PAWLEY, S.J.
Domesday watermills in Lincolnshire; Medieval maritime trade and fishing; Medieval trade and fishing 1500-1700, in S. Bennett & N. Bennett, ed. *An Historical Atlas of Lincolnshire*, Hull University Press, 1993, 44-45, 56-57, 58-59.

RAVENSDALE, J.R.
The china clay labourers' union, *H.S.*, I, 1968, 51-62.

The 1913 china clay strike and the workers' union, J.H. Porter, ed. *Provincial Labour History*, Exeter Papers in Economic History, 6, University of Exeter, 1972, 73pp.

REED, M.A.
Markets and fairs in medieval Buckinghamshire, *Records of Bucks*, 20, 1981 for 1978, 563-585.

RHODES, J.N.
The London Lead Company in North Wales, 1693-1792, Leicester Ph.D. thesis, 1970.

SMITH, H.B.
Communities of butchers and tanners of the Borough of Leicester, 1520-1640, Leicester M.A. dissertation, 1992.

SNELL, K.D.M.
The apprenticeship system in British history: the fragmentation of a cultural institution, *History of Education*, 25, 4 1996, 303-321.

SNELL, K.D.M. (with Houston, R.)
Proto-industrialisation? Cottage industry, social change and the Industrial Revolution, *Historical Journal,* 27, 1984, 473-492.

SPUFFORD, H.M.
*The Great Reclothing of Rural England: Petty Chapmen and their Wares in the
Seventeenth Century*, Hambledon, 1984, 258pp.

Buying and selling, in L.M. Smith, ed. *The Making of Britain: 1500-1750*, Macmillan,
1986, 113-25.

THIRSK, J.
Roots of industrial England, in A.R.H.Baker and J.B.Harvey, ed. *Man Made the Land*,
David and Charles, 1973, 93-108.

The fantastical folly of fashion: the English stocking knitting industry, 1500-1700,
N.B. Harte and K.G. Ponting, ed. *Textile History and Economic History*, Manchester
University Press, 1973, 50-73.

Industries in the countryside, F.J. Fisher, ed. *Essays in the Economic and Social
History of Tudor and Stuart England in Honour of Professor R.H. Tawney*,
Cambridge University Press, 1961, 70-88.

Roots of industrial England, *Geog.Mag.*, Aug. 1970, 816-826.

*Economic Policy and Projects: the Development of a Consumer Society in Early
Modern England* (The James Ford Lectures for 1975), Clarendon Press, 1978, 199pp.

Reflections. Luxury trades and consumerism, in R. Fox and A. Turner, ed. *Luxury
Trades and Consumerism in Ancien Régime Paris. Studies in the History of the Skilled
Workforce*, Aldershot, 1998.

TRINDER, B.S.
Industrial conservation and industrial history: reflections on the Ironbridge Gorge
Museum, *H.W.*, II, 1976, 171-176.

Ironbridge: industrial archaeology in England, *Archaeology*, New York, 1980, 44-52.

The Industrial Revolution in Shropshire, 2nd edn, Phillimore, 1981, 308pp.

Industrial archaeology in Britain, *Archaeology*, New York, 1981, 8-16.

*The Most Extraordinary District in the World: Ironbridge and Coalbrookdale: an
Anthology of Visitors' Impressions*, Phillimore, 1977, 126pp., 2nd edn, 1988, 138pp.

The development of the integrated ironworks in the eighteenth century, *Institute of
Metals Handbook*, Institute of Metals, 1988-89, 20-36.

The Darbys of Coalbrookdale, 2nd edn, Phillimore, 1992, 76pp.

Ditherington flax mill - a re-evaluation, *T.H.*, XXIII, 1992, 189-224.

Editor, *The Blackwell Encyclopedia of Industrial Archaeology*, Blackwell, 1992, 964pp.

The archaeology of the British food industry 1660-1960: a preliminary survey, *I.A.R.*, XV, 1993, 119-39.

The archaeology of mills: a review article, *T.H.*, XXV, 1994, 115-19.

Revolutions in the food industry, in L.Trottier, ed. *From Industry to Industrial Heritage*, Canadian Society of Industrial Heritage, 1998, 111-18.

The Industrial Archaeology of Shropshire, Phillimore, 1996, 278pp.

TRINDER, B.S. (with Stratton, M.)
Stanley Mill, Gloucestershire, *P.-Med.Arch.*, XXII, 1988, 68-85.

Industrial England, Batsford/English Heritage, 1997, 128pp.

WALKEY, G.
Occupations as indices of industrialization and social change, St Helens, 1751-1840, Leicester M.A. dissertation, 1986.

WHITE, H.J. (with Trudgeon, R.)
Birmingham's gun quarter: a skilled trade in decline, *Oral History*, 11, 2, 1983, 69-83.

WILLIAMS, M.I.
Aberthaw - the port of the Vale, S. Williams and D.Brown, ed. *Saints and Sailing Ships*, Cambridge University Press, 1962, 11-22.

Carmarthenshire's maritime trade in the sixteenth and seventeenth centuries, *Carm.Ant.*, XIV, 1978, 61-70.

F Transport

ALDRED, D.H.
Country carriers, Cheltenham, 1880, *Gloucestershire Community Council Local History Bulletin*, 36, 1977, 8-10.

CLARKE, J.S.
Turnpike roads in Shropshire: part of the development of communications in the West Midlands, Leicester M.A. dissertation, 1997.

COX, R.C.W.
The railways that didn't come, *Bourne Society Local History Records*, III, 1964, 31-36.

EDEN, P.
Waterways of the Fens, University Printing House Cambridge, 1972.

EVERITT, A.M.
Country carriers in the nineteenth century, *J.T.H.*, n.s., III, 1976, 179-202.

Town and country in Victorian Leicestershire: the role of the village carrier, A. Everitt, ed. *Perspectives in English Urban History*, Macmillan, 1973, 213-240, 62.

FLETCHER, S.M.
The Melton Mowbray navigation, in S. Fletcher and D.H. Tew, *The Melton Mowbray Navigation and the Oakham Canal*, East Midlands Group of the Railway and Canal Historical Society, 1990, 1-6.

FLETCHER, S.M. (with Miller, M.G.)
The Melton Mowbray Navigation, Railway and Canal Historical Society, 1984.

FRIEL, I.
The documentary evidence for maritime technology in later medieval England and Wales, Keele Ph.D. thesis, 1990. Short form in *The Good Ship: Ships, Shipbuilding and Technology in England 1200-1520*, London, 1995.

Archaeological sources and the medieval ship: some aspects of the evidence, *International Journal of Nautical Archaeology*, XII, 1983, 41-62.

The three-masted ship and Atlantic voyages, in J.Youings, ed. *Raleigh in Exeter 1985: Privateering and Colonisation in the Reign of Elizabeth I*, Exeter, 1985, 21-37.

The building of the Lyme galley, 1294-1296, *P.D.N.H.A.S.*, CVIII, 1986, 41-4.

Henry V's *Grace Dieu* and the wreck in the River Hamble near Bursledon, Hampshire, *International Journal of Nautical Archaeology*, XXII, 1993, 3-19.

Winds of change? Ships and the Hundred Years War, in A.Curry and M.Hughes ed. *Arms, Armies and Fortifications*, Woodbridge, 1994, 183-93.

The carrack: the advent of the full rigged ship, in R.W. Unger, ed. *Cogs, Caravels and Galleons*, Woodbridge, 1994, 77-90.

GOODACRE, J.D.
The new rail roads, or, the delight and pleasure of travelling by hot water, *Leics.H.*, II, x, 1979/80, 26-30.

GRAHAM, M.
Roads around Botley, *Top Oxon*, 21, 1976-7.

Hurry along please! Trams and Buses in Oxfordshire, 1881-1981, Oxfordshire County Council, 1981.

HAMPTON, S.J.S.
Country carriers of West Surrey: a study of the Guildford area, Leicester M.A.
dissertation, 1972.

HARRISON, J.D.
The Somerset and Dorset Railway in Public Archives, Somerset and Dorset Railway
Trust, 1988, 71pp.

The Bridgwater Railway, Oakwood Press, 1990, 96pp.

Celebrations to sources: an investigation into 2-2-2 well tanks of the Bristol and
Exeter Railway, *Historical Model Railway Society Journal,* 14, 1, 1991, 3-9.

Essex plus '91', *Historical Model Railway Society Journal,* 14, 10, 1993, 323.

HEY, D.G.
*Packmen , Carriers and Packhorse Roads: Trade and Communications in North
Derbyshire and South Yorkshire*, Leicester University Press, 1980, 279pp.

HILL, T.G.
From packhorse to railway: changing transport systems from the seventeenth to
nineteenth centuries and their impact upon trade and industry in the Shropshire area,
Leicester Ph.D. thesis, 1998.

JENKINS, S.C.
Victorian Witney and its railway, Leicester M.A. dissertation, 1976.

The Great Western and Great Central Joint Railway, Oakwood Press, 1978, 51pp .

The Witney and East Gloucestershire Railway (Fairford Branch), Oakwood Press,
1975, 52pp.

Witney passenger station, *R.W.*, 4, 1978, 7-8.

Witney country carriers in 1903, *R.W.*, 16, 1983, 4-9.

The River Windrush, *R.W.*, 16, 1983, 11-15.

The Fairfield Branch, Oakwood Press, 1985, 152pp.

The Lynn & Hunstanton Railway, Oakwood Press, 1987, 140pp.

The Woodstock Branch, Wild Swan Press, 1987, 104pp.

The Wells-next-the-Sea Branch, Oakwood Press, 1988, 108pp.

Cromer Branch, Oakwood Press, 1989, 144pp.

The Moretonhampstead & South Devon Railway, Oakwood Press, 1989, 120pp.

The Northampton & Banbury Junction Railway, Oakwood Press, 1990, 112pp.

The Watford to St Albans Branch, Oakwood Press, 1990, 96pp.

The Alston Branch, Oakwood Press, 1991, 120pp.

The Leek to Manifold Railway, Oakwood Press, 1991, 104pp.

The Cork Blackrock & Passage Railways, Oakwood Press, 1991, 104pp.

The Rothbury Branch, Oakwood Press, 1991, 96pp.

The Melton Constable to Cromer Branch, Oakwood Press, 1991, 152pp.

The Helston Branch Railway, Oakwood Press, 1992, 120pp.

The Lynn & Dereham Railway, Oakwood Press, 1993, 176pp.

The Wensleydale Branch: A New History, Oakwood Press, 1993, 192pp.

The Bideford, Westward Ho! and Appledore Railway, Oakwood Press, 1993, 144pp.

The Fairford branch, *R.M.*, XXVII, 1976, 246.

Cromer Beach, *R.M.*, XXVIII, 1977, 116, 118.

Culm Valley, *R.M.*, XXVIII, 1977, 210-211.

The directors, promoters and early years of the Witney Railway, *R.W.*, II, 1977, 13-14.

The Isle of Wight, *R.M.*, XXIX, 1978, 18-19.

The Lakeside branch, *R.M.*, XXVII, 1976, 213.

London Transport, *R.M.*, XXIX, 1978, 114-115.

South Leigh, *R.M.*, XXIX, 1978, 304-305.

Staines West, *R.M.*, XXIX, 1978, 84.

West London link, *Railway Magazine,* April 1982, 168-170.

Rails to Brentford dock, *Railway Magazine,* August 1982, 359-361.

Leamington to Coventry, *Railway Magazine,* October 1982, 438-439.

By LMS to Oxford, *Railway World,* September 1983, 461-485.

The Uxbridge Vine Street branch, *Railway World,* March 1984, 126-127.

The Hunstanton branch, *Railway World*, June 1984, 298-300.

Two Lincolnshire byways, *Railway World*, August 1985, 404-408.

The Shipston-on-Stour branch, *British Railways Journal*, 12, 1986, 112-121.

The Glasson Dock branch, *British Railways Journal*, 16, 1987, 267-274.

The Fawley branch, *Back Track*, 1, 1987, 28-32.

The Cromer branch, *Back Track*, Vol.1, 2, 1987, 78-84.

The St Albans Abbey branch, *British Railways Journal*, 21, 1988, 47-58.

The Falmouth branch, *British Railways Journal*, 27, 1989, 325-339

The Helston branch, *Back Track*, 3, 5, 1989.

The Faringdon branch, *Back Track*, 5, 5, 1991, 225-231.

The West Norfolk branch of the G.E.R., *British Railway Journal*, 35, 1991.

The Lymington branch, *British Railway Journal*, 42 & 43, 1992, 90-102, 158-175.

The St Ives branch, *Great Western Journal* (Special Cornish Issue) 1992, 2-34.

The Marlborough branch, *Great Western Journal*, 6, 1993, 222-239, 260-263.

Uxbridge Vine Street, *Great Western Journal*, 13, 1995, 530-561.

JENKINS, S.C. (with Quayle, H.I.)
The Lakeside and Haverthwaite Railway, Dalesman Publishing Co., 1977, 72pp.

The Oxford, Worcester and Wolverhampton Railway, Oakwood Press, 1977, 128pp.

Branch Lines into the Eighties, David & Charles, 1980, 96pp.

JENKINS, S.C. (with Strange, J.M.)
The Gobowen & Oswestry line, *Great Western Journal*, 22, 1997

JENKINS, S.C. (with Turner, C.J.)
Denham to Uxbridge (High Street), *Great Western Journal*, 1, 1992, 2-20.

The Yealmpton Branch, *Great Western Journal*, 9, 1994, 354-383.

JENKINS, S.C. (with Carpenter, R.S.)
The Shipston-on-Stour Branch, Wild Swan Press, 1997, 106pp.

KAYE, D.
British Battery Electric Buses, Oakwood Press, 1976, 20pp.

Buses and Trolleybuses before 1919, Blandford, 1972, 152pp.

Discovering Old Buses and Trolleybuses, Shire Publications, 1972, 60pp.

KAYE, D. (with Cormack, I.)
Illustrated History of Trams and Trolleybuses, Spur Books, 1977, 160pp.

MORRIS, C.I.
Gloucester Railway Carriage and Wagon Company Ltd, 1860, Gloucester Folk
Museum Information Sheet, 1982.

MOSS, C.A.
The carriers of Nottinghamshire 1834-1936. A study of the growth and decline of the
country carrier and the effects of the change in transport upon the networks, Leicester
M.A. dissertation, 1982.

NIX, M.
The Cruel Coast of North Devon, Badger Books, 1982.

Wreckers galore: the tale of the Johanna, in R.A. Lauder, ed. *An Anthology for North
Devon*, Badger Books, 1983, 10-15.

The Sjofna service, in E.Thompson, ed. *Sea Stories of Devon*, Bossiney Books, 1984,
49-57.

English ship registers: a source for genealogists, *The Genealogical Helper*, May-June
1988, 9-11.

NIX, M. (with Myers, M.)
Guide to the Coast and Shipwrecks: South from Hartland Quay, Hartland Quay
Museum, 1981.

Hartland Quay: the Story of a Vanished Port, Hartland Quay Museum, 1982.

NIX, M. (with Greenhill, B.)
North Devon shipping, trade and ports, 1786-1939, in M. Duffy *et al.*, ed. *The New
Maritime History of Devon*, 2, Conway Maritime Press, 1994, 48-59.

PEBERDY, R.B.
Navigation on the River Thames between London and Oxford in the late Middle
Ages: a reconstruction, *Ox.*, LXI, 1996, 311-340.

REED, M.A.
Kanalen en aquaducten: de binnenlandse waterwegen van Groot-Brittainnie, in
W. Blckmans, ed. *De Mens in Bewegen*, being vol. 10 of *De wording van Europe*,
Hilversum, 1993, 81-92, English edn, 1994.

SCOTT, P.
The railways' influence on place-names in suburbia: Harrow Borough, Leicester
M.Phil. thesis, 1995.

SHERRINGTON, M.
Preston carriers, 1841-1932: from the railway to the motor age, Leicester M.A.
dissertation, 1973.

TRANTER, E.M.
Editor, *By Water, Road and Rail: a History of Transport in Weston on Trent,* Weston
on Trent Local History Society, 1993, 38pp.

Introduction; Before the nineteenth century; Steam comes to Weston; Conclusion,
ibid., 2-9, 21-30, 37.

TRINDER, B.S.
Transport in Shropshire, *The County of Shropshire*, Salop County Council, 1978,
35-36.

The Severn Navigation at Dowles, *T.S.A.S.*, LXIV, 1983-4, 29-34.

WILLIAMS, M.I.
A note on ship-building in Aberystwyth, 1800-1816, *Cer.*, III, 1957, 183-184.

G Urban Societies and Economies

1 General

COURTNEY, P. (with Newman, R.)
Report on an excavation in Union St. Worcester, *Worcestershire Archaeology and
Local History Newsletter,* 32, 1984, 2-5.

EVERITT, A.M.
Editor, *Perspectives in English Urban History*, Macmillan, 1973, 271pp, including
Introduction, 1-15.

FINBERG, H.P.R.
Four articles on Tavistock history, *Tavistock Gazette,* 14 May, 21 May, 28 May, 18
June, 1943.

GENT, F.J.R.
The development of Strangeways, 1768-1868, Leicester M.A. dissertation, 1973.

HART, C.E.
Coleford: the History of a West Gloucestershire Forest Town, Alan Sutton
Publishing, 1983, 573pp.

HART, Clive R.
Bolsover. A Town is Born: its Origins, Change and Continuity, Bolsover District Council, 1998.

HEY, D.G.
Sheffield on the eve of the Industrial Revolution, *T.H.A.S.*, 14, 1987, 1-10.

The post-medieval town, in P.C.Buckland *et al., The Archaeology of Doncaster, 2: the Medieval and Later Town*, B.A.R., British Series 202, 1, 1989, 62-66.

Doncaster people of ten generations ago, in B.Elliott, ed. *Aspects of Doncaster*, Wharncliffe Publishing, 1997, 119-52.

HEY, D.G (with Olive, M. and Liddament, M.)
Foraging the Valley, Sheffield Academic Press, 1993, 143pp.

HILLIER, K.A.
Ashby-de-la-Zouch: the Spa Town, Ashby Museum, 1983, 49pp.

The Book of Ashby-de-la-Zouch, Barracuda Books, 1984, 148pp.

HOSKINS, W.G.
The Heritage of Leicestershire, Edgar Backus, 1946, 88pp.

British towns and cities, IV: Exeter, *H.T.*, I, v, 1951, 28-37.

British towns and cities, VII: Leicester, *H.T.*, I, ix, 1951, 48-56.

Leicester, Eileen Molony, ed. *Portraits of Towns*, Dobson, 1952, 97-107.

Two Thousand Years in Exeter, Townsend & Sons, 1960, 164pp.

JAMES, T.M.
The Falcon Inn, Croydon, *C.N.H.S.S. Archaeology Newsletter*, 25, 1974, 1-2.

Croydon's fairs: some thoughts, *ibid.*, 30, 1975, 3-4.

In pursuit of an archbishop, *C.N.H.S.S. Proceedings*, 16, 2, 1975, 72-4.

The George Inn, Croydon, *C.N.H.S.S. Archaeology Newsletter*, 33, 1976, 1-2.

The Ship at Croydon, *ibid.*, 37, 1977, 3-4.

Additional comment on the Surrey Street excavation (1966) report, *C.N.H.S.S. Arch.*, 54, 1982.

JENKINS, S.C.
Notes on local government in Witney 1600-1978, *R.W.*, 6, 1979, 7.

LORD, E.
Derby Past, Phillimore, 1996, 134pp.

McKINLEY, R.A.
Editor, *The Victoria History of the County of Leicester, IV, The City of Leicester*, Oxford University Press, 1958, xx + 484pp.

Topography [of Leicester], *ibid.*, 338-458.

McKINLEY, R.A. (with Smith, C.T.),
Social and administrative history since 1835, *ibid.*, 251-302.

MIDGLEY, L.M.
Some notes on old Stafford and 'Old Staffordians', *Transactions of the Stafford Historical and Civic Society* for1974-76, 1977, 9-13.

MOSS, S.R.
The community of Towcester, 1750-1842, Leicester M.A. dissertation, 1976.

REDMONDS, G.
The Heirs of Woodsome, and other Essays, GR Books, 1982, 64pp.

SAUNDERS, A.L.
Editor, *The Mercers' Hall*, by J. Imray, The London Topographical Society, 1991, 509pp.

Editor, *The Mercers' Company*, by I.Doolittle, The Mercers' Company, 1994, 248pp.

SHETTLE, M.
The development of fire protection in Surrey 1666-1941 with especial reference to south-west Surrey, Leicester M.A. dissertation, 1990.

SNELL, L.S.
Essays Towards a History of Bewdley, Department of Extra-Mural Studies, University of Birmingham, 1972, 122pp.

SPUFFORD, H.M. (with Spufford, P.)
Eccleshall: the Story of a Staffordshire Market Town and its Dependent Villages, Department of Extra-Mural Studies, University of Keele, 1964, 68pp.

TEALL, D.G.
The corporation and tradesmen of Stamford, 1461-1649 (with an indication of developments until 1750), Leicester Ph.D. thesis, 1975.

THIRSK, J.
Popular consumption and the mass market in the sixteenth to eighteenth centuries, *Material History Bulletin*, National Museum of Science and Technology, Ottawa, Canada, 31, 1990, 51-58.

2 Origins and Medieval

BURGESS, L.A.
The Origins of Southampton, D.E.L.H. Occasional Papers, 16, Leicester University Press, 1964, 31pp.

COURTNEY, P.
The first Welsh mints and the origins of Cardiff, *Morgannwg,* 30, 1986, 65-9.

The Marcher town in medieval Gwent: a study in regional history, *Scottish Archaeological Review*, 1988, 103-9.

Medieval and Later Usk, University of Wales Press, 1994.

EDWARDS, E.
The medieval market town of Solihull - 1200-1580, Leicester M.A. dissertation, 1992.

EVERITT, A.M.
The Banburys of England, *U.H.Y.B.*, 1974, 28-38.

The primary towns of England, *L.H.*, XI, 1975, 263-277.

FINBERG, H.P.R.
The borough of Tavistock: its origin and early history, *T.D.A.*, LXXIX, 1947, 129-153. Reprinted in W.G. Hoskins and H.P.R. Finberg, *Devonshire Studies*, Jonathan Cape, 1952, and H.P.R. Finberg, *West-Country Historical Studies*, David and Charles, 1969.

The boroughs of Devon, *D.C.N.Q.,* XXIV, 1951, 203-209.
The boroughs of Devon, *D.C.N.Q.,* XXVII, 1956, 54-55.

The genesis of the Gloucestershire towns, in H.P.R. Finberg, ed. *Gloucestershire Studies,* Leicester University Press, 1957, 52-88.

The skelving-stool, *D.C.N.Q.,* XXII, 1946, 368-369.

FINBERG, H.P.R. (with Beresford, M.W.)
English Medieval Boroughs: a Hand List, David and Charles, 1973, 200pp.

FOX, H.S.A.
Going to town in thirteenth-century England, *Geog.Mag.*, XLII, 1970, 658-67.
Reprinted in A.R.H. Baker and J.B. Harley, ed. *Man Made the Land*, David and Charles, 1973, and as Development of towns and market places in England, *Ekistics*, XXI, 1971, 47-50.

Medieval towns and town foundation, in R.J.P.Kain and W.L.D.Ravenhill, ed. *An Historical Atlas of South-West England*, University of Exeter Press, forthcoming.

HART, Clive R.
Excavations in Tynemouth, Tyne & Wear, *Archaeologica Aeliana*, XXV, 1995.

HART, Clive R. (with Stetka, J.)
The Burh of Edward the Elder at Bakewell, Derbyshire, Derbyshire Archaeological Journal and Bakewell Historical Society, 1997.

HART, Cyril R.
The early history of Wisbech, *The Wisbech Society 34th Annual Report*, 1973, 8-10.

HOSKINS, W.G.
Chagford and Moreton markets, *D.C.N.Q.*, XXIII, 1947-9, 21-22.

Exeter: the south-western area, *Arch. Jnl.*, CXIV, 1957, 167-171.

The origins and rise of Market Harborough, *T.L.A.S.*, XXV, 1949, 56-68.

LAUGHTON, J.
Prolegomena to a societal history of late-medieval Chester, Leicester M.A. dissertation, 1987.

The alewives of later medieval Chester, in R.E.Archer, ed. *Crown, Government and People in the Fifteenth Century*, Stroud,1995, 191-208.

The port of Chester in the Middle Ages, in P. Carrington, ed. *'Where Deva spreads her wizard stream': Trade and the Port of Chester*, Chester, 1996, 66-71.

MARTIN, G.H.
The Early Court Rolls of the Borough of Ipswich, University College of Leicester, D.E.L.H. Occasional Papers, 5, 1954, 45pp.

NEWTON, K.C.
Thaxted in the Fourteenth Century: an Account of the Manor and Borough, with Translated Texts, Essex County Council, 1960, 108pp.

PEBERDY, R.B.
The economy, society, and government of a small town in late medieval England: a study of Henley-on-Thames from *c.*1300 to *c.*1540, Leicester Ph.D. thesis, 1994.

PETCHEY, W.J.
Ripon market place research: the medieval origins of the ' Marketstead', *The Ripon Historian*, I, VIII, 7-8.

PHYTHIAN-ADAMS, C.V.
Jolly cities: goodly towns: the current search for England's urban roots, *U.H.Y.B.*, 1977, 30-39.

Urban decay in late medieval England, in P. Abrams and E.A. Wrigley, ed. *Towns in Societies: Essays in Economic History and Historical Sociology*, Past and Present Publications, Cambridge University Press, 1978, 159-185.

Dr Dyer's urban undulations, *U.H.Y.B*, 1979, 73-76.

Desolation of a City: Coventry and the Urban Crisis of the Later Middle Ages, Past and Present Publications, Cambridge University Press, 1979, 350pp.

REDMONDS, G.
Settlement in Huddersfield before 1800, in E.A.H. Haigh, ed. *Huddersfield, a Most Handsome Town*, Kirklees Cultural Services, 1992, 17-36.

RICHARDSON, P.
Market vills and the development of boroughs in medieval Suffolk, Leicester M.A. dissertation, 1997.

STEDMAN, J.O.
Portsmouth rebuilt: studying postwar reconstruction, *Local History*, 50, 1995, 16-19.

TRANTER, E.M.
Of cows and churches: reflections on the origin of Derby, *M.S.R.G. Annual Report*, 4, 1989, 21-4.

Burton Abbey holdings and the origins of Derby - a comment, *Derbyshire Miscellany*, XII, III, Spring 1990, 82 -3.

Early medieval settlement: problems, pitfalls and possibilities, *Derbyshire Miscellany*, 12, 1991, 159-163.

WATSON, I.G.
Career and community: a study of the officeholders of the town council of Leicester, 1485-1535, Leicester M.A. dissertation,1988.

WRIGHT, S.J.
A study of the Gild of High Cross, the Blessed Mary and St John the Baptist of Stratford-upon-Avon from 1406 to 1545, Leicester M.A. dissertation, 1978.

3 Early Modern

ALLDRIDGE, N.J.
Hearth and home: a three-dimensional reconstruction, in N.J.Alldridge, ed. *The Hearth Tax: Problems and Possibilities*, C.O.R.A.L., Hull, 1983, 84-105.

Decline with dignity: the case of early modern Chester, *Neuvième Congrès International d'Histoire Economique*, Berne, 1986, 1-23.

Loyalty and identity in Chester parishes, 1540-1640, in S. Wright, ed. *Parish, Church and People: Local Studies in Lay Religion, 1350-1750,* 1988, 85-124.

BERRYMAN, P.A.
The manufacturing crafts in York, 1740-1784, Leicester M.A. dissertation, 1978.

BIRD, S.C.
Watlington 1660-1740 - a market town?, Leicester M.A. dissertation, 1991.

BONE, R.D.
The inns of Leicester in the reign of George III, 1760-1820, Leicester M.A. dissertation, 1976.

The inns of Nottingham, Derby and Leicester, 1720-1820, Leicester M.Phil. thesis, 1986.

BOWEN, P.
The inns and public houses of Birmingham, 1767-1812, Leicester M.A. dissertation, 1978.

CARTER, M.P.
An urban society and its hinterland: St Ives in the seventeenth and early eighteenth centuries, Leicester Ph.D. thesis, 1989.

Town or urban society? St Ives in Huntingdonshire, 1630-1740, in C. Phythian-Adams, ed. *Societies, Cultures and Kinship, 1580-1850,* 1993, 77-130.

COURTNEY, P.
Parliamentarians divided or fear and loathing at the siege of Leicester 1645, *Leics.H.,* 4, 2, 1994, 3-10.

COURTNEY, P. (with Courtney, Y.)
A siege examined: the Civil War archaeology of Leicester, *P.-Med.Arch.,* 26, 1992, 47-89.

EVERITT, A.M.
The English urban inn, 1560-1760, A. Everitt, ed. *Perspectives in English Urban History,* Macmillan, 1973, 91-137.

The food market of the English town, 1660-1760, *Troisième Conférence Internationale d'Histoire Economique, Munich, 1965,* Mouton, 1968, 57-71.

Leicester and its markets: the seventeenth century, A.E. Brown, ed. *The Growth of Leicester,* 1970, 39-45.

The market towns, Peter Clark, ed. *The Early Modern Town: a Reader,* Longman, 1976, 168-204.

Urban growth, 1570-1770, *L.H.,* VIII, 1968, 118-125.

Urban growth and inland trade, 1570-1770: Sources, *L.H.*, VIII, 1969, 196-204.

GOODACRE, J.D.
Lutterworth in the sixteenth and seventeenth centuries: a market town and its area, Leicester Ph.D. thesis, 1977.

The Transformation of a Peasant Economy: Townspeople and Villagers in the Lutterworth Area, 1500-1700, Scolar Press, 1994, 342pp.

The distress of an eighteenth century apothecary: Simon Mason in Market Harborough, *Leics.H.*, II, xi, 1980/1, 11-22.

GREENWOOD, J.J.
Reigate, 1700-1821: its turnpikes and its economy, Leicester M.A. dissertation, 1980.

HALEY, D.
Aspects of the economic history and the demography of the parish of Buckingham, *c*.1560-1710, a preliminary study, Leicester M.A. dissertation, 1982.

HEY, D.G.
Introduction, in J.M. Bestall and D.V. Fowkes, ed. *Chesterfield Wills and Inventories 1521-1603*, 1977, xi-xxxii.

The Cutlers of Hallamshire, 1624-1699, University of Sheffield, 1993, 132pp.

The establishment of a legal profession in Sheffield, 1660-1740, *T.H.A.S.*, 16, 1991, 16-23.

HOSKINS, W.G.
Banking in Exeter, *D.C.N.Q.*, XIX, 1937, 175.

Elizabethan merchants of Exeter, in S.T. Bindoff, J. Hurstfield, C.H. Williams, ed. *Elizabethan Government and Society*, Athlone Press, 1961, 163-187. Reprinted in W.G. Hoskins, *Old Devon*, David and Charles, 1966.

An Elizabethan provincial town: Leicester, in J.H. Plumb, ed. *Studies in Social History: a Tribute to G.M. Trevelyan*, Longman, 1955, 33-67. Reprinted in W.G. Hoskins, *Provincial England*, Macmillan, 1963.

English provincial towns in the early sixteenth century, *T.R.H.S.*, 5th ser., VI, 1956, 1-19. Reprinted in W.G. Hoskins, *Provincial England*, Macmillan, 1963.

Editor, *Exeter in the Seventeenth Century: Tax and Rate Assessments, 1602-1699*, Devon and Cornwall Record Society, n.s., II, Devonshire Press, 1957, 154pp.

Industry, Trade and People in Exeter, 1688-1800, with Special Reference to the Serge Industry, Manchester University Press, History of Exeter and the South-West Research Group, Monograph VI, 1935, 189pp.

Mol's Coffee House, *D.C.N.Q.*, XXI, 1941, 25.

HUNT, H.M.J.
The ruling elite in Coventry, 1675-1720, Leicester M.A. dissertation, 1975.

JAMES, T.M.
The inns of Croydon, 1640-1830, Leicester M.A. dissertation, 1970.

The inns of Croydon, 1640-1840, *S.A.C.*, LXVIII, 1971, 109-129.

LAITHWAITE, J.M.W.
1523-1642: merchants, money and markets, in M. Bridge and J. Pegg, ed. *The Heart of Totnes*, AQ & DJ Publications, 1998, 132-143.

LORD, E.
Trespassers and debtors: Derby at the end of the sixteenth century, *Derbyshire Archaeological Journal*, 117, 1997, 97-109.

MOORE, P.
Rothwell: town or village? 1750-1850. A case-study of the changing pattern of urban status in the small town, Leicester M.A. dissertation, 1986.

PEET, S.J.
The magisterial elite of Southampton, 1550-1600, Leicester M.A. dissertation, 1992.

PETCHEY, W.J.
The borough of Maldon, Essex, 1500-1688, Leicester Ph.D. thesis, 1972.
A Prospect of Maldon 1500-1698, Essex Record Office, 113, 1991, 300pp.

Some properties of the Duchy of Lancaster in Ripon, 1547-1576, *The Ripon Historian*, II, vi, 256-260.

'Through the keyhole' and 'built environment' at Ripon 1592-1674, *The Ripon Historian*, II, x, 256-260.

PHYTHIAN-ADAMS, C.V.
The economic and social structure, *The Fabric of the Traditional Community* (Open University Course A.322, *English Urban History 1500-1780*, Block II, Unit 5), 1977, 9-40.

Urban crisis or urban change?, *The Traditional Community under Stress* (Open University Course A.322, *English Urban History 1500-1780*, Block III, Unit 9), 1977, 9-25.

PHYTHIAN-ADAMS, C.V. (with Wilson, K.)
The Market Town, Open University Television production for Course A322, 1977.

POUND, J.F.
Government and society in Tudor and Stuart Norwich, 1525-1675, Leicester Ph.D.
thesis, 1974.

The social and trade structure of Norwich, 1525-1575, *P.& P.*, XXXIV, 1966, 49-69.
Reprinted in P. Clark, ed. *The Early Modern Town*, Longman, 1976, 129-147.

The validity of freemen's lists: some Norwich evidence, *E.H.R.*, 2nd ser., XXXIV,
1981.

Tudor and Stuart Norwich, Phillimore, 1988.

The distribution of wealth in the sixteenth century, in P. Wade-Martins, ed. *An
Historical Atlas of Norfolk*, 1993, 96-7.

REED, M.A.
Ipswich in the seventeenth century, Leicester Ph.D. thesis, 1973.

Economic structure and change in seventeenth-century Ipswich, in P. Clark, ed.
Country Towns in Early Modern Britain: Economic and Social Change, Leicester
University Press, 1981, 88-141.

Decline and recovery in a provincial urban network: Buckinghamshire towns, 1350-
1800, in J. van der Vries, ed. *The Dynamics of Urban Decline in the late Middle Ages
and Early Modern Period: Economic Response and Social Effects*, 9th International
Economic History Congress, Debates and Controversies, 2, Berne, 1986, 405-422.

La rete urbana inglese: crescita e camiamento in una gerarchia urbana tradizionale,
1600-1800, *Storia Urbana*, 59, 1992, 5-34.

London and its hinterland: the view from the provinces, in P.Clark and B.Lepetit, ed.
Capital Cities and their Hinterlands in Early Modern Europe, Scolar Press,
Aldershot, 1996, 51-83.

ROBSON, D.G.
Scarborough in the reign of George III: the town, its people and trade, Leicester M.A.
dissertation, 1975.

SMITH, J.R.
The borough of Maldon, 1688-1768, Leicester M.Phil. thesis, 1981.

The Origins and Failure of New South End, Essex Record Office, 1991.

STEDMAN, J.O.
A very indifferent small city: economy of Carlisle, 1550-1700, Leicester Ph.D thesis,
1989.

THIRSK, J.
Stamford in the sixteenth and seventeenth centuries, in A. Rogers, ed. *The Making of Stamford*, Leicester University Press, 1965, 58-76.

The fashioning of the Tudor-Stuart gentry, *Bulletin of the John Rylands University Library of Manchester*, 72, 1, 1990, 69-85.

THORNBOROW, P.
Mortality crisies in Northampton, 1571 to 1640, Leicester M.A. dissertation, 1997.

UPTON, A.A.
Sixteenth-century Foleshill: population, economy and religion in a Coventry suburban parish, Leicester M.A. dissertation, 1997.

WEEDON, R.
Co-editor with A.S.Milne, *Aspects of English Small Towns in the 18th and 19th Centuries*, C.U.H.U.L., Working Paper 6, 1993.

WILLIAMS, M.I.
Cardiff: its trade and its people, 1660-1720, *Morgannwg*, VII, 1963, 74-97.

The port of Aberdyfi in the eighteenth century, *N.L.W.J.*, XVIII, 1973, 95-134.

4 Modern

ADAMS, N.C.
The local Coventry society as revealed by five autobiographies, Leicester M.A. dissertation, 1992.

Who are the Coventry kids?, *Newsletter*, Friends of D.E.L.H., 5, 1992, 22-23.

ALDIS, M.
One man's Nuneaton, 1810-1854, Leicester M.A. dissertation, 1992.

ALLAN, J.D.
Pickering: the community of a Yorkshire market town in the nineteenth century, Leicester M.A. dissertation, 1970.

AUTTON, A.P.
The forgotten boroughs of Devon: a study of the structure and composition of the village boroughs of Bow, Colyford, Newton Poppleford and South Zeal during the nineteenth century, Leicester M.A. dissertation, 1988.

BRITTON, C.J.
Thornbury, 1841-1851: a study of a small market town in Gloucestershire, Leicester M.A. dissertation, 1976.

BROWN, J.
The nineteenth century industrialization of a primary market town: Grantham, Lincolnshire, Leicester M.A. dissertation, 1994.

BROWN, J.L.
South Highfields, Leicester: the evolution of a suburb, Leicester M.A. dissertation, 1992.

CHRISTMAS, E.
The growth of Gloucester 1820-1852. Tradition and innovation in a county town, Leicester Ph.D. thesis, 1989.

Samuel Baker and Gloucester, *Gloucestershire History*, 1991, 10.

COLTMAN, S.F.
The role of decayed minor market towns in the mid-Victorian countryside: two Oxfordshire examples, Hook Norton and Charlbury, Leicester M.A. dissertation, 1985.

COOPER, A.W.
Newark in 1830, *T.T.S.*, LXXIV, 1970, 38-44.

The Newark-on-Trent Permanent Building Society, Dec. 1868-May 1904, *N.A.L.H.S.N.*, LX, 1975, 1-2.

Victorian Newark, *T.T.S.*, LXXV, 1971, 103-114.

William Cafferata, 1812-1874, *N.A.L.H.S.N.*, XLIV, 1973, 2.

William Midworth, 1817-1899, *N.A.L.H.S.N.*, XLIV, 1973, 2.

COX, R.C.W.
Across the road: contrasts in urban development in south Croydon, *Proceedings of the Croydon Natural History and Scientific Society*, XIII, 4, 1965.

Some aspects of the urban development of Croydon, 1870-1940, Leicester M.A. thesis, 1967.

Urban development and redevelopment in Croydon, 1835-1940, Leicester Ph.D. thesis, 1970.

Middle Row: Victorian decay and renewal, in J.B. Gent, ed. *Croydon: the Story of a Hundred Years*, C.N.H.S.S., 1970, 38-42.

The old centre of Croydon: Victorian decay and redevelopment, in A. Everitt, ed. *Perspectives in English Urban History*, Macmillan, 1973, 184-212.

EATON, M.D.
Victorian Market Harborough: the structure and functions of a nineteenth-century market town, Leicester M.A. dissertation, 1970.

EDWARDS, L.E.
A study of Coalville from the census returns, Leicester M.A. dissertation, 1992.

FLETCHER, S.J.C.
Crime in Cheltenham 1848-1851, Leicester M.A. dissertation, 1989.

FLEMING, A.J.
Newport Pagnell: a hundred town, 1825-1875, Leicester M.A. dissertation, 1972.

FLEMING, D.
Homes for People: the Story of Council Housing in Hull, Hull Museums, 1986.

GLASSON, M.O.J.
City Children: Birmingham Children at Work and Play, 1900-1930, Birmingham Museums, 1985.

GOODACRE, J.D.
Lord Macaulay on the Leicester Parliamentary Election of 1826, *Leics.H.*, II, xi, 1980/1, 24-27.

Lenin on the 1913 Leicester election, *Leics.H.*, III, viii, 1990, 21-24.

GRAHAM, M.
Tavistock, 1825-1875, Leicester M.A. dissertation, 1971.

Oxford in the 1850s: reminiscences of Henry Taunt, *Top Oxon*, 18, 1972.

Henry Taunt of Oxford: Victorian Photographer, Oxford Illustrated Press, 1973.

Oxford and the Licensing Act, 1872, *Top Oxon*, 19, 1973/74.

When the lights went out: Oxfordshire 1939-1945, Oxfordshire County Council, 1979.

The suburbs of Victorian Oxford: growth in a pre-industrial city, Leicester Ph.D. thesis, 1985.

Oxford City apprentices, 1697-1800, *Oxford Historical Society*, n.s., 31, 1987.

Housing development on the fringe of Oxford, 1850-1914, *Ox.*, 54, 1989.

A short-lived messenger: the Oxford Mercury and Midland Counties Chronicle, 1795-96, *Oxfordshire Local History*, 3, 5, Autumn 1990.

Images of Victorian Oxford, Alan Sutton Publishing, 1992.

Oxfordshire at War, Alan Sutton Publishing, 1994.

Policing the community: the Oxfordshire career of Thomas Hawtin, 1857-91, *Oxfordshire Local History*, 4, 5, Autumn 1994.

Hill View Road, Oxford: a Centenary History, Hill View Road Centenary Committee, 1996.

The Changing Faces of West Oxford, Robert Boyd Publications, 1998.

HEMMING, A.C.
A study of social relationships in late-Victorian London: the diaries of Hannah Cullwick and Arthur Munby, Leicester M.A. dissertation, 1987.

HEY, D.G.
A History of Sheffield, Carnegie Press, 1998.

HEY, D.G. (with Binfield, C. *et al.*,)
The History of the City of Sheffield, 1843-1993, 3 vols, Sheffield Academic Press, 1993.

HILL, T.G.
The trading community of Shifnal and its geographical and genealogical linkages: a case study, 1841-1861, Leicester M.A. dissertation, 1989.

HOBSON, M.
The occupational structure of West Malling, 1841-1871, Leicester M.A. dissertation, 1978.

HODGKINSON, J.S.
Changing standards of living in the smaller house in the Northampton area 1850-1940, Leicester M.A. dissertation, 1991.

HOSKINS, W.G.
Exeter Today, *The Listener*, LXXII, 1964, 842-843.

JACKSON, P.
Sawley, from principal settlement to suburb: a study of rural decline in the nineteenth century, Leicester M.A. dissertation, 1993.

JENKINS, S.C.
The industrial archaeology of Witney, *R.W.*, III, 1978, 18-22.

The night Hitler bombed Witney, *R.W.*, I, 1977.

KENNEDY, P.J.B.
The air raids on Smethwick and Oldbury 1940-1942, Leicester M. A. dissertation,1993.

KINGMAN, M.J.
Chester, 1801-1861, Leicester M.A. dissertation, 1970.

LORD, E.
Conflicting interests: public health, Lammas lands and pressure groups in nineteenth-century Kingston-upon-Thames, *Southern History,* 13, 1991, 22-31.

LOWNDES, M.
The Caldmore district of Walsall in the nineteenth century with special reference to the decade 1861-1871, Leicester M.A. dissertation, 1976.

MILES, J.
The rise of suburban Exeter and the naming of its streets and houses *c.*1801-1907, Leicester Ph.D. thesis, 1990.

MITCHELL, J.W.
The population and industries of Victorian Melton Mowbray, 1851-1871, Leicester M.A. dissertation, 1975.

MUSSON, E.
Retail trading in Chesterfield, 1835-1872, Leicester M.A. dissertation, 1975.

PAGE, D.
Ashby de la Zouch: the social structure of a mid-Victorian market town, Leicester M.A. dissertation, 1974.

PAWLEY, S.J.
'Democracy and proper drains': public health and landed influence in late nineteenth century Sleaford, *Lincolnshire Past and Present*, 7, 1992, 8-11.

PHYTHIAN-ADAMS, C.V.
Foreword, in R.Gill, *The Book of Leicester,* Barracuda Books, 1985, 9.

POTTS, R.A.J.
Job-creation projects in Newcastle upon Tyne, 1816-1817, *Tyne & Tweed* (Bulletin of the Association of Northumberland Local History Societies), 52, 1978, 11-15.

REDMONDS, G. (with Pearce, C.)
Self-help in house-building 1799, *O.W.R.*, 2, 2 , 1982, 2.

ROLES, J.
'The dull haunts of business': a study of retailing in Cheltenham 1800-1851, Leicester M.A. dissertation, 1982.

ROGERSON, M.
People, poverty and occupations: Worcester 1779-1821, Leicester M.A. dissertation, 1981.

SCOTT, H.L.
The changing fortunes of the Royal Arcade Newcastle-upon-Tyne, 1830-1882, Leicester M.A. dissertation, 1997.

SNELL, K.D.M.
Leicester in the 1840s, in B. Abbott, ed. *Follow the Man from Cooks*, 1991, 10-11.

STEDMAN, J.O.
Aspects of the economic history of Winchester 1770-1810, Leicester M.A. dissertation, 1979.

Portsmouth Reborn: Destruction and Reconstruction, 1939-1974, Portsmouth Paper 66, City of Portsmouth, 1995, 24pp.

STUTTARD, R.
People with small means and high hopes - co-operators in Leicester, 1860-1990, Leicester M.A. dissertation, 1991.

Putting it down to posterity, *Co-operative News*, n.s., 3750, 1991, 5.

SURGEY, J.R.
Transport, trade, and industry in Mansfield, 1800-1850, Leicester M.A. dissertation, 1973.

TOOLE, S.
Liverpool in the mid-Victorian era - its pride and shame, Leicester M.A. dissertation, 1993.

TRINDER, B.S.
The distant scene: Banbury and the United States in the mid-nineteenth century, *C.& C.*, VII, 1978, 163-173.

Victorian Banbury, Phillimore, 1982, 235pp.

Editor, *Victorian Shrewsbury: Studies in the History of a County Town*, Shropshire Libraries, 1984, 128pp.

The Shropshire coalfield, in P.Clark and P.Corfield, ed. *Industry and Urbanisation in Eighteenth Century England*, C.U.H.U.L., 1994, 33-40.

The textile industry in Shrewsbury in the late eighteenth century, in P.Clark and P.Corfield, ed. *Industry and Urbanisation in Eighteenth Century England*, C.U.H.U.L., 1994, 80-92.

TRINDER, B.S. (with Jones, K., Hunt, M. & Malam, J.)
Holywell Lane: a squatter community in the Shropshire coalfield, *I.A.R.*, VI, 1982, 163-85.

WILLSHAW, E.M.
The inns of Chester 1775-1832. The functions of provincial inns and their importance to the local community, Leicester M.A. dissertation, 1979.

WISDOM, J.
The making of a West London suburb: housing in Chiswick, 1861-1914, Leicester M.A. dissertation, 1977.

WISE, R.
Corby: the growth and decline of a steel town 1930-1990, Leicester M.A. dissertation, 1995.

WISE, S.E.
Coalville: the origins and growth of a nineteenth-century mining town, Leicester M.A. dissertation, 1969.

H The Poor and Social Problems

ADAMS, J.S.
Crisis in Crippledom: some aspects of the history of the Rowley Bristow Orthopaedic Hospital, Pyrford, Surrey, 1908-1962, Leicester M.A. dissertation, 1993.

From Crippledom to orthopaedic nursing: Pyrford 1908-1945, *International History of Nursing Journal*, 2, 4, 1997, 23-37.

ALDIS, M. (with Inder, P.)
The ailments and medical remedies of Susanna Ingleby of Basford Hall, *Staffordshire Studies*, 9, 69-79.

ALDRED, D.H.
Poor relief in Winchcombe, Gloucestershire 1800-1851, Leicester M.A.dissertation, 1973.

AMBROSE, G.R.
The administration of the Old Poor Law in Wells from 1776, Leicester M.A. dissertation, 1971.

CAMERON, J.
The lives of female vagrants in the casual ward of St Mary's workhouse, Nottingham, April 1899-1900, Leicester M.A. dissertation, 1994.

CHRISTMAS, E.
The poor at Stow-on-the-Wold 1836, *Gloucestershire Historical Studies*, III, 1969, 69.

HAYES, W.F.G.
The working poor in mid-nineteenth century Torquay, Leicester M.A. dissertation, 1991.

HILL, T.G.
Shropshire and Birmingham settlement certificates, 1686-1726, *Shropshire Family History Journal,* 11, 1990, 78-79.

More Shropshire to Birmingham settlement certificates, 1727-1757, *ibid,* 118-119.

HILLIER, K.A.
The welfare and education of working-class children in Ashby de la Zouch in the nineteenth century, Leicester M.A. dissertation, 1996.

HOARE, N.F.
The community of Colyton and its poor, 1800-1850, Leicester M.A. dissertation, 1974.

HOSKINS, W.G.
Epidemics in English history, *The Listener* LXXII, 1964, 1044-1046.

HUTCHIN, J.D.
Attitudes to the relief of poverty in Leicester, 1901-14, Leicester M.A. dissertation, 1994.

INDER, P.M. (with Aldis, M.)
The ailments and medical remedies of Susanna Ingleby of Basford Hall, *Staffordshire Studies*, 9, 69-70.

OWEN, T.E.
Enclosure, poor relief expenditure and the labouring poor in Leicestershire, 1750-1830, Leicester M.A. dissertation, 1991.

PINCHES, S.
Roman Catholic charities and voluntary societies in the diocese of Birmingham, 1834-1945, Leicester M.A. dissertation, 1997.

Father Hudson's Society, Archdiocese of Birmingham Historical Commission, 1998.

POUND, J.F.
The Norwich Census of the Poor, 1570, Norfolk Record Society, XL, 1971, 118pp.

Debate: vagrants and the social order in Elizabethan England, *P.& P.*, LXXI, 1976, 126-129.

Poverty and Vagrancy in Tudor England, Seminar Studies in History, Longman, 1971, 120pp.

Poverty and public health in Norwich, 1845-1880, in C.Barringer, ed. *Norwich in the Nineteenth Century,* Gliddon, 1984.

Clerical poverty in early sixteenth century Suffolk: some East Anglian evidence, in *Journal of Ecclesiastical History*, 37, 3, July 1986, 389-96.

The great social divide, in R.A.Smith, ed. *Royal Armada: 400 Years*, Manorial Research (Armada) Ltd., 1988.

McDERMOTT, M.B.
The administration of the Poor Law in the Somerset parish of Langford Budville during the periods 1657-1730 and 1782-1836, Leicester M A. dissertation, 1974.

SMITH, J.R.
The Speckled Monster: Smallpox in England, 1670-1970, with particular reference to Essex, Essex Record Office, 1987.

SNELL, K.D.M.
Pauper settlement and the right to poor relief in England and Wales, *Continuity and Change*, 6, 3, 1991, 375-415.

Settlement, poor law and the rural historian: new approaches and opportunities, *R.H.E.S.C.*, 3, 2, 1992, 145-172.

SNELL, K.D.M. (with J.Millar)
Lone-parent families and the Welfare State: past and present, *Continuity and Change*, 2, 1987, 387-422.

WATSON, A.F.
The Chesterfield Poor Law Union: the first ten years, 1837-1847, Leicester M.A. dissertation, 1976.

IV POPULATION, FAMILY and KINSHIP

A Population

DOREE, S.G.
Aspects of mortality crises in eleven parishes in East Hertfordshire between 1560 and 1670, Leicester M.A. dissertation, 1977.

FOX, H.S.A.
Exploitation of the landless by lords and tenants in early medieval England, in Z.Razi and R.Smith, ed. *Medieval Society and the Manor Court*, Clarendon Press, 1996, 519-68.

Servants, cottagers and tied cottages during the later Middle Ages: a regional dimension, *R.H.E.S.C.*, 6, 2, 1995, 125-54.

Farmworkers' accommodation in later medieval England: three case studies from Devon, in D.A. Postles, ed. *Name, Time and Place*, Leopard's Head Press, forthcoming.

HOSKINS, W.G.
Population of Exeter, *D.C.N.Q.*, XX, 1939, 242-247.

The population of an English village 1086-1801, *T.L.A.S.*, XXXIII, 1957, 15-35. Reprinted in W.G. Hoskins, *Provincial England*, Macmillan, 1963.

JENKINS, S.C.
The population of seventeenth-century Witney, *R.W.*, 6, 1979, 8-12.

MORLEY, I.M.
A demographic study of the parish of Otley in the seventeenth and eighteenth centuries, Leicester M.A. dissertation, 1969.

NEWEY, R.G.
East Hendred, Berkshire. A social and demographic study, 1800-1840, Leicester M.A. dissertation, 1979.

PEEBLES BROWN, R.A.
Population changes and the railway. Aspects of the railway industry's influence on two localities of south Cheshire, 1850-1875, Leicester M.A. dissertation, 1981.

POUND, J.F.
Population in the sixteenth century, in P.Wade-Martins, ed. *An Historical Atlas of Norfolk*, 1993, 94-5.

THOMPSON, M.G.
Demographic aspects of thirteenth- and fourteenth-century Shapwick with Moorlinch, *Shapwick Project: the Eighth Report*, University of Bristol, 1998, 171-80.

THORNBOROW, P.
Mortality crises in Northampton 1571 to 1640, Leicester M.A. dissertation, 1996.

WEST, F.
Mortality in the parishes of Leake and Wrangle, *L.P.S.*, XIII, 1974, 41-44.

WILLIAMS, M.I.
Population changes in Glamorgan, 1800-1900, *Glam.H.*, I, 1963, 109-120.

Population movements in Cardiganshire, 1800-1900, *Llawlyfr Cymdeithas Ceredigion Llundain*, 1964-5, 22-27.

B Migration and Minorities

BROWN, G.P.
Population and mobility: a study using marriage registers of the Leicester and Nottinghamshire borders during the eighteenth and nineteenth centuries, Leicester M.A. dissertation, 1986.

DAVIES, V.E.L.
A sweet prison: aspects of the origin and establishment of the Leicester Asian community, Leicester M.A. dissertation, 1993.

Older people and the environment, Leicester City Council, 1995, 39pp.

ELLIOTT, B.S.
English immigration to Prince Edward Island, *The Island Magazine,* 40, 1996-7, 3-11: 41, 1997, 3-9.

'The Protestant Irish' and `The English', in *The Peoples of Canada: an Encyclopaedia for the Country,* The Multicultural History Society of Ontario, forthcoming 1998, 80pp. and 100pp.

FRYE, J.
Population migration in a selected region of north-east Leicestershire in the mid-nineteenth century, Leicester M.A. dissertation, 1974.

GARRISON, L.
The Black historical past in British education, in P. Stone and R. Mackenzie, ed. *The Excluded Past: Archaeology in Education,* Unwin Hyman, 1990, 31-44.

From Africa to Britain: mapping a heritage, *1992 and the New World: 500 years of Resistance,* 1992, 12-15.

Post-war immigration and settlement of West Indians in Nottingham, 1948-1968, Leicester M.A. dissertation, 1992.

Introduction: where are our monuments?, in *The Black Presence in Nottingham* (catalogue of the exhibition held 2 Oct. - 14 Nov. 1993), The Castle Museum, Nottingham.

HUME, J.A.
Settlement and migration in Dorset 1704-1862: a study of the migrational patterns of paupers, Leicester M.A. dissertation, 1989.

LORD, E.
Spatial and social mobility in east Surrey, 1750-1850, *Historical Social Sciences Newsletter*, Winter 1986, 1-2.

LUXTON, S.
A small Poland? A portrait of the Polish community in Leicester, Leicester M.A. dissertation, 1994.

POSTLES, D.
The pattern of migration in a Midlands county: Leicestershire, *c*.1270-1350, *Continuity and Change*, 7, 1992, 139-62.

REDMONDS, G.
West Riding emigrants, 1843, *O.W.R.*, 1/1,1981, 3pp.

THIRSK, J.
Rural migration in England: the long historical perspective, in J.A. Mollett, *Migrants in Agricultural Development. A Study of Intrarural Migration*, Macmillan, London, 1991, 32-55.

WILLIAMS, M.I.
Seasonal migrations of Cardiganshire harvest gangs to the Vale of Glamorgan in the nineteenth century, *Cer.*, III, 1957, 156-160.

C Personal names

CAMSELL, M.
Devon locative names in the fourteenth century, *Nomina,* 10, 1986, 137-147.

EVERITT, A.M.
Foreword, R.A. McKinley, *Norfolk and Suffolk Surnames in the Middle Ages*, Phillimore, 1975, vii-xiv.

HEY, D.G.
Editor, *The Origins of One Hundred Sheffield Surnames*, University of Sheffield, 1992, 66pp.

The Local History of Family Names, British Association for Local History, 1997, 20pp.

Mahlon Stacy: an early Sheffield immigrant, in M. Jones, ed. *Aspects of Sheffield*, 1, Wharncliffe Publishing, 1997, 39-47.

The distinctive surnames of Staffordshire, *Staffordshire Studies*, 1998.

HOSKINS, W.G.
The homes of family names, *H.T.*, XII, 1962, 189-194.

McKINLEY, R.A.
The distribution of surnames derived from the names of some Yorkshire towns, in F.Emmison and R.Stephens, ed. *Tribute to an Antiquary* [Dr Marc Fitch], Leopard's Head Press, 1976, 165-175.

Norfolk and Suffolk Surnames in the Middle Ages, Phillimore, 1975, 153pp.

Norfolk Surnames in the Sixteenth Century, D.E.L.H. Occasional Papers, 2nd ser., 2, Leicester University Press, 1969, 60pp.

The Surnames of Oxfordshire, English Surnames Series, Leopard's Head Press, 1977, 212pp.

The Surnames of Lancashire, English Surnames Series, Leopard's Head Press, 1981, 501pp.

The Surnames of Sussex, English Surnames Series, Leopard's Head Press, 1988, 483pp.

The survey of English surnames, *L.H.*, VIII, 1969, 299-302.

Survey of English surnames, *The Study of Personal Names of the British Isles*, ed. H. Voitl, University of Erlangen, 1976, 119-125.

British surnames, in M. Rubincam, ed. *Genealogical Research: Methods and Sources*, 1, American Society of Genealogists, 555-564.

A History of British Surnames, Longman, 1990, 230pp.

Medieval Latin translations of English personal names: their value for surname history, *Nomina,* 14, 1992, 1-6.

The evolution of hereditary surnames in Devon, in D.Postles, ed. *The Surnames of Devon,* Leopard's Head Press, Oxford, 1995.

NEWMAN, E.
Surname development 1279-1332 in the Kineton Hundred of Warwickshire, Leicester M.A. dissertation, 1995.

POSTLES, D.
Personal naming patterns of peasants and burgesses in late medieval England, *Medieval Prosopography*, 12, 1991, 29-56.

The baptismal names in thirteenth-century England: processes and patterns, *Medieval Prosopography*, 13, 1992, 1-52.

Surnames and the composition of local populations: Rutland, thirteenth to seventeenth centuries, *East Midlands Geographer*, 16, 1993, 27-38.

The changing pattern of male forenames in medieval Leicestershire and Rutland to c.1350, *L.P.S.*, 51, 1993, 54-61.

At Sørensen's request: the formation and development of patronyms and metronyms in late medieval Leicestershire and Rutland, *Nomina*, 17, 1994, 55-70.

Notions of the family, lordship and the evolution of naming processes in medieval English rural society: a regional example, *Continuity and Change*, 10, 1995, 169-98.

Noms de personnes en langue française dans l'Angleterre du moyen âge, *Le Moyen Age*, CI, 1995, 7-21.

The Surnames of Devon, English Surnames Series, Leopard's Head Press, 1995, xx + 332pp..

Cultures and peasant naming in twelfth-century England, *Medieval Prosopography*, 18, 1997, 25-54.

The Surnames of Leicestershire and Rutland, Leopard's Head Press, forthcoming, 1999.

Editor, *Name, Time and Place,* Leopard's Head Press, forthcoming.

REDMONDS, G.
The development of West Riding surnames from the thirteenth century to the twentieth century, Leicester Ph.D. thesis, 1969.

English surnames research, H. Voitl, ed. *The Study of Personal Names of the British Isles*, University of Erlangen, 1976, 75-82.

Lancashire surnames in Yorkshire, *Gen.Mag.*, XVIII, 1975, 13-18.

Noms d'origine Française dans le Yorkshire, *Vie et Langage*, 235, 1971, 588-593.

Problems in the identification of some Yorkshire filial names, *Gen.Mag.,* XVII, 1974, 205-212.

Surname heredity in Yorkshire, *L.H.*, X, 1972, 171-177.

Surnames and place-names, *L.H.*, X, 1972, 3-6.

Yorkshire, West Riding, English Surnames Series, I, Phillimore, 1973, 314pp.

The origins of Yorkshire 'royd' surnames, *O.W.R.*, 1, 1, 1981.
Amer: a rare personal name, *O.W.R.*, 9, 1989.

Yorkshire Surnames Series Part I Bradford and District, GR Books, 1990, 62pp.

Yorkshire Surnames Series Part II Huddersfield and District, GR Books, 1992, 64pp.

Surnames and Genealogy: a New Approach, New England Historic Genealogical
Society, 1997, 310pp.

SEKULLA, M.F.
Patterns of naming in the parish of Dry Drayton, Cambridgeshire, 1550-1850,
Leicester M.A. dissertation, 1993.

THOMAS, K.
The surnames of Warwick 1185-1500, Leicester M.A. dissertation, 1986.

D Family and Kinship

ALDIS, M. (with Inder, P.M.)
Muskets and Mining: the 1844 Diary of John William Sneyd, Churnet Valley Books,
1996.

Thirty Pieces of Silver: the Diary of the Rev. John Sneyd 1815-1871, Churnet Valley
Books, 1998.

*A Scandal in the Parish. Consistory Court hearing into the Bastardy Case brought
against the Rev Gustavus Sneyd 1881*, Oxford Record Office, 1998.

DOREE, S.G.
The Sassoons of Trent Park, *Heritage*, Edmonton Hundred Historical Society, 1,
1982, 1-12.

DRINKALL, J.T.
The life and interests of the Rev. Sir Richard Kay, Bt., LL.D., F.R.S., F.S.A: an
eighteenth-century pluralist, Leicester Ph.D. thesis, 1966.

EVERITT, A.M.
Kentish family portrait, in C.W. Chalklin and M.A. Havinden, ed. *Rural Change and
Urban Growth, 1500-1800: Essays in English Regional History in Honour of W.G.
Hoskins*, Longman, 1974, 169-199.

FAITH, R.J.
Peasant families and inheritance customs in medieval England, *A.H.R.*, XIV, 1966, 77-95.

FINBERG, H.P.R.
The ancestry of J.M.W. Turner, R.A., *D.C.N.Q.*, XXIV, 1950, 97.

The Gostwicks of Willington, Bedfordshire Historical Record Society Publications, XXXVI, 1956, 92pp.

Prideaux of Tavistock and Altarnun, *D.C.N.Q.*, XXI, 1941, 337-345.

Three studies in family history: Berkeley of Berkeley; Kingscote of Kingscote; Holder of Taynton, in H.P.R. Finberg, ed. *Gloucestershire Studies*, Leicester University Press, 1957, 145-183.

GOODACRE, J.D.
Letters from a seventeenth-century rector of Lutterworth: Nathaniel Tovey as marriage agent, *Leics.H.*, III, ii, 1983/4, 9-16.

HART, Cyril R.
John Clarke, M.D., *c.*1583-1653: President of the College of Physicians, 1645-1650, *St Bartholomew's Hospital Journal*, LV, 1951, 34-40.

Two queens of England, *A.J.*, LXXXII, ii, 1977, 10-15.

William Malet and his family, *Anglo-Norman Studies*, 19, 1996, 123-165.

HEY, D.G.
The Oxford Guide to Family History, Oxford University Press, 1993, 246pp. (Paperback 1998).

HOSKINS, W.G.
The Baring family, *D.C.N.Q.*, XIX, 1937, 173.

A history of the Humberstone family, *T.L.A.S.*, XX, 1939, 241-289.

George Wightwick and John Foulston, *D.C.N.Q.*, XXVI, 1955, 40-41.

Leicestershire yeoman families and their pedigrees, *T.L.A.S.*, XXIII, 1947, 29-63.

George Oliver, D.D., 1781-1861, *D.R.*, LXXIX, 1961, 334-348.

Richard Thornton, 1776-1865: a Victorian millionaire, *H.T.*, XII, 1962, 574-579.

Leicestershire Yeoman Families and their Pedigrees, Leicester Research Services, 1974, 28pp.

INDER, P.M. (with Aldis, M.)
Muskets and Mining: the 1844 Diary of John William Sneyd, Churnet Valley Books, 1996.

Thirty Pieces of Silver: the Diary of the Rev. John Sneyd 1815-1871, Churnet Valley Books, 1998.

A Scandal in the Parish. Consistory Court hearing into the Bastardy Case brought against the Rev Gustavus Sneyd 1881, Oxford Record Office, 1998.

IREDALE, D.A.
Our family tree, *St Andrew's Church Magazine*, Chester, Oct. 1966, 4-6.

Discovering Your Family Tree: a Handbook on Tracing Ancestors, Shire Publications, 1970, 2nd edn, 1973; 3rd edn, 1977, 63pp.
Discovering Your Family Tree, Shire Publications, 1985.

LORD, E.
Spatial and social interaction in S.E.Surrey, 1750-1850, Leicester Ph.D. thesis, 1989.

The Cornwall-Leghs of High Legh: approaches to the inheritance patterns of north-west England, *Bulletin of the John Rylands University Library of Manchester*, 73, 2, 1991, 21-36.

Communities of common interest: the social landscape of south-east Surrey, 1750-1850, in C.V. Phythian-Adams, ed. *Societies, Culture and Kinship, 1580-1850*, Leicester University Press, 1993, 131-199.

MARKS, R.
Padbury: kinship and community *c.* 1538-1634, Leicester M.A. dissertation, 1994.

MITSON, A.
Social, economic and kinship networks in rural south-west Nottinghamshire *c.* 1580-1700, Leicester Ph.D. thesis, 1987.

The significance of kinship networks in the seventeenth century: south-west Nottinghamshire, in C.V.Phythian-Adams, ed. *Societies, Cultures and Kinship, 1580-1850*, Leicester University Press, 1993, 24-76.

PHYTHIAN-ADAMS, C.V.
Introduction, in C.V.Phythian-Adams, ed. *Societies, Cultures and Kinship, 1580-1850*, Leicester University Press, 1993, 1-23.

PHYTHIAN-ADAMS, H.V.
Thomas-Jones-Gwynne of Monachty, *Journal of South Wales Family History Society*, II, iv, 1978, 2-5.

Lords of Towyn, *South Wales Family History Society Journal*, III, ii, Summer 1979, 9-15.

The Lords of Towyn - corrigenda and addenda, *South Wales Family History Society Journal,* IV, i, Spring 1980, 3-4.

Royal roots of a Cardiganshire parson's wife, *South Wales Family History Society Journal,* V, ii, Summer 1981, 39-45.

POSTLES, D.
Choosing witnesses in twelfth-century England, *Irish Jurists,* XXIII, n.s., 1991 for 1988, 330-46.

Personal pledging: medieval 'reciprocity' or 'symbolic capital' ?, *Journal of Interdisciplinary History,* XXVI, 1996, 419-35.

Reviewing social networks: using Ucinet, *History and Computing,* 6, 1994, 1-11.

POTTS, R.A.J.
A Leicestershire link [Leics. branches of the Carlyons of Cornwall and Winstanleys of Lancs.], *D.C.N.Q.,* XXX, 1967, 293-295.

SHORT, C.D.
Hearths, people and status: a study of the social structure of three areas of Hertfordshire in the late seventeenth century, Leicester M.A. dissertation, 1986.

STORM, A.
Family and maritime community: Robin Hood's Bay *c.*1653 - *c.*1867, Leicester Ph.D. thesis, 1991.

SPUFFORD, H.M. (with Takahashi, M.)
Families, will witnesses and economic structure in the fens and on the chalk: sixteenth- and seventeenth-century Willingham and Chippenham, *Albion,* XXXVIII, 1996, 379-411.

THIRSK, J.
The family, *P. & P.,* XXVII, 1964, 116-122.

Editor, (with Goody, J. and Thompson, E.P.), *Family and Inheritance: Rural Society in Western Europe, 1200-1800,* Cambridge University Press., 1976, 337pp.

THOMAS, C.M.
Population, poverty and partible inheritance.......?, Leicester M.A. dissertation, 1991.

WATSON, A.F.
The Edensor Friendly Benefit Society, *Derbyshire Miscellany,* 10, 2, Autumn 1983, 44-47.

WICKES, M.J.L.
The Tucker Family of Devon, M. Wickes Publications, 1984, 81pp.

WILLIAMS, M.I.
Huw Williams (1796-1874), *Llenfer*, XXVI, 1975-76, 24-30.

WRIGHT, S.J.
Family life and society in sixteenth- and early seventeenth-century Salisbury,
Leicester Ph.D. thesis, 1982.

Sojourners and lodgers in a provincial town: the evidence from Ludlow, *U.H Y.B.,*
1990, 14-35.

The elderly and the bereaved in eighteenth-century Ludlow, in M. Pelling and
R. Smith, ed. *Life, Death and the Elderly: Historical Perspectives*, Routledge, 1991,
102-133.

E Gender

ALDIS, M. (with Inder, P.M.)
Body-linings, braids, bones and buttons: a Staffordshire lady and her dress-maker,
Staffordshire History, 25, Spring 1997.

ANDREWS, K.
World War II: its effect on the work of working-class women in Boston, Lincolnshire,
Leicester M.A. dissertation, 1998.

BHATT, J.S.
Margaret Miller and the campaign for the right of the married woman to earn,
Leicester M.Phil. thesis, 1995.

DeLONG, R.E.
Women, widows and witches. A study of four Huntingdonshire villages, 1630-1650,
Leicester M.A. dissertation, 1987.

EDWARDS, H.
Farmers' wives of Leicestershire and Northamptonshire: their working lives 1918-
1950, Leicester M.A. dissertation, 1988.

Pitching stooks and making tea: farming wives of Leicestershire and
Northamptonshire, *Common Voice,* 4, 1989, 7-9.

INDER, P.M. (with Aldis, M.)
Body-linings, braids, bones and buttons: a Staffordshire lady and her dress-maker,
Staffordshire History, 25, Spring 1997.

LAUGHTON, J.
Women in court: some evidence from fifteenth-century Chester, in N. Rogers, ed.
England in the Fifteenth Century: Proceedings of the 1992 Harlaxton Symposium,
Stamford, 1994, 89-99.

LORD, E.
A good archbishop: the Countess of Huntingdon, *Arch.*, XIX, 86, 1991, 423-432.

Weighed in the balance and found wanting: female friendly societies, self-help and economic virtue in the East Midlands in the eighteenth and nineteenth centuries, *M.H.*, XXII, 1997, 100-112.

POSTLES, D.
The distinction of gender? Women's names in the thirteenth century, *Nomina*, 19, 1996, 79-90.

SIMKIN, A.
Community participation and the role of women in the court rolls of the manor of Wakefield, 1274-1352, Leicester M.A. dissertation, 1993.

SNELL, K.D.M.
Agricultural seasonal unemployment, the standard of living and women's work in the South and East, 1690-1860, *Ec.H.R.*, XXXIII, 1981, 407-437.

Editor (with Bellamy, L. and Williamson, T) *R.H.E.S.C.*, 5, 2, October 1994, 112 pp. (Nine-article issue entitled `Women and Rural History' including introduction by the joint editors, 123-127).

Agricultural seasonal unemployment, the standard of living and women's work in the South and East, 1690-1860, in P. Sharpe, ed. *Women's Work: the English Experience, 1650-1914*, 1998.

SPUFFORD, H.M.
Women teaching reading to poor children in the sixteenth and seventeenth centuries, in M. Hilton, M. Styles and V. Watson, ed. *Opening the Nursery Door. Reading, Writing and Childhood 1600-1900*, Routledge, 1997, 47-62.

STEWART, S.
The status of women in Surrey *c*.1235-1348, Leicester M.A. dissertation, 1997.

THIRSK, J.
Foreword, in M. Prior, ed. *Women in English Society, 1500-1800*, Methuen, 1985, 1-21.

THORNTON, M.
Women peasants in Bedfordshire and Huntingdonshire before the Black Death, Leicester M.A. dissertation, 1997.

VERDON, N.
Women's work in the inter-war period: a study of Nottingham, Leicester M.A. dissertation, 1996.

WRIGHT, S.J.

'Churmaids, huswyfes and hucksters': the employment of women in Tudor and Stuart Salisbury, in L.Charles and L. Duffin, ed. *Women and Work in Pre-Industrial England*, Croom Helm, 1985, 107-116.

'Holding up half the sky': women, and their occupations in eighteenth-century Ludlow, *M.H.*, XIV, 1989, 54-74.

V CULTURE

A Religious History

1 Medieval and Reformation

ARNOLD, B.
The saints' dedications of Somerset, M.A. dissertation, 1986.

BATEMAN, J.
Those who fought, those who prayed, those who worked: the secular clergy and laity in the archdeaconry of Northampton in the late Middle Ages, Leicester M.A. dissertation, 1997.

COOPER, N.
The church in Anglo-Saxon Northumberland, Leicester M.A. dissertation, 1994.

DOREE, S.G.
The Bassingbourn St George Play of 1511, *Hertfordshire's Past*, 33, Autumn 1992, 36-44.

The popular religion in Hertfordshire before the Reformation, *Hertfordshire's Past*, 35, Autumn 1993, 17-28.

The early Bishops Stortford churchwardens' accounts, *Hertfordshire's Past*, 37, Autumn 1994, 9-11.

FINBERG, H.P.R.
Abbots of Tavistock, *D.C.N.Q.*, XXII, 1943, 159-162, 174-175, 186-188.

Abbots of Tavistock, *D.C.N.Q.*, XXII, 1944, 194-197.

A Cellarer's Account Book, *D.C.N.Q.*, XXIII, 1948, 253-255. Reprinted in W.G. Hoskins and H.P.R. Finberg, *Devonshire Studies*, Jonathan Cape, 1952 and in H.P.R. Finberg, *West-Country Historical Studies*, David and Charles, 1969.

Church and state in twelfth-century Devon: some documentary illustrations, *T.D.A.*, LXXV, 1943, 159-162. Reprinted in H.P.R. Finberg, *West-Country Historical Studies,* David and Charles, 1969.

Prelude to Abbot Bonus, *D.C.N.Q.*, XXIII, 1948, 184-187.

St Michael's, Brentor, *Tavistock Ruri-decanal Magazine*, XXXVIII, 1947.

The tragi-comedy of Abbot Bonus, *D.C.N.Q.*, XXII, 1946, 341-347. Enlarged and reprinted in W.G. Hoskins and H.P.R. Finberg, *Devonshire Studies*, Jonathan Cape, 1952, and in H.P.R. Finberg, *West-Country Historical Studies*, David and Charles, 1969.

A vice-archdeacon's legacies, *D.C.N.Q.*, XXII, 1945, 285-287. Reprinted in W.G. Hoskins and H.P.R.Finberg, *Devonshire Studies,* Jonathan Cape, 1952, and in H.P.R. Finberg, *West-Country Historical Studies*, David and Charles, 1969.

FOX, D.E.
The spread of Christianity and Christian churches in the wapentake of Langbargh, North Riding of Yorkshire, 600-1300, Leicester M.A. dissertation, 1993.

HART, Cyril R.
The church of St Mary, Huntingdon, *P.Camb.A.S.*, LIX, 1966, 105-111.

The foundation of Ramsey Abbey, *Revue Bénédictine*, 104, 1994, 295-327.

KAYE, D.
Church dedications in Lincolnshire, Leicester M.A. dissertation, 1974.

JAMES, T.M.
English churchyards, *C.N.H.S.S. Archaeology Newsletter,* 49, 1980, 6.

JENKINS, S.C.
West Oxfordshire church dedications, *R.W.*, 10, 1980, 8-12.

JONES, G.R.
Holy wells and the cult of St Helen, *Landscape History,* 8, 1986, 59-76.

Church dedications and landed units of lordship and administration in the pre-reformation diocese of Worcester, Leicester Ph.D. thesis, 1996.

New departmental research programme. Saints settlements and culture, *Newsletter,* Friends of D.E.L.H., 9, 1996, 6-7.

A summer of research in Catalonia, *Newsletter*, Friends of D. E. L.H., 10, 1997, 27-28.

Leverhulme research programme. Saints' Cults: towards a national electronic atlas, *Newsletter*, Friends of D.E.L.H., 11, 1998, 7-8.

What's in a name? St Michael, patron saint and cosmic guardian, in E. Bailey, ed. *Small is Cosmic: Millenial Issues in Parochial Perspective*, Winterbourne PCC, 1998, 13-22.

Authority and identities in three undiscussed saints' cults in Gloucestershire, in R. Purdie, and I.Wei, ed. *Authority and Community in the Middle Ages*, Alan Sutton Publishing, forthcoming.

Penda's footprint? Place-names containing personal names associated with those of early Mercian kings, *Nomina*, 21, 1998, 29-62.

LLOYD, P.
A study of the dedications given to religious buildings in Leicestershire before the Reformation, Leicester M.A. dissertation, 1974.

MASTERS, P.J.
The minsters, territories and proprietary churches of Saxon West Sussex, Leicester M.A. dissertation, 1993.

PETCHEY, W.J.
The fabric works of Ripon Minster (1512-13, 1520-21), *The Ripon Historian*, I, v, 6-10.

POSTLES, D.
Gifts in frankalmoign, warranty of land, and feudal society, *Cambridge Law Journal*, 50, 1991, 330-46.

Tenure in frankalmoign and knight service in twelfth-century England: interpretation of the charters, *J. Soc. Arch.*, 13, 1992, 18-28.

Monastic burials of non-patronal lay benefactors, *Journal of Ecclesiastical History*, 47, 1996, 620-37.

The Austin canons in English towns, *Historical Research*, 66, 1993, 1-20.

Some ambiguities of late medieval religion in England, *Electronic Seminars in History*, Institute of Historical Research, April 1998.

Lay Piety in Transition: Local Society and New Religious Houses in England 1100-1280, Friends of D.E.L.H., Paper 1, 1998.

Heads of religious houses as administrators, in W.M.Ormrod, ed. *England in the Thirteenth Century*, Harlaxton Medieval Studies, 1, 1991, 37-50.

Lamps, lights and layfolk: lay piety and religious houses before 1348, *Journal of Medieval History,* 1998.

The foundation and early patronage of Garendon Abbey, in B.J. Thompson, ed. *Monasteries and Society in Medieval England*, Harlaxton Medieval Studies, 1998.

REED, H.
The Cornish saints in their background, Leicester M.A. dissertation, 1996.

SNELL, L.S.
Editor, *Chantry Certificates for Devon and the City of Exeter*, Townsend, 1961, 98pp.

London chantries and chantry chapels, *Collectenea Londiniensia Studies Presented to Ralph Merrifield*, London and Middlesex Archaeological Society, Special Publication, 1978, 216-222.

The suppression of the religious foundations of Devon and Cornwall, Leicester M.A. thesis, 1964.

The Suppression of the Religious Foundations of Devon and Cornwall, Wordens, 1967, 200pp.

2 Post-Reformation

ALEXANDER-MACQUIBAN, T.S.
History of Priory Place Methodist Church, Doncaster: 1832-1978, 1978, 15pp.

BATES, W.
The churches' mission in South Derbyshire and North West Leicestershire, 1901-1911, Leicester M.A. dissertation, 1997.

BOWER, W.
The congregation of the Dover General Baptist Church, 1660-1700, Leicester M.A. dissertation, 1983.

COOPER, A.
Patterns of nonconformity and social change in nineteenth-century Cardiganshire, Leicester M.A. dissertation, 1993.

COURTNEY, P. (with Grey, M.)
Tintern Abbey after the Dissolution, *Bulletin, Board of Celtic Studies*, 38, 1991, 145-58.

CROCKETT, A.
A secularising geography? Religious change in England and Wales, 1676 - 1851, Leicester Ph.D. thesis, 1998.

CROCKETT, A. (with Snell, K.D.M.)
From the Compton Census of 1676 to the 1851 Census of Religious Worship: religious continuity or discontinuity?, *R.H.E.S.C.*, 8, 1, 1996, 55-89.

CROMPTON, J.
The pattern of dissent in Staffordshire in 1851, Leicester M.A. dissertation, 1987.

The Methodist sects, part 1: the origins of schism, *Five Arches*, 32, Summer 1998, 16-18.

DE WAAL, E.A.L.
Revolution in the Church, *V.S.*, X, 1967, 435-439.

ELL, P.S.
A quantitative analysis of variables allegedly influencing the pattern of religious observance in 1851: a case study in Warwickshire, Leicester M.A. dissertation, 1987.

The geography of religious worship in England and Wales: the 1851 census, *GIMMS Newsletter,* 12, 1991, 6-7.

ELLIOTT, B.
The early quakers of Monk Bretton, 1657-1700: a study of dissent in a south Yorkshire village, *T.H.A.S.,* X, 1977, 260-272.

EVERITT, A.M.
Nonconformity in country parishes, in Joan Thirsk, ed. *Land, Church, and People: Essays Presented to Professor H.P.R. Finberg, A.H.R.,* XVIII, Supplement, 1970, 178-199.

Nonconformity in the Victorian countryside, in T.G. Cook, ed. *Local Studies and the History of Education,* Methuen, 1972, 37-62.

The Pattern of Rural Dissent: the Nineteenth Century, D.E.L.H. Occasional Papers, 2nd ser., 4, Leicester University Press, 1972, 92pp.

Philip Doddridge and the evangelical tradition, in R. Greenall, ed. *Philip Doddridge, Nonconformity and Northampton,* 1981, 31-53. Reprinted in *Landscape and Community in England* (Collected Essays), 1985.

GLADDEN, D.H.
Nonconformity in Newark, 1850-1882, Leicester M.A. dissertation, 1976.

HARRATT, S.R.
Leicestershire parish clergy during the archdeaconate of Andrew Burnaby, 1786-1812: origins, education and intellectual pursuits, Leicester M.A. dissertation, 1982.

Queen Anne's Bounty and the augmentation of Leicestershire livings in the age of reform, *T.L.A.S.,* 61, 1987, 8-23.

HENDY, S.
Bedfordshire in 1851: an exploration of the patterns of worship of the major religious denominations in the registration district of Bedfordshire at the time of the religious census, Leicester M.A. dissertation, 1994.

HEY, D.G.
History of Bullhouse Chapel, 1692-1976, published by the chapel, 1977, 10pp.

The pattern of nonconformity in South Yorkshire, 1660-1851, *N.H.,* VIII, 1973, 86-118. Reprinted as The changing pattern of nonconformity, 1660-1851, in S. Pollard and C. Holmes, ed. *Essays in the Economic and Social History of South Yorkshire,* South Yorkshire County Council, 1976, 204-217.

The riches of Bullhouse: a family of Yorkshire dissenters, *N. H.,* XXXI, 1995, 178-93.

HOGAN, C.J.
The distribution of puritanism in Norfolk and Suffolk, 1603-1642, Leicester M.A. dissertation, 1975.

HOSKINS, W.G.
The Leicestershire country parson in the sixteenth century, *T.L.A.S.*, XXI, 1940, 89-115. Reprinted in W.G. Hoskins, ed. *Essays in Leicestershire History*, Liverpool University Press, 1950.

IREDALE, D.A.
Mary and her child: Mary Burgess of Barnton at Christmas 1817, *Methodist Recorder*, Dec. 1964; *Northwich Guardian*, Jan. 1965.

Records of the Richmond monthly meeting of the Religious Society of Friends, *North Riding Record Office Report*, 1966, 25-38.

JONES, K.
Aspects of society in the Vale of Belvoir in the first half of the ninteenth century, looking particularly at the relationship between the Nonconformist and Established sectors of society, Leicester M.A. dissertation, 1998.

LLOYD, P. (with Cocks, T.Y.)
50 Years - 30 Centuries: a History of the Church and Some Churchmen in Leicestershire, Leicester Diocesan Golden Jubilee Committee, 1976, 88pp.

MOIR, E.A.L.
The architecture of dissent, *H.T.*, XIII, 1963, 383-389.

New churches in east London in the early eighteenth century, *Renaissance and Modern Studies*, IX, 1965, 98-114.

MOIR, M.
Church and society in sixteenth-century Herefordshire, Leicester M.Phil. thesis, 1984.

NEAVE, G.R.
The clergy of the Gartree deanery in the diocese of Leicester, *c.*1600-1640, Leicester M.A. dissertation, 1974.

NIX, M.
Heaven and Helling Stones: the Story of St John's, Hartland, St John's Art and Music Centre, 1978.

SNELL, K.D.M.
Church and Chapel in the North Midlands: Religious Observance in the Nineteenth Century, D.E.L.H. Occasional Papers, 4th ser., 3, Leicester University Press, 1991, 77pp.

SNELL, K.D.M. (with Crockett, A.)
From the Compton Census of 1676 to the 1851 Census of Religious Worship: religious continuity or discontinuity?, *R.H.E.S.C.*, 8, 1, 1996, 55-89.

SPUFFORD, H.M.
The dissenting churches in Cambridgeshire, 1660-1700, *P.Camb.A.S.*, LXI, 1968, 67-95.

The quest for the heretical laity in the visitation records of Ely in the late sixteenth and early seventeenth centuries, *S.C.H.*, IX, 1972, 223-230.

The social status of some seventeenth-century rural dissenters, *S.C.H.*, VIII, 1971, 203-210.

Puritanism and social control?, in A.J. Fletcher and J. Stevenson, ed. *Order and Disorder in Early Modern England*, Cambridge University Press, 1985, 41-57.

Can we cut on the 'Godly' and the 'Comfortable' in the seventeenth century, *Journal of Ecclesiastical History*, 36, 3, 1985, 428-38.

The importance of the Lord's Supper to seventeenth-century dissenters, *Journal of the United Reformed Church History Society*, V, 1993, 62-80.

Editor, *The World of Rural Dissenters 1520-1725*, Cambridge University Press, 1994, 429pp.

The importance of religion in the sixteenth and seventeenth centuries, *ibid.*, 1-102.

Religion and society in early modern England, *Rikkyo University International Exchange Series*, Occasional Paper 12, Tokyo, 1996.

THORNTON, C.
Tudor and Stuart Colchester: religious life, in J. Cooper, ed. *The Victoria History of the County of Essex, IX: The Borough of Colchester,* Oxford University Press, 1994, 121-32.

TRANTER, E.M.
Aspects of the development of dissent in rural Derbyshire, 1662-1851, Leicester M.A. dissertation, 1975.

Landlords, labourers, local preachers: rural nonconformity in Derbyshire, 1772-1851, *Derbyshire Archaeological Journal*, CI, 1981, 139-50.

Many and diverse dissenters: the 1829 religious returns of Derbyshire, *L.H.*, 18, 4, Nov.1988, 162-67.

Editor, *The Derbyshire Returns to the 1851 Religious Census*, Derbyshire Records Society, 1995, 238pp.

Introduction (with contributions from D.A.Barton and P.S.Ell), *ibid.*, vii-lxxvi.

WICKES, M.J.L.
John Wesley in Devon 1739-1789, M.Wickes Publications, 1985, 78pp.

John Wesley in Devon 1739-1789, Plymouth & Exeter Methodist District, 1988, 43pp.

Devon in the Religious Census of 1851, M.Wickes Publications, 1990, 157pp.

The West Country Preachers, a History of the Bible Christians 1815-1907, M.Wickes Publications, 1987, 104pp.

WILLIS, S.R.
The Stroudwater Primitive Methodist circuit, Leicester M.A. dissertation, 1988.

WRIGHT, S.J.
Editor, *Parish, Church and People. Local Studies in Lay-religion 1350-1750*, Century Hutchinson, 1988.

Catechism, confirmation and communion: the role of the young in the post-Reformation Church, in S.J. Wright, ed. *Parish, Church and People. Local Studies in Lay-religion 1350-1750*, Century Hutchinson, 1988, 203-227.

B   Education and Culture

BAINBRIDGE, J.
The social and cultural life of Great Malvern in 1871, Leicester M.A. dissertation, 1989.

BATES, D.
All manner of natural knowledge: the Northampton Philosophical Society, *N.P.P.*, VIII, 4, 1992-3, 363-374.

BOURNE, J.M.
Leicester Museums Department of Education, *Newsletter,* Friends of D.E.L.H., 3, 1990.

BROWN, E.
Leicester Mechanics' Institute, 1833-1870, studied in its local and national context, Leicester M.A. dissertation, 1996.

COX, R.C.W.
Croydon School Archives: a Report, London Borough of Croydon Education Department, 1985, 390pp.

Croydon School Archives: a Second Report, London Borough of Croydon Education., Department, 1992, 340pp.

BULLEN, S.C.
The cultural life of Preston, 1742-1842, Leicester M.A. dissertation, 1971.

CROMPTON, J.
Three in One: the birth of a school, *Five Arches*, 16, 1993, 10-11.

CROSS, M.C.
The Free Grammar School of Leicester, University College of Leicester, D.E.L.H. Occasional Papers, 4, 1953, 51pp.

FAITH, R.J. (with Aston, T.H.)
University and college endowments, in J. Catto, ed. *The Early Oxford Schools* [The History of the University of Oxford, I], 1984.

FAITH, R.J. (with Evans, T.A.R.)
College estates and university finances, in J. Catto and T.A.R. Evans, ed. *Later Medieval Oxford* [The History of the University of Oxford, II], 1992.

FLEMING, D.
Survival! 400 Years of Hull's Old Grammar School, Hull Museums, 1988.

FREEBODY, N.K.
The History of the Collegiate Girls' School, Leicester, 1867-1967, Armstrong-Thornley, 1967, 64pp .

GRAHAM, M.
School Days: Elementary Education in Oxfordshire, 1800-1914, Oxfordshire County Council, 1980.

Oxfordshire at School in Old Photographs, Alan Sutton Publishing, 1996.

GREWCOCK, C.E.S.
Social and intellectual life in Leicester, 1763-1835, Leicester M.A. dissertation, 1973.

HARRIS, K.S.
Some aspects of education and society in Market Harborough 1869-1913 as seen through schools' log books, Leicester M.A. dissertation, 1991.

HARRATT, S.R. (with Gurman, S.J.)
Revd Dr William Pearson (1767-1847): a founder of the Royal Astronomical Society, *Quarterly Jnl. Royal Astronomical Society*, 35, 1994, 271-292.

HILLIER, K.A.
Ashby Church of England Infant School 1836-1986, Ashby Museum, 1986, 64pp.

Ashby Grammar School: a Centenary of Girls' Education, Ashby Museum, 1989, 61pp.

Packington School: a History, Ashby Museum, 1993, 72pp.

HOSKINS, W.G.
Exeter bookseller's stock in 1615, *D.C.N.Q.*, XXI, 1941, 36-38.

IREDALE, D.A.
A Victorian schoolmistress, *Cheshire Round*, 1966, 195-199.

KAYE, D.
Editor, *Monk's Dyke, 1929-1979*, 1979.

McKINLEY, R.A.
Education in Leicestershire; charity schools, elementary education in the nineteenth and twentieth centuries, in W.G. Hoskins and R.A. McKinley, ed. *The Victoria History of the County of Leicester*, III, Oxford University Press, 1955, 243-251.

PETCHEY, W.J.
Centenary Notes, *The Riponian*, n.s., XXIX, 1974, 11-15.

PETFORD, A.J.
Matthew Broadley's benefactions and the origins of the Grammar School at Hipperholme, *Transactions of the Halifax Antiquarian Society*, 6, n.s., 1998, 30-5.

POUND, J.F.
The social and geographical origins of the English Grammar school pupil: Bury St Edmunds and Manchester Grammar schools in the reign of George II, *History of Education Society Bulletin*, 37, Spring 1986.

REED, M.A.
A footnote to the history of English music: The will and probate inventory of George Hudson, *The Music Review*, 41, 1980, 169-171.

The cultural role of small towns in England, 1600-1800, in P. Clark, ed. *Small Towns in Early Modern Europe*, Cambridge University Press, 1995, 121-147.

Cities and the transmission of cultural values in the late Middle Ages and Early Modern period: the case of London, 1500-1800, in *17th International Colloquium: Cities and the Transmission of Cultural Values in the Late Middle Ages and Early Modern Period*, Crédit Communal: Collection Histoire, 96, 1996, 85-100.

SPUFFORD, H.M.
The schooling of the peasantry, 1575-1700, in J. Thirsk, ed. *Land, Church and People: Essays Presented to H.P.R. Finberg, A.H.R.*, XVIII, Supplement, 1970, 112- 147.

First steps in literacy: the reading and writing experiences of the humblest seventeenth-century spiritual autobiographers, *Social History*, 4, 3, Oct 1979, 407-35. Reprinted in E.Graff, ed. *Literacy and Social Development in the West*, Cambridge University Press, 1981, 125-50.

Literacy, trade and religion in the commercial centres of Europe, in J. Lucassen and

K. Davids, ed. *A Miracle Mirrored: the Dutch Republic in European Perspective*, Cambridge, 1996, 229-283.

WARNER, P. (with Edwards, E.)
Homerton 1894-1994: One Hundred Years in Cambridge, The Trustees of Homerton College, 1993.

WEST, F.
The Charity School in Wrangle, *Lincs.H.*, II, x, 1963, 1-13.

WILLIAMS, M.I.
Did Handel visit Cardiganshire?, *Cer.*, III, 1959, 337-343.

Edward Lhuyd in Glamorgan, *Glam.H.*, VI, 1969, 95-104.

C Popular Culture (including folklore)

BATES, D.
When earth her entrails shook: the earthquake of 1750, *N.P.P.*, IX, 1, 1994-5, 55-68.

BENNETT, C.I.
A devouring nostalgia and an infinite repulsion: the impact of D.H.Lawrence on the town and country of Eastwood, Leicester M.A. dissertation, 1994.

COX, R.C.W.
`At the going down of the sun': an Account of Croydon's War Memorials, C.N.H.S.S., 1992, 60pp.

GOODACRE, J.D.
Wyclif in Lutterworth: myths and monuments, *Leics.H.*, III, ii, 1983/4, 25-35.

KING, J.
George Eliot's legacy: local history revisited, Leicester M.A. dissertation, 1992.

PETCHEY, W.J.
The Intentions of Thomas Plume, Trustees of the Plume Library, 1985, 41pp.

PHYTHIAN-ADAMS, C.V.
Ceremony and the citizen: the communal year at Coventry, 1450-1550, in P. Clark and P. Slack, ed. *Crisis and Order in English Towns, 1500-1700*, Routledge and Kegan Paul, 1972, 57-85. Reprinted in P. Clark, ed. *The Early Modern Town: a Reader*, Longman, 1976. 106-128, and in R. Holt and G. Rosser, ed. *The Medieval Town: a Reader in English Urban History*, Longman, 1990, 238-264.

Local History and Folklore: a New Framework, The National Council of Social Service for the Standing Conference for Local History, 1975, 40pp.

Ceremony and the citizen, Open University Television production for Course A322, 1977.

Rural culture, in G.E.Mingay, ed. *The Victorian Countryside*, Routledge and Kegan Paul, 1981, II, 76-86.

Milk and soot: the changing vocabulary of a popular ritual in Stuart and Hanoverian London, in D. Fraser and A. Sutcliffe, ed. *The Pursuit of Urban History*, Arnold, 1983, 83-104.

Rural culture, in G.E.Mingay, ed. *The Vanishing Countryman*, Routledge, 1989, 76-86.

Rituals of personal confrontation in late medieval England (J.E. Neale Memorial Lecture for 1988, University of Manchester), *Bulletin of the John Rylands University Library of Manchester*, LXXIII, 1991, 65-90.

Calendar Customs; Civic Ritual; Customs; Folklore; Popular Culture; in D.G. Hey, ed. *The Oxford Companion to Local and Family History*, Oxford University Press, 1996, 63-64, 93-95, 123-125, 186-188, 363-370.

Environments and identities: landscape as cultural projection in the English provincial past, in P. Slack, ed. *Environment and Historical Change*, Linacre Lectures for 1998, Oxford University Press, forthcoming.

PHYTHIAN-ADAMS, H.V.
Three Winchcombe ghosts, *Cotswold Life*, 180, Oct 1983, 38-39.

SMITH, J.R.
The suppression of pestiferous dancing in Essex, *English Dance and Song*, XXXVI, i, 1974, 9-11.

SNELL, K.D.M.
Editor (with Bellamy, L and Williamson, T), *R.H.E.S.C.*, 4, 1, April 1993, 109 pp. (Six-article issue entitled 'Rural History and Popular Culture').

Folklore and rural history, *Folklore Society News*, January, 1990.

Rural history and folklore studies: towards new forms of association, *Folklore,* 100, 2, 1989, 218-220.

Editor, *The Regional Novel in Britain and Ireland, 1800-1990*, Cambridge University Press, 1998, 319 pp.

The regional novel: themes for interdisciplinary research, *ibid., 1-53.*

SPUFFORD, H.M.
Small Books and Pleasant Histories: Popular Fiction and its Readership in Seventeenth-Century England, Methuen, 1981, 261pp. Acquired by Cambridge University Press for re-issue as a paperback, Past and Present Publications, Summer 1985, reprinted 1989.

The contents of Samuel Pepys's collection, and the Bibliotheque Bleue, *Scienze, Credenze, Occulte Livelli di Cultura,* Instituto Nazionale di Studi Sul Rinascimento, 1982, 147-158.

The pedlar, the historian, and the folklorist: seventeenth-century communications' 10th Katherine Briggs Memorial Lecture, *Folklore*, CV, 1994, 13-24.

Drukwerk voor de armen, in Engeland en Nederland, 1450-1700, in T.Bijvoet *et al.,* ed. *Bladeren in Andermans Hoofd: over Lezers en Leescultuur*, Nijmegen, 1996, 67-80

STEDMAN, J.O.
Portsmouth's favourite artist: W.L.Wyllie, *Hampshire*, XXXVI, x, Aug 1996, 38-40.

THOMPSON, M.G.
Edwardian excursions, *Newsletter*, Friends of D.E.L.H., 11, 1998, 23-24.

D Recreations

ALDRED, D.H.
George Stevens: superstar in the shadows, *Gloucestershire and Avon Life,* March 1979, 30-32.

Christmas Day in the workhouse, *ibid.,* Dec. 1979, 4-9.

No return trip to Winchcombe, *ibid.,* Feb., 1980, 24-27.

Bishop's Cleeve, *ibid.,* Nov., 1981, 41-44.

Guilt and gingerbread at the pre-Prestbury races, *ibid.,* March, 1982, 46-49.

BOASE, S.
The Leicester pleasure fairs in Humberstone Gate 1837-1904, Leicester M.A. dissertation, 1979.

The Humberstone Gate pleasure fairs in the late nineteenth century, *Leics.H.,* II, x, 1979/80, 16-25.

GENT, K.S.
Leisure activities in Leicester, 1870-1901, with special reference to the working class, Leicester M.A. dissertation, 1977.

GRAHAM, M.
Public library facilities in Oxford before 1914, *Ox.,* 43, 1978.

The building of Banbury Library in 1884, *C. & C.,* 9, 8, Spring 1985.

A lost resort: the lock cottages at Nuneham Courtenay, *Oxfordshire Local History,* 3, 4, Spring 1990.

Oxfordshire at Play in Old Photographs, Alan Sutton Publishing, 1997.

JENKINS, S.C.
Some memories of the Palace Cinema, Witney, *R.W.,* n.s., 2, 6, 1994, 105-111.

KILBURN, T.
West Bromwich theatres, Part 1, *The Blackcountryman,* 20, 3, 1987, 54-60

West Bromwich theatres, Part 2, *ibid.,* 20, 4, 1987, 44-50.

The West Bromwich Theatre Royal, 1875-1900, *Staffordshire History,* 6, 1987. Drinking, gambling and illegal activities in West Bromwich, 1875-1900, part 1, *The Blackcountryman,* 21, 2, 1988.

Drinking, gambling and illegal leisure activities in late-Victorian West Bromwich, *Staffordshire History,* 12, 1990, 34-51.

McINTOSH, T.
The decline of Stourbridge Fair 1770-1934: deliberate suppression or inevitable collapse?, Leicester M.A. dissertation, 1992. Published by Friends of D.E.L.H. as Friends Paper, 2, 1998.

PHYTHIAN-ADAMS, H.V.
A formidable challenger, William Vevers (1782-1858), *Country Life,* CLXVIII, Nov. 13, 1980.

E   Representations (in print, song, picture, etc.)

BURNS, H.
Aspects of the Portsmouth area in fiction: from 1814, Leicester M.A. dissertation, 1995.

HALL, J.
Poems and songs of Staffordshire in the modern period and their depiction of people and region, Leicester M.A. dissertation, 1996.

HART, Cyril R.
The Canterbury contribution to the Bayeux Tapestry, in Guy de Boe and Frans Verhaeghe, ed. *Papers of the Medieval Europe Brugge 1997 Conference Vol.5, Art and Symbolism in Medieval Europe*, Institute of the Archaeological Heritage of Flanders, 1997.

HEATHCOTE BALL, J.
An attempt to analyse the development of the alabaster effigy tombs of Leicestershire 1350-1605, Leicester M.A. dissertation, 1998.

HILLIER, K.A.
Around Ashby-de-la-Zouch in Old Photographs, Alan Sutton Publishing, 1994, 124pp.

INDER, P.M.
Topographical prints and the development of seaside resorts: case studies of Scarborough and Sidmouth, Leicester M.A. dissertation, 1992.
KING, J.
George Eliot's legacy: local history revisited, Leicester M.A. dissertation, 1992

MERRALL, I.
The sense of belonging amongst people in the Midlands, Leicester M.A. dissertation, 1993.

ORME, P.
Alabaster monuments as a reflection of changes in liturgy, Leicester M.A. dissertation, 1994.

PAGETT, K.
Image problems: the ambiguous identity of Birmingham as represented in novels set in the city, *c*.1870-1950, Leicester M.A. dissertation, 1992.

PHYTHIAN-ADAMS, C.V.
Environments and identities: landscape as cultural projection in the English provincial past, in P. Slack, ed. *Environment and Historical Change*, Linacre Lectures for 1998, Oxford University Press, forthcoming.

PARR, M.
The churchyard in the modern period: function, idea and place, Leicester M.A. dissertation, 1994.

REED, M.A.
La rappresentazione pittorica delle Citta Inglesi dal XVII al XIX secolo, in Cesare de Seta, ed. *Citta d'Europa: Iconografia e Vedutismo dal XV al XVIII secolo*, Naples, 1996, 61-71.

REEVE, D.
Pity the poor labourer: English protest folksongs and their effects on the study of popular culture during the Industrial Revolution, Leicester M.A. dissertation, 1989.

SNELLING, J.
Early-modern and modern society reflected in memorials: a local perspective - the Welland valley, Leicester M.A. dissertation, 1996.

Welland valley society reflected in memorials, *The Harborough Historian*, 15, 1998.

TOWNSEND, S.N.
George Morland: a source for rural social conditions in southern England, 1790-1800 Volumes I and II, Leicester M.A. dissertation, 1986.

WALLACE, J.
Newspapers in Leicester, 1850-1900, Leicester M.A. dissertation, 1994.

WILLARS, G.
A view from the one-and-nines: a sense of place: the English regional novel in film, Leicester M.A. dissertation, 1996.

VI   LOCAL HISTORY and MUSEUMS

COURTNEY, P.
In small things forgotten: the Georgian world view, material culture and consumer revolution, *R.H.E.S.C.*, 7, 1, 1996, 87-95.

'Different strokes for different folks', the trans-Atlantic development of historical and post-medieval archaeology, R. Michael and G. Egan, ed. *Old and New Worlds: Proceedings of the 1997 S.H.A./S.P.M.A. joint conference,* Oxford.

CRESSWELL Y.M. (with Neale, K.)
The House of Manannan, *S.H.C.G. Journal,* 23, 1997-8, 41-45.

FLEMING, D.
Photographic collections - a strategy for information retrieval, *M.D.A. Information*, 9, 11, 1985, 14-24.

From shepherd's smocks to EEC: interpretation in rural museums, *Museums Journal,* 85, 4, 1985, 179-186.

Exploring Museums in the North East, H.M.S.O., 1989.

Cain's people: museums and the urban enviroment, *S.H.C.G. Journal,* 19, 1992, 37-44.

Social History in Museums, D. Fleming, C. Paine, J. Rhodes, ed. HMSO, 1993.

Documents, in D. Fleming *et al.*, ed. *Social History in Museums*, 104-110.

Making city histories, in G.Kavanaugh, ed. *Making Histories in Museums*, 1996, 131-142.

JENKINS, S.C.
Some thoughts on museums, *R.W.*, 20, 1988, 3-7.

HAYHURST, Y.M.
Co-author, *Samplers in the Collections of the Manx Museum*, Manx Museum and National Trust, 1988, 60pp.

MORRIS, C.I.
Articles Made by the French Prisoners of War at Norman Cross, and Life in the Barracks, Norris Museum Information Sheet, 1, 1976, 4pp.

Clay tobacco pipes, Norris Museum Information Sheet, 2, 1976, 6pp.

NIX, M.
Interpreting objects: a milk churn, *Tiverton Museum Newsletter*, 1, 1993.

Under fire: the Virginie story, *Tiverton Museum Newsletter*, 6, 1995.

Cruel Copinger: fact and fiction, *North Devon Heritage*, 7, 1995, 24-5.

TRINDER, B.S.
Industrial conservation and industrial history: reflections on Ironbridge Gorge Museum, *H.W.*, II, 1976, 171-6.

Museum projects as a means of community education, *Papers of the Second International Congress of Friends of Museums*, Brussels, 1976, 136-141.

A philosophy for the industrial open air museum, *Report of the 1984 Conference of the Association of European Open Air Museums*, Westfalischer Frielichtmuseum, ed. C. Ahrens, 1985, 87-105.

Industry or fantasy: a review of industrial history as presented to tourists, in U. Georgeacopol-Winischhofr, P. Swittalek & M. Wehdorn, ed. *Industrial Heritage - Austria 1987 Transactions* II, 1990, 16-20.

Authenticity in the industrial heritage, in K.E. Larsen, ed. *Proceedings of the Nara Conference on Authenticity in relation to the World Heritage Convention*, UNESCO, 1995, 403-6.

Industry and the world heritage, *World Heritage Review*, II, 1996, 52-63.

WHITE, H.J.
Snuff Bottles from China, V&A, Bamboo, 1992, 291pp.

VII BEYOND ENGLAND AND WALES

CRESSWELL, Y.M.
A recent find of a horse skull in a house at Ballaugh, Isle of Man, *Folklore*, 100, 1989, 105-109.

Living With the Wire: Civilian Internment in the Isle of Man during the Two World Wars, Manx National Heritage, 1994, 72pp.

EDWARDS, E.J.M.
Australia in Oxford, Oxford Pitt Rivers Museum Monograph 4, in Morphy and Edwards, ed. *Australia in Oxford,* 1988.

Guest editor, A question of image, *Journal of Museum Ethnography,* 1, 1989.

Images of the Andamans: the photography of E.H.Man, *ibid.,* 71-78.

African photographs in the collections of the Pitt Rivers Museum, Oxford, in A.Roberts, ed. *Photographs as Sources for African History,* London: S.O.A.S., 1989.

Photographic types: the pursuit of method, *Visual Anthropology,* 3, 2-3, 239-258.

Wamo: Jenness' photographs of D'Entrecasteaux Island, *Pacific Arts,* 5, 1992, 53-56,.

A reflection on four Australian postcards, *Tourism in Focus,* 6, 1992, 4-5,.

Editor, *Anthropology and Photography 1860-1920,* Yale University Press,1992.

Science visualised: E.H.Man in the Andaman Islands, *ibid.*

Wilfred Thesiger's Photographs: a Most Cherished Possession, Oxford Pitt Rivers Museum, 1993.

Axel Poignant's photographs: a review essay, *Pacific Arts,* 7, 1994, 120-123.

Jorma Puranen: imaginary homecoming, *Social Identities,* 2, 1995, 317-322.

Seeing how others die: an historical perspective from anthropological photography, in V.Williams, ed. *The Dead,* Manchester: Cornerhouse, 1995.

Photography in ethnographic museums: a reflection, *Journal of Museum Ethnography,* 7, 1995, 131-139.

Visuality and history: a contemplation on two photographs by Captain W.A.D. Acland, in C. Blanton, ed. *Picturing Paradise: Colonial Photography in Samoa,* Daytona Beach: Southeast Museum of Photography, 1995.

Visualität und Geschichte: Eine Betrachtung zweier Somoa-Fotographien von Acland, Kapitän der Royal Navy, in J. Engelhard and P. Mesenhöller, ed. *Bilder aus dem Paradies*, Marburg Jonas Verlag, 1995.

Visualising history: Diamond Jenness' photographs of Massim, 1911-12, a case study in re-engagement, *Canberra Anthropology*, 17, 2, 1995, 1-26.

Postcards: greetings from another world, in T. Selwyn, ed. *The Tourist Image*, London: John Wiley, 1996.

Photography, in T. Barfield, ed. *Blackwell Dictionary of Anthropology*, Oxford: Blackwell, 1996.

Photo-objects, *Martor*, 2, 1997, 85-93.

Mohini Chandra:'Travels in a New World 2', Liverpool Bluecoat Gallery, 1997.

Ordering others: photography, anthropologies and taxonomies, in R.Roberts, ed. *Visible Light: Classification and Photography in Art, Science and the Everyday*, Oxford Museum of Modern Art, 1997.

Guest editor, 'Anthropology and Colonial Endeavor', *History of Photography*, 21, 1, 1997.

Beyond the boundary: ethnography and photographic expression, in M. Banks and H. Morphy, ed. *Rethinking Visual Anthropology*, Yale University Press, 1997, 53-80.

Impossible science of being, *Visual Anthropology Review*, 13, 2, 1998, 79-84.

Preface, degree show 'Catalogue', Department of Photography, Royal College of Art, London, 1998.

Performing science: the cultural currency of photographs and the Torres Strait Expedition, in A. Herte and S. Rouse, ed. *The Torres Strait Expedition: Cambridge and the Development of Anthropology*, Cambridge University Press, 1998, 106-136.

The Cambridge Torres expedition, 1898: making histories, *Journal of Pacific Studies*, 1998.

Photographic facts and imperial fictions, *J.Hist.Geog.*, 1998.

The resonance of anthropology, in *Native Nations: American Photographs from the Edge 1850-1914*, London Barbican Art Gallery, 1998.

Encounter at Ngalarrambe: a review essay, *Pacific Arts*, 1998.

EDWARDS, E.J.M. (with Coote, J.)
Images of Benin at the Pitt Rivers Museum, *African Arts*, 30, 4, 1997, 26-35.

EDWARDS, E.J.M. (With Mowat, L.)
Terminology at the Pitt Rivers Museum: a pragmatic approach, in D.A. Roberts, *Terminology in Museums*, Cambridge, Museums Documentation Association, 1990.

ELLIOTT, B.S.
The City Beyond: a History of Nepean, Birthplace of Canada's Capital, 1792-1990, Corporation of the City of Nepean, 1991, xiv + 461pp.

Editor (with C.A.Heald), *The Carleton Election, or the Tale of a Bytown Ram,* Pinhey's Point Foundation, 1989.

Irish Migrants in the Canadas: a New Approach, McGill Queen's University Press and Institute of Irish Studies, 1988, xxviii + 371pp. Paperback edition 1989.

Editor, *Index to the 1871 Census of Ontario,* O.G.S., 1986-92, 30 vols.

Editor, *The McCabe List: Early Irish in the Ottawa valley,* O.G.S., 1991, 64pp.

Editor (with Dan Walker and Fawne Stratford-Devai), *Men of Upper Canada: Militia Nominal Rolls, 1828-1829,* O.G.S., 1995, xvii + 356pp.

The Bell family of Nepean township, in A.C.Hare, *Tales of the Hares: the Story of Henry Hare and his Descendants, 1823-1976,* 1977.

Immigration from South Leinster to Eastern Upper Canada, in K. Whelan, ed. *County Wexford: History and Society,* Dublin Geography Publications, 1987, 422-26. Reprinted in D.H. Akenson, ed. *Canadian Papers in Rural History, VIII,* 1992, 277-305.

Regionalized migration and settlement patterns of the Irish in Upper Canada, in R.O'Driscoll, ed. *The Untold Story: the Irish in Canada,* 1988, 308-18.

Canadian sources for Irish genealogy, in M.D. Evans and E. O'Duill, ed. *Aspects of Irish Genealogy,* Irish Genealogical Congress, 1993, 105-22.

'The famous township of Hull': image and aspirations of a pioneer Quebec community, *Histoire Sociale/Social History,* 12, 24, 1979, 339-67.

Ritualism and the beginnings of the reformed episcopal movement in Ottawa, *Journal of the Canadian Church Historical Society,* 27, 1, 1985, 18-41.

Sources of bias in nineteenth-century Ontario wills, *Histoire Sociale/Social History,* 18, 35, 1985, 125-32.

Kanata, in *Canadian Encyclopaedia,* 2nd edn, Hurtig Publishers, 1988, 2, 1126.

The Moffatt family, in *Aylmer Sunday Reporter,* 9 Sept, 1973.

The Pink and Moffatt families of Hull, in *Up the Gatineau!,* 1, 1975.

The Bonell family, *The Midland Ancestor, Journal of the Birmingham and Midland Society for Genealogy and Heraldry,* 1977.

Gleanings from Britain: the ancestry of the Hon. Hamnett Kirkes Pinhey, *O.G.S. Ottawa Branch News,* Jan 1978.

Utility and variety of early church records, *Families,* 16, 4, 1977, 207-24.

Tracing your Ottawa Family, City of Ottawa Archives, 1980, 2nd revised edn, 1986.

The Bucks of Hull and Merrickville, *O.G.S. Ottawa Branch News,* March/April, 1981.

Arthur Hopper of Merivale, his children and grandchildren, in J.Kennedy, ed. *The Merivale Cemeteries,* O.G.S., 1981.

The Hopper family, *The Irish Ancestor,* 1982, 2, 59-73.

More on the family of Sgt John Johnston, Merrickville lockmaster, *O.G.S. Ottawa Branch News,* Nov-Dec, 1982.

How to write a book review, *Families,* 21, 4, 1982, 167-9.

Philemon Wright 1769-1839, in *L'Outaouais: Proceedings of the Forum on the Regional Identity of Western Quebec,* Institut d'Histoire et de Recherche sur l'Outaouais, 1982, 12-14.

The George Blackwell family of Renfrew Co. Ontario, *Blackwell Newsletter,* 4, 2, 1982, 24-28.

Symposium: access to census records, in B.D. Merriman, ed. *Seminar Annual 1983,* O.G.S., 1983, 114-26.

Tipperary? Well, just barely...the Donnellys located, *Families,* 22, 2, 1983, 91-96.

Pink and Rolston; the Elliotts; the Scrivens family; the Stanleys and Mossops, articles in *Pioneer Families of Osgoode Township,* VI, VII, VIII.

Irish and Scottish relations of some West Carleton families, *O.G.S. Ottawa Branch News,* Jan 1986.

Computerization of the 1871 Ontario census, *Machine Readable Archives Bulletin,* 4, 1, 1986, 1.

Editor (with G.L.S.Buell), The family of Judge William Buell of Gates, near Rochester, New York, in *Families,* 23, 2, 1896, 85-94.

The North Tipperary settlements of Upper Canada, *Irish Family History,* 3, 1987, 21-23.

History sheds light on origins of Kanata's old homes, *Kanata Standard,* 1987, 11 June, 4; 18 June, 4.

The building of Horaceville, *Horaceville Herald,* 8 March 1987; 9 June 1987.

Landmarks in Ontario genealogy: a 25 year retrospective, *Families,* 26, 4, 1987, 195-200.

Irish settlement in Eastern Ontario and Western Quebec, in *Proceedings of the O.G.S.,* 1988, 1-21.

Urban History in Canada, *U.H.N.L.,* second ser., 5, 1988, 4.

The Bradley farms, *The Log Farm Gazette,* 3, 1, 1989, 1,3,4.

Old St Mary's church, parish of March, city of Kanata, *The Pinhey's Point Foundation for the City of Kanata,* 1991.

The place of Grosse-Ile in the story of Irish immigration, in *Grosse Ile National Historic Site: Public Consultation: Briefs presented in Toronto,* 1993.

High School yearbooks as genealogical sources, *O.G.S. Ottawa Branch News,* 1994.

CIHM for historians: prospects and limitations, *Facsimile,* 12, 1994, 5-7. reprinted in *Microform Review,* 24, 3, 1995, 130-32.

Township Council minutes and Poor Relief, *O.G.S. Ottawa Branch News,* 28, 3, 1995, 90-92.

H.W.Monk: the prophet of March, *Kanata Kourier-Standard,* 23 June,1995, 33.

Heritage highways: our forced roads then and now, *Horaceville Herald,* 27, 1995, 3-4.

J.C.Pinhey, R.C.A.: Canadian Artist, *Horaceville Herald,* 27, 1996.

Canada's Irish, in *Ireland of the Welcomes,* 41, 4, 1992, 21-23.

1861 Census of Eardley Township, C.E., O.G.S., 75, 9.

Canada Company remittance books, *O.G.S. Ottawa Branch News,* 1981.

Index to Torbolton township wills, *O.G.S. Ottawa Branch News,* 1981.

Carleton County case files: Second Heir and Devisee Commission, 1804-1895, *O.G.S. Ottawa Branch News,* 1982.

Perth Independent Examiner and Bathurst District Advertiser, 1829-30, *O.G.S. Ottawa Branch News,* 1982.

1842 and 1851 Census of Renfrew County, C.W., 1, Horton, O.G.S. Ottawa Branch, no. 83.

Editor, *1851 Census of Renfrew County, C.W., 2, Stafford and Pembroke,* O.G.S. Ottawa Branch, no. 84.

Early Ottawa Wesleyan Methodist registers, *O.G.S. Ottawa Branch News,* 1984.

Clarendon and Bristol Methodist baptisms, 1830-1849, *O.G.S. Ottawa Branch News,* 1984.

Upper Canada marriage licence bonds of residents of Carleton County and Western Quebec, 1826-1832, *O.G.S. Ottawa Branch News,* 1984, 1985.

The `McCabe List': early Irish in the Ottawa valley, *Families,* 29, 1990, 3, 145-57; 4, 209-21. 30, 1991, 1, 19-31; 2, 77-78.

Pink's Cemetery (Mountain View), O.G.S. Ottawa Branch no. 73-3.

Bells Corners Cemetery, O.G.S. Ottawa Branch, no.73-5.

Two cemeteries of Masham Township, Quebec, O.G.S. Ottawa Branch no. 73-10.

Centre Eardley Cemetery (near Aylmer, Quebec), O.G.S. Ottawa Branch, no. 74-15.

St James Anglican Cemetery, Hull, Quebec, O.G.S. Ottawa Branch no.77-6.

ELLIOTT, B.S. (with Acres, D.P.)
The Acres families of Carleton county, *Families,* 20, 3, 1981, 131-45.

ELLIOTT, B.S. (with Brown, D.L. and McLean, L.R.)
Historical research using computer files from the 1871 census of Ontario, *Archivaria,* 33, 1991-2, 161-72.

ELLIOTT, B.S. (with Evans, P.M.O.)
St Stephen's Roman Catholic Cemetery, Old Chelsea, Quebec, O.G.S. Ottawa Branch, no. 80.

ELLIOTT, B.S. (with Moodie, E.M.)
The Hazeldean Cemeteries, O.G.S. Ottawa Branch, no. 80-6.

St John's Anglican Cemetery, South March, with a History of the Church and Burying Ground, O.G.S. Ottawa Branch, no.85-2.

ELLIOTT, B.S. (with Stratford-Desai, F.)
Upper Canada land settlement records: the Second District Land District Boards, 1819-1825, *Families,* 34, 3, 1995, 132-37.

Alphabetical list of locations by the Land Board, Newcastle District, 1819-25, *Families,* 34, 1995, 3, 138-47; 4, 208-21; 35, 1996, 1, 26-39; 2, 88-99

FAITH, R.J.
The peasants of St Victor de Marseille during the 'other transition', in R. Evans, ed. *Lordship and Learning: Studies in Memory of Trevor Aston*, forthcoming.

GRAHAM, M.
Local studies: a new approach, *Public Library Journal*, 7, 3, May/June 1992.

IREDALE, D.A.
Leask leaks: the secret agenda for archives in the 1990s, *J.Soc.Arch.*, 10, 1, Jan 1989, 9-13.

Hunt the motte - a search for Norman conquerors, *Scots Magazine*, 1997.

The Lowland clearances, *Scots Magazine*, Sept 1992, 633-40.

Culloden - a Scottish landscape, *Scots Magazine*, April 1996, 373-382.

Building royal burghs, *Scots Magazine*, Jan 1995, 10-22.

JENKINS, S.C.
Ireland and the Great Western Railway, *British Railway Journal*, Special edn, 112-119.

LORD, E.
Fairs, feasts and fertility in Alkmaar North Holland 1650-1810, *L.P.S.,* 42, 1989, 43-53.

The moral, political and cultural construction of the North Sea landscape, in J. Roding ed. *The North Sea and Culture*, Verloren Hilversum, 1996, 64-77.

A vadon megszelitiese: tag mint allegoria, *Liget*, Irodalm, Es Okologiai IX Evfolyam, 11, 1996.

MASSAM, M.
Ballads and the nineteenth-century transition from Britain to Australia, Leicester M.A. dissertation, 1992.

MOIR, E.A.L.
Pattern book Georgian: English architecture in the U.S.A., *H.T.*, XII, 1962, 576-579.

NURSS, K.
The transmission of culture: process of naming, marriage and death in the American colonial Chesapeake, Leicester M.A. dissertation, 1991.

RAVENSDALE, J.R.
Impressions on the study of the making of the Australian landscape, *The Bulletin of the Australian Historical Association*, 13, December 1977.

REDMONDS, G.
David Bower M.P., *O.W.R.*, 7, 2, 1987.

A voyage from the West Indies, *O.W.R.*, 6, 1, 1986.

SMITH, J.R.
Pilgrims and Adventurers: Essex (England) and the making of the United States of America, Essex Record Office, 1992.

SNELL, K.D.M.
Editor, Alexander Somerville, *Letters from Ireland During the Famine of 1847*, Irish Academic Press, Dublin, 1994, 219 pp. Published in hardback and paperback editions, as part of the commemoration of the 150th anniversary of the Great Irish Famine.

German translation of Alexander Somerville, *Letters from Ireland During the Famine of 1847,* introduced by German editors and translated as *Irlands Grosser Hunger: Briefe und Reportagen aus Irland Während der Hungersnot 1847,* Unvast-Verlag, Munster, 1996, 336 pp.

Famine letters and eye-witness accounts, in G.R. Barterian and D. Evans, ed. *Nineteenth-Century Literature Criticism*, Detroit, 1998, 245-254.

SNELL, K.D.M. (with Tomida, H.)
Japanese women and oral history: European comparison and Japanese development, in G. Daniels and H. Todd, ed. *Japanese Information Resources*, Sheffield, 1994, 31 pp.

Japanese oral history and women's historiography, *Oral History: the Journal of the Oral History Society,* 24, 1, Spring 1996.

THIRSK, J.
The European debate on customs of inheritance, 1500-1700, in J. Goody, J. Thirsk, and E.P. Thompson, ed. *Family and Inheritance: Rural Society in Western Europe, 1200-1800*, Cambridge University Press, 1976, 177-191.

Economic and social development on a European-world scale, *American Journal of Sociology*, LXXXII, v, 1977, 1097-1102.

Policies for retrenchment in seventeenth-century Europe, *Comparative Studies in Society and History*, XXII, iv, 1980, 626-38.

TRINDER, B.S. (with Stratton, M.)
Hermoupolis: the archaeology of a Mediterranean industrial city, *I.A.R.,* XVI, 1994, 119-39.

WILLIAMS, M.I.
A note on Welsh emigration to America 1697-1707, *N.L.W.J.*, XVII, 1971, 210-212.

VIII   MISCELLANEOUS

BENNETT, J.
The Wildlife Garden: Month by Month, David and Charles, Newton Abbott, 1993, 139pp.

BURT, J.
The Silsoe Perspective: From the National College of Agricultural Engineering to the Cranfield Rural Institute, Cranfield Press, 1989.

COX, R.C.W.
Oh Captain Shaw: The Life Story of the First and Most Famous Chief of the London Fire Brigade, 1861-1891, Paramount Printing, 1984, 191pp, 2nd edn 1988.

Captain Shaw: the first and most famous chief of the London Fire Brigade, *Transactions of the Lewisham Local History Society,* 1987-88, 8-30.

From Cradle to Conscription: the First 18 Years of my Life: 1924-1942, privately printed, 1990, 376pp.

Gone but not forgotten, *Bourne Society Bulletin,* 144, May 1991, *et seq.*

CRESSWELL, Y.M.
Man, mutiny and motorcycles, *Newsletter,* Friends of D.E.L.H., 4, 1991, 24-25.

HART, C.E.
Alternative Silvicultural Systems to Clear Cutting in Britain: a Review, The Forestry Commission, Bulletin 115, H.M.S.O., 1995, 93pp.

HART, Cyril R. .
Religio Medici: an Autobiography and Personal Philosophy, Mellen, 1997, ix + 229pp

HILLIER, K.A.
The early years, *Ashby Hospital: a Century of Caring 1897-1997,* 1997, 3-11.

INDER, P.M.
Yoghurt pots and all that, *Newsletter,* Friends of D.E.L.H., 5, 1992, 23.

JAMES, T.M.
The East India Company college gymnasium, *C.N.H.S.S. Archaeology Newsletter,* 20, 1973, 1-2.

JENKINS, S.C.
The night Hitler bombed Witney, *R.W.,* 1, 1977, 5-7.

West Oxfordshire at war, *R.W.,* 5, 1978, 8-12.

The Titanic, seventy years on, *R.W.*, 14, 1982, 5-10.

World War Two aerodromes of Oxfordshire, *Wing Span*, Autumn 1983, 5-7.

World War Two aerodromes of Oxfordshire: Part 2 - North Oxon, *Wing Span*, Autumn 1984, 4-6.

World War Two aerodromes of Oxfordshire: Part 3 - South Oxon, *Wing Span*, Autumn 1985, 22-25.

Aerodromes of Oxfordshire, *R.W.*, 19, 1985, 8-13.

Some neglected aspects of Witney's military history, *R.W.*, n.s., 2, 7, 1997, 125-130.

KISSOCK, J.A.
Archaeology and its place in the primary school curriculum, *Archaeological Review from Cambridge*, 6, 1987, 119-128.

Challenging centipede - archaeologists of the century, *Guardian*, 22 September 1992, 33.

LORD, E.
Derbyshire friendly societies and the paradox of thrift, *Journal of Regional and Local Studies*, 16, 1996, 11-18.

PAUL, E.D.
Public demand threatens to outstrip resources, *L.H.*, XV, 1982, 3-5.

Reference and information work in local history: training for librarians, *Education for Information*, VI, 1988, 323-338.

The expansion of local history: its impact on libraries, *Library Review*, XXXVIII, i, 1989, 34-44.

Training 2000? local and family history in libraries, *Librarian Career Development*, III, iv, 1995, 4-9.

Local studies collections in academic libraries, in M.D. Dewe, ed. *Local Studies Collections. A Manual*, Vol.1. (Originally published as *A Manual of Local Studies Librarianship*, Gower Press, 52-69.

PETCHEY, W.J.
A Ripon armorial, *The Ripon Historian*, I & II.

PETFORD, A.J.
'Can I shake your hand, man, for having such a smashing car?', *Boldness Be My Friend, Remembering Bob Cryer*, Bradford Libraries, 1996, 117-129.

REED, M.A.
Artefacts, archives and knowledge, in A.J. Meadows, ed. *Knowledge and Communication*, Library Association, 1991, 19-44.

SMITH, J.R.
Jesty, Benjamin; Sutton, Daniel; Sutton, Robert, *The Dictionary of National Biography Missing Persons*, Oxford University Press, 1993-4, 355-356, 651-652, 653-654.

IX REVIEWS

COURTNEY, P.
The Archaeology of Inequality, ed. R. Paynter, in *P-Med.Arch.,* 26, 1992, 175-6.

P. Greene, *The Archaeology of Monasticism,* in *Landscape History,* 14, 1992, 78-9.

Approaches to Material Culture Research for Historical Archaeologists G.L. Miller, O.R. Jones, L.A. Ross and T. Majewski, ed., and C.R.Ewen, *The Archaeology of Spanish Colonialism in the Southeastern United States and the Caribbean,* both in *P.-Med. Arch.,* 27, 1993, 315-6.

S. Rees, *Cadw. A Guide to Ancient and Historic Wales: Dyfed,* and E. Whittle, *Cadw. A Guide to Ancient and Historic Wales: Glamorgan and Gwent,* both in *P.-Med. Arch.,* 27, 1993, 317-8.

The Meta Incognita Project: Contributions to Field Studies, S.Alsford, ed. in *P.-Med. Arch.,* 28, 1994, 194.

J.L.Cotter, D.G.Roberts and M.Parrington, *The Buried Past: An Archaeological History of Philadelphia,* in *P.-Med. Arch.,* 28, 1994, 196.

E.L.Bell, *Vestiges of Mortality and Remembrance,* in *P. Med. Arch.,* 29, 1995, 206.

Puerto Real: the Archaeology of a 16th Century Spanish Town in Hispaniola, K.Deagan, ed. in *P. Med. Arch.,* 29, 1995, 207-8.

A.Yentsch, *A Chesapeake Family and their Slaves,* in *P. Med. Arch.,* 30,1996, 340.

EDEN, P.
H.C. Darby, *Domesday Geography of Eastern England,* in *Arch.Jnl.,* CIX, 1952, 162.

M W. Barley, *Lincolnshire and the Fens,* in *Arch.Jnl.,* CIX, 1952, 161.

G.H. Cook, *The English Medieval Church,* in *Ant.Jnl.,* XXXV, 1955, 119.

H.C. Darby, *The Draining of the Fens,* in *Arch.Jnl.,* CXIII, 1956, 174-175.

J.M. Richards, *The Functional Tradition in Early Industrial Buildings,* in *Ant.Jnl.,* XXXIX, 1959, 310.

N. Pevsner, *The Buildings of N.E. Norfolk and Norwich* and *The Buildings of N.W. and S. Norfolk,* in *Arch.Jnl.,* CXX, 1963, 321-322.

The Victoria History of the County of Oxford, VII, ed. Mary Lobel, in *Ant.Jnl.,* XLIII, 1963, 150-159.

F. Burgess, *English Churchyard Memorials,* in *Ant.Jnl.,* XLV, 1965, 295-296.

D. Portman, *Exeter Houses, 1400-1700*, in *U.H.N.L.*, IX, 1967, 29.

The Victoria History of the County of Stafford, II, ed. M.W. Greenslade and J.D. Jenkins, in *Ant.Jnl.*, XLIX, 1969, 437-438.

V. Parker, *The Making of King's Lynn*, in *P.-Med. Arch.*, VI, 1972, 226-227.

EVERITT, A.M.
F.W. Jessup, *A History of Kent*, in *Ec.H.R.*, 2nd ser., XI, 1958, 172.

C. Read, *Bibliography of British History: Tudor Period, 1485-1603*, in *A.H.R.*, VIII, 1960, 121-122.

Kentish Sources, II: Kent and the Civil War, ed. E. Melling, in *Arch.*, V, 1961, 54-56.

Essays in the Economic and Social History of Tudor England in Honour of R.H. Tawney, ed. F.J. Fisher, in *A.H.R.*, X, 1962, 128-129.

Kentish Sources, III: Aspects of Agriculture and Industry, ed. E. Melling, in *A.H.R.*, X, 1962, 128-130.

The Letterbooks, 1644-5, of Sir Samuel Luke, Parliamentary Governor of Newport Pagnell, in *Arch.*, VII, 1965, 113-114.

R. Church, *Economic and Social Change in a Midland Town: Victorian Nottingham*, in *U.H.N.L.*, VI, 1966, 8-10.

C.W. Chalklin, *Seventeenth Century Kent: a Social and Economic History*, in *A.H.R.*, XIV, 1966, 65-69.

The Victoria History of the County of Leicester, V, ed. J.M. Lee and R.A. McKinley, in *Ant.Jnl.*, XLVI, 1966, 139-140.

G.H. Green and M.W. Green, *Loughborough Markets and Fairs (through 7½ centuries)*, in *A.H.R.*, XV, 1967, 120-129.

Worcestershire Historical Society, n.s., V, *Miscellany II*, 1967, ed. A.D. Dyer, R.D. Hunt, and B.S. Smith, in *Arch.*, VIII, 1968, 216-217.

M.W. Beresford, *New Towns of the Middle Ages: Town Plantation in England, Wales and Gascony*, in *T.L.S.*, 6 June 1968.

W. Herbert, *The History of the Twelve Great Livery Companies of London*, in *I.A.*, VI, 1969, 286-288.

H.P.R. Finberg and V.H.T. Skipp, *Local History: Objective and Pursuit*, in *Ec.H.R.*, 2nd ser., XXII, 1969, 552-553.

The Victoria History of the County of Gloucester, VIII, ed. C.R. Elrington, in *T.L.S.*, 13 Mar. 1969.

The Victoria History of Shropshire, VIII, ed. A.T. Gaydon, in *T.L.S.*, 13 Mar. 1969.

Bulletin for Local History Tutors and Students: East Midlands Region, ed. A. Rogers, in *A.H.R.*, XVIII, 1970, 77-78.

Historic Towns: Maps and Plans of Towns and Cities in the British Isles with Historical Commentaries, from Earliest Times to 1800, I, ed. M.D. Lobel and W.H. Johns, in *Geog.Jnl.*, CXXXVI, 1970, 428-430.

F. Alderson, *The Inland Resorts and Spas of Britain,* in *U.H.Y.B.*, 1974, 52-53.

The Victoria History of the County of Cambridge, V, ed. C.R. Elrington, in *E.H.R.*, XC, 1975, 837-839.

A.J. Fletcher, *A County Community in Peace and War: Sussex 1600-1660*, in *T.L.S.*, 17 Sept. 1976.

A New Historical Geography of England, ed. H.C. Darby, in *E.H.R.*, XCI, 1976, 121-123.

T.S. Willan, *The Inland Trade: Studies in English Internal Trade in the Sixteenth and Seventeenth Centuries*, in *Ec.H.R.*, 2nd ser., XXX, 1977, 701-703.

P. Clark, *English Provincial Society from the Reformation to the Revolution: Religion, Politics, and Society in Kent 1500-1640*, in *T.L.S.*, 1 Sept. 1978, 968-969.

K.P. Witney, *The Jutish Forest, a Study of the Weald of Kent from 450-1380 A.D.*, in *J-Hist.Geog.*, IV, 1978, 407-408.

The Victoria History of the County of Cambridge and the Isle of Ely, VI, ed. A.P.M.Wright, in *E.H.R.*, XCIV, 1979, 437-39.

The Victoria History of the County of Oxford, IV, the City of Oxford, ed. A.Crossley, in *U.H.Y.B.*, 1981, 196-98.

The Victoria History of the County of Stafford, VI, ed. M.W.Greenslade and D.A.Johnson, in *Ec.H.R.*, XXXIII, 1980, 4, 622-23.

The Victoria History of the County of Essex, VII, ed. W.R.Powell, in *E.H.R.*, XCVII, 1982, 877-78.
P. Corfield, *The Impact of English Towns, 1700-1800*, in *Ec.H.R.*, XXXVI, 4, 631-32.

A.Kussmaul, *Servants in Husbandry in Early-Modern England*, in *E.H.R.*, XCIV, 1984, 383-386.

The Victoria History of the County of Essex, VIII, ed. W.R.Powell, in *E.H.R.,* CI, 1986, 470-71.

The Southwold Diary of James Maggs, 1818-1876, vol. 1, 1818-1848, ed. A.Farquhar Bottomley, in *E.H.R.,* CII, 1987, 240.

The Victoria History of the County of Cambridge and the Isle of Ely, IX, ed. A.P.M.Wright & C.P.Lewis, in *E.H.R.,* CVIII, 1993, 275-76.

The Diary of Isaac Fletcher of Underwood, Cumberland, 1756-1781, ed. Angus J. I.Winchester, in *A.H.R.,* 44, 1996, 241-42.

John Goodacre, *The Transformation of a Peasant Economy: Townspeople and Villagers in the Lutterworth Area, 1500-1700,* in *R.H.E.S.C.,* 7 Oct. 1996, 244-45.

Kenneth Cameron, *English Place Names,* in *English Place-Name Society Journal,* 29, 1996-1997, 89-94.

Nigel Yates, Robert Harne, and Paul Hastings, *Religion and Society in Kent, 1640-1914,* in *E.H.R.,* CXII, 1997, 486-87.

Seasonal Settlement. Papers presented to a meeting of the Medieval Settlement Research Group, ed. H.S.A.Fox, in *A.H.R.,* 45, 1997, 99-100.

The Victoria History of the County of Essex, IX, *The Borough of Colchester,* ed. Janet Cooper, in *E.H.R.,* CXIII, 1998, 253-55.

FAITH, R.J.
P.D.A. Harvey, *A Medieval Oxfordshire Village: Cuxham, 1240-1400,* in *A.H.R.,* XIV, 1966, 131-133.

The Oxfordshire Eyre, 1241, ed. J. Cooper, in *Ox.*

Medieval Society and the Manor Court, ed. Z. Razi and R. Smith;
J.A. Raftis, *Peasant Economic Development within the Manorial System;*
E.B. Fryde, *Peasants and Landlords in Later Medieval England;*
all in *Journal of British Studies,* 37, 3, 1998.

The Salt of Common Life: Individuality and Choice in the Medieval Town, Countryside and Church. Essays presented to J. Ambrose Raftis, ed. E.B. De Windt, in *E.H.R.,* 113, 452, 1998.

FINBERG, H.P.R.
J. Fowler, *Saint Aldhelm,* in *D.C.N.Q.,* XXIII, 1948, 190-191.

J. Thorp, *B.H. Newdigate, Scholar-Printer, 1869-1944,* in *The Month,* CXCI, 1951, 179-181.

D.M. Stenton, *English Society in the Early Middle Ages*, in *Ec.H.R.*, 2nd ser., V, 1952-53, 284.

English Historical Documents, II, 1042-1189, ed. D.C. Douglas and G.W. Greenaway, in *The Month*, CXCV, 1953, 364-366.

R. Douch, *A Handbook of Local History: Dorset*, in *Ec.H.R.*, 2nd ser., VI, 1953, 217. *Local Records, their Nature and Care*, ed. L.J. Redstone and F.W. Steer, in *Ec.H.R.*, 2nd ser., VI, 1953, 339.

G.J. Copley, *The Conquest of Wessex in the Sixth Century*, in *Ant.*, CIX, 1954, 43.

M.M. Postan, *The Famulus*, in *A.H.R.*, II, 1954, 62.

D. Knowles and R.N. Hadcock, *Medieval Religious Houses*, in *T.L.A.S.*, XXX, 1954, 135.

Victoria History of the County of Sussex, IV, ed. L.F. Salzman, in *Ant.Jnl.*, XXXIV, 1954, 103.

L. Fox, *The Borough Town of Stratford on Avon*, in *H.*, XL, 1955, 175.

B. Little, *The City and County of Bristol: Study in Atlantic Civilization*, in *B.T.R.*, III, 1955, 386-387.

J. Rowe, *Cornwall in the Age of the Industrial Revolution*, in *H.*, XL, 1955, 167.

H.C. Darby and I.B. Terrett, *The Domesday Geography of Midland England*, in *T.L.A.S.*, XXXI, 1955, 71-72.

C.S. and C.S. Orwin, *The Open Fields*, in *A.H.R.*, III, 1955, 54-55.

The Victoria History of the County of Leicester, II, ed. W.G. Hoskins and R.A. McKinley, in *Ant.Jnl.*, XXXV, 1955, 114-115.

J. Youings, *Devon Monastic Lands: a Calendar of Particulars for Grants*, in *A.H.R.*, IV, 1956, 63.

R.B. Pugh, *How to Write a Parish History*, in *H.*, XLI, 1956, 327.

The Victoria History of Wiltshire, II, ed. R.B. Pugh and E. Crittall, in *Ant.Jnl.*, XXXVI, 1956, 126.

A.H Smith, *English Place-Name Elements*, in *A.H.R.*, V, 1957, 117-118.

Ministers' Accounts of the Manor of Petworth, 1347-53, ed. L.F. Salzman, in *A.H.R.*, V, 1957, 58.

F.W. Jessup, *A History of Kent*, in *Ant.Jnl.*, XXXVIII, 1958, 266.

M.W. Beresford, *History on the Ground*, in *Ant.Jnl.*, XXXVIII, 1958, 122.

M.W. Beresford and J.K. St Joseph, *Medieval England: an Aerial Survey*, in *A.H.R.*, VI, 1958, 116-117.

The Victoria History of the County of Oxford, V, ed. M.D. Lobel, in *Ec.H.R.*, 2nd ser., XI, 1958, 170-171.

O.M. Griffiths, *Daglingworth*, in *The Village*, XIV, 1959, 116.

D. Sylvester and G. Nulty, *The Historical Atlas of Cheshire*, in *A.H.R.*, VII, 1959, 60.

Medieval England, ed. A.L. Poole, in *A.H.R.*, VII, 1959, 121.

H.L. Gray, *English Field Systems*, in *A.H.R.*, VIII, 1960, 51.

Lord Rennell of Rodd, *Valley on the March*, in *E.H.R.*, LXXV, 1960, 328-329.

H.M. Colvin, *A History of Deddington*, in *A.H.R.*, XI, 1963, 120.

The Victoria History of the County of Wiltshire, VI, ed. E. Crittall, in *Ant.Jnl.*, XLIV, 1964, 78.

A.H. Smith, *The Place Names of Gloucestershire*, in *Arch. Jnl.*, CXXII, 1965, 252.

F.W. Maitland, *Township and Borough*, in *A.H.R.*, XIV, 1966, 73.

The Victoria History of the County of Gloucester, VI, ed. C.R. Elrington, in *A.H.R.,* XIV, 1966, 74.

M. Twyman and W. Rollinson, *John Soulby, Printer, Ulverston*, in *A.H.R.*, XVI, 1968, 75.

Town Origins: the Evidence from Medieval England, ed. J.F. Benton, in *U.H.N.L.*, X, 1968, 15.

J. Lancaster, *Godiva of Coventry* in *E.H.R.*, LXXXIV, 1969, 379.

H.M. Porter, *The Saxon Conquest of Somerset and Devon,* in *L.H.* VIII, 1969, 299-302.

Anglo-Saxon Charters: an Annotated List and Bibliography, ed. P.H. Sawyer, in *Ant.Jnl.*, L, 1970, 148-149.

V. Skipp, *Medieval Yardley*, in *M.H.*, I, 1971, 59-60.

Leofric of Exeter, in *D.C.N.Q.*, XXXII, 1971-73, 187.

A General Introduction to the Victoria County Histories, ed. R.B. Pugh, in *E.H.R.*, LXXXVIII, 1973, 233.

Charters of Rochester, ed. A. Campbell, in *Ant.Jnl.*, LIV, 1974, 346-347.

W.B. Stephens, *Sources for English Local History*, in *Ant.Jnl.*, LIV, 1974, 128.

FLETCHER, S.M.
H. Household, *The Thames and Severn Canal*, in *I.A.R.*, VII, 1, Autumn 1984, 105-6.

H. Hanson, *The Canal Boatmen, 1760-1914*, in *I.A.R.*, VII, 1, Autumn 1984, 106.

FOX, H.S.A.
Court Rolls of the Wiltshire Manors of Adam de Stratton, ed. R.B. Pugh, in *Arch.*, 10, 1970, 208-209.

Exeter Essays in Geography, ed. K.J. Gregory and W.L.D. Ravenhill, in *D.C.N.Q.*, 32, 1972, 156-157.

J.C. Russell, *Medieval Regions and their Cities*, in *Geog. Mag.*, 44, 1972, 502-503.

University of Chicago Library, *The Sir Nicholas Bacon Collection: Sources on English Society 1250-1700*, in *P.S.I.A.*, 32, 1972, 279-281.

N.J.G. Pounds, *An Historical Geography of Europe 450 B.C.-A.D.1330*, in *T.L.S.*, 24 August, 1973

Capital Accumulation in the Industrial Revolution, ed. B L. Anderson;
W. Minchinton, *Devon at Work: Past and Present*;
W. Pennington, *A History of British Vegetation*;
R.C. Russell, *The Logic of Open Field Systems: 15 Maps of Groups of Common Fields on the Eve of Enclosure*;
J.M. Steane, *The Northamptonshire Landscape*; all in *J.Hist.Geog.*, I, 1975, 325-326.

M.W. Beresford and H.P.R. Finberg, *English Medieval Boroughs: a Handlist*;
English Rural Communities: the Impact of a Specialised Economy, ed. D.R. Mills;
W.B. Stephens, *Sources for English Local History*; all in *J.Hist.Geog.*, I, 1975, 129-130.

J.F. Hart, *The Look of the Land*, in *Geog.Mag.*, 48, 1975, 61.

P. Brandon, *The Sussex Landscape*, in *T.L.S.*, 24 Oct. 1975.

B.W. Blouet, *Sir Halford Mackinder, 1861-1947: some New Perspectives*;
I. Scargill, *The Dordogne Region of France*;
J. Vaughan, *The English Guide Book, c.1780-1870: an Illustrated History*;
R.J.A. Wilson, *A Guide to the Roman Remains in Britain*; all in *J.Hist.Geog.*, II, 1976, 194-195.

W. Ravenhill, *John Norden's Manuscript Maps of Cornwall and its Nine Hundreds*, in *J.Hist.Geog.*, II 1976, 80-81.

J. Hatcher, *Plague, Population, and the English Economy 1348-1530*, in *Geog.Mag.*, 50, 1977, 148.

B.K. Roberts, *Rural Settlement in Britain*, in *Geog.Mag.*, 49, 1977, 732.

A.R.H. Baker, *Historical Geography and Geographical Changes*;
A New Historical Geography of England, ed. H.C. Darby;
H.P.R. Finberg, *The Gloucestershire Landscape*;
R. Grove, *The Cambridgeshire Coprolite Mining Rush*; all in *J.Hist.Geog.*, 4, 1978, 330-2..

Historical Geography Newsletter, 6, 1; *Journal of Transport History*, n.s., 3, 3, 1976;
Sir James Marshall-Cornwall, *History of the Geographical Club*;
Arthur Young and his Times, ed. G.E. Mingay; all in *J.Hist.Geog.*, 4, 1978, 426-8.

Bodfan Gruffydd, *Protecting Historic Landsapes: Gardens and Parks*, in *Geog. Mag.*, L, 1978, 418-419.

J. Patten, *English Towns 1500-1700*; in *Geog.Mag.*, 51, 1979, 316.

R.E. Glasscock, *The Lay Subsidy of 1334*, in *Arch.*, 14, 1979, 31-3.

P. Brandon and R.Millman, *Historic Landscapes: identification. recording and management*;
B. Campbell, *Register of Research and List of Theses and Dissertations Relating to the Historical Geography of Ireland*;
H.C. Darby, *Medieval Cambridgeshire*;
W.G. Hoskins, *The Making of the English Landscape*;
I.S. Maxwell, *Historical Atlas of West Penwith*; all in *J.Hist.Geog.*, 6, 1980, 110-12.

M. Harvey, *The Morphological and Tenurial Structure of a Yorkshire Township: Preston in Holderness*;
Medieval Village Research Group, *Twenty-sixth annual report*, both in *J. Hist.Geog.*, 7, 1981, 128.

Landscape History, 1;
J. Sheppard, *The Origin and Evolution of Field and Settlement patterns in the Herefordshire Manor of Marden*;
W. Upcott and J.Simmons, *A Bibliographical Account of the Principal Works Relating to English Topography*, all in *J.Hist.Geog.*, 7, 1981. 445-6.

M. Gelling, *Signposts to the Past: Place-names and the History of England*, in *Geographical Review*, New York, 71, 1981, 231-2.

T. Rowley, *Villages in the Landscape*, in *Bulletin of the Society of University Cartographers*, 15, 1981, 47-8.

F.H.A. Aalen. *Man and the Landscape in Ireland*, in *U.H.Y.B.*, 1982, 136-7.

F.A. Aberg, *Medieval Moated Sites*: in *A.H.R.*, 30, 1982, 84.

C. Dyer, *Lords and Peasants in a Changing Society: the Estates of the Bishopric of Worcester, 680-1540*, in *J.Hist.Geog.*, 8, 1982, 413-4

H.E. Hallam, *Rural England 1066-1348*; in *J.Hist.Geog.*, 9, 1983, 315-7.

W. Minchinton, *Agricultural Improvement: Medieval and Modern*, in *D.C.N.Q.*, 35, 1984, 237-9.

Collected Papers of the Permanent European Conference for the Study of the Rural Landscape;
C. Dyer, *Warwickshire Farming, 1349-c.1520*;
N.J.G. Pounds, *The Parliamentary Survey of the Duchy of Cornwall*;
The Open Field Village of Laxton (being East Midland Geographer, 7, 6);
R. Morgan, *Dissertations on British Agrarian History*: all in *J.Hist.Geog.*, 10, 1984, 456-8.

D. Hall, *Medieval Fields*, in *N.P.P.*, 7, 1984-5, 126-7.

M. Havinden, *The Somerset Landscape*; in *A.H.R.*, 33, 1985, 91-2.

D.W. Howell, *Land, Family and Inheritance in Transition*, in *Ant.Jnl.*, 67, 1987.

G. Platts, *Land and People in Medieval Lincolnshire*, in *Lincs.H.A.*, 21, 1987, .45-6.

V. Hall, *History of the Yorkshire Agricultural Society 1837-1987*, in *Ambix*, 36, 1989, 158-9.

C. Holdsworth, *Domesday Essays*, in *Geog.Jnl.*, 155, 1989, 117.

J. Bond and L. Over, *Ordnance Survey Historical Guides: Oxfordshire and Berkshire*, in *Bulletin of the Society of University Cartographers*, 14, 1990.

G. Astill and A. Grant, *The Countryside of Medieval England*, in *Landscape History*, 12, 1990, 74-5.

D. Austin, *Tin and Agriculture in the Middle Ages and Beyond*, in *Annual Report of the Medieval Settlement Research Group*, 5, 1990, 45-6.

A. Fleming, *The Dartmoor Reaves: Investigating Prehistoric Land Divisions*, in *Transactions of the Ancient Monuments Society*, 35, 1991, 194-5.

G. Sivery, *Terroirs et communautés rurales dans l'Europe occidentale au moyen age*, in *Ec.H.R.*, 45, 1992, 616-7.

L. Abrams and J.P. Carley, *The Archaeology and History of Glastonbury Abbey: Essays in Honour of the Ninetieth Birthday of C.A.Ralegh Radford*, in *Early Medieval Europe*, 2, 1993, 75-76.

Change and Continuity: Rural Settlement in North-West Lincolnshire, ed. P.L. Everson, C.C. Taylor, and C.J. Dunn, in *Lincs.H.A.*, 28, 1993, 77-78.

Maps and History in South-West England, ed. K.Barker and R.Kain, in *A.H.R.*, 41, 1993, 196-97.

C.M. Woolgar, *Household Accounts from Medieval England*, in *A.H.R.*, 45, 1997, 101-2.

M.W. Beresford and J. Hurst, *Wharram Percy Deserted Medieval Village*, in *A.H.R.*, 42, 1994, 84-5.

K. Batten and F. Bennett, *The Printed Maps of Devon*, in *Imago Mundi: the International Journal for the History of Cartography*, 49, 1997, 166-7.

M. Kowaleski, *Local Markets and Regional Trade in Medieval Exeter*, in *A.H.R.*, 46, 1998, 228-229.

D. Hall, *The Open Fields of Northamptonshire*, in *Landscape History*, forthcoming.

GOODACRE, J.D.
Leics. Ecology Action Group, *Leicester: Transport & Environment*;
Susanna Watts, *A Walk Through Leicester*;
Town and Country Planning Association, *Leicester Town Trail*, all in *Leics.H.*, II, 1972, 26-27.

W. Kidd, *Leicester Old and New*, in *Leics.H.*, II, vi, 1975, 34-35.

Leicester City Council, *Leicestershire's Architectural Heritage*, and *The Local Tradition*, in *Leics.H.*, II, vi, 1975, 33, 35.

P.G. Lindley, *The Town Library of Leicester*, in *Leics.H.* II, vi, 1975, 32, 34.

Bygone Loughborough in Photographs, I and II, in *Leics.H.*, II, vii,1976, 33.

E. Swift, *The Inns of Leicestershire*, in *Leics.H.*, II, vii, 1976, 33.

J. Daniell, *Leicestershire Clockmakers: Directory of Watch and Clock Makers Working in Leicestershire before 1900*, in *Leics.H.*, II, vii, 1976, 37.

J.D. Bennett, *Who was Who in Leicestershire*, in *Leics.H.*, II, vii, 1976, 36.

B. & J. Wilford, *Bygone Barrow upon Soar*;
Castle Donington, 1841, Wilden Ferry and the Cavendish Bridges, Inns and Taverns of Castle Donington, Castle Donington Local History Society;

V.N. & R.P.Jarrett, *History of Narborough and Littlethorpe*;
Walks around Shepshed; `Padge owling' or Messing Around after Dark, all in
Leics.H., 2, 12, 1981-2, 49, 50, 51-2.

T.H.McK. Clough, *Oakham Castle: a Guide and History*;
C.Page, *Foundations of Fashion, the Symington Collection: Corsetry from 1856 to the
Present Day*, both in *Leics.H.*, 2, 12, 1981-2, 46.

Turnpikes and Royal Mail of Rutland, Rutland Local History Society, 2, 12, 1981-2,
45.

N.Moon, *The Windmills of Leicestershire and Rutland*, in *Leics.H.*, 2, 12, 1981-2, 43-
44.

M.Todd, *The Iron Age and Roman Settlement at Whitwell, Leics.*;
P.Clay, *Two multi-phase Barrow sites at Sproxton and Eaton, Leics*;
C.E.Allin, *The Medieval Leather Industry in Leicester*, all in *Leics.H.*, 2, 12, 1981,
2, 42.

A.M.Everitt and M.Tranter, *English Local History at Leicester, 1948-1978: a
Bibliography of Writings by Members of the Department of English Local History,
University of Leicester*, in *Leics.H.*, 2, 12, 1981-2, 42.

Rutland Record: the Journal of the Rutland Record Society, 1, 1980, 2, 1981, in
Leics.H., 2, 12, 1981-2, 40-41.

C.V.Phythian-Adams, *Re-thinking English Local History*, in *Leics.H.* III, vi, 1988,
35-6.

HART, Clive R.
J.Barnatt & K.Smith, *The Peak District: Landscapes Through Time*, in *Arch.Jnl.*,
1998

HART, Cyril R.
E. John, *Orbis Britanniae and Other Studies*, in *A.H.R.*, XVII, 1969, 148-150.

The Victoria History of the County of Dorset, III, ed. R.B. Pugh, in *T.L.S.*, 13 March
1969.

Ordering back the waves, *The Reign of Cnut, King of England, Demark and Norway*,
A.Rumble ed. in *British Archaeology*, 1995.

HAYDON, E.S.
D.Stuart, *Latin for Local and Family Historians*, in *L.H.*, 26, 3, 1978.

HEY, D.G.
J.S. Roper, *Dudley: The Medieval Town; The Town in the Sixteenth Century; The
Town in the Seventeenth Century; The Town in the Eighteenth Century*, in *U.H.N.L.*,
XVI, 1971, 22.

F.W. Steer, *Farm and Cottage Industries of Mid-Essex, 1635-1749*, in *Ec.H.R.*, 2nd ser., XXIV, 1971, 146.

P. Horn, *Joseph Arch: the Farmworkers' Leader*, in *N.P.P.*, IV, 1971-72, 394-395.

G. Jackson, *Hull in the Eighteenth Century: a Study in Economic and Social History*, in *U.H.N.L.*, XVIII, 1972, 48-49.

A. Rogers, *This was their World - Approaches to Local History*, in *L.H.*, X, 1972, 201-202.

D. Jenkins, *The Agricultural Community in South-West Wales at the Turn of the Twentieth Century*, in *L.H.*, X, 1973, 316-317.

J.R. Smith, *Foulness: a History of an Essex Island Parish*, in *A.H.R.*, XXI, 1973, 76-77.

Industrial Archaeology, IX and X, ed. J. Butt;
M.I. Thomis, *Luddism in Nottinghamshire*, both in *U.H.Y.B.*, 1974, 50-51.

B. Trinder, *The Industrial Revolution in Shropshire*;
J.H. Smith, *The Great Human Exploit: Historic Industries of the North-West*, both in *U.H.Y.B.*, 1974, 49-50.

The Victoria History of the County of Oxford, X, ed. A. Crossley, in *A.H.R.* XXII, 1974, 190-191.

G. Mee, *Aristocratic Enterprise*, in *E.M.L.H.B.*, XI, 1976, 93-94.

E.J. Evans, *The Contentious Tithe*, in *T.H.E.S.*, 248, 23,7, 1976, 16.

The Early Records of the Bankes Family at Winstanley, ed. J. Bankes and E. Kerridge, in *A.H.R.*, XXIV, 1976, 77.

C C Taylor, *Fields in the Landscape*, in *P.-Med.Arch.*, X, 1976, 187.

J.D. Marshall, *Kendal 1661-1801: the Growth of the Modern Town*, in *U.H.Y.B.*, 1976, 77-78.

Village Life and Labour, ed. R. Samuel, in *Lore and Language*, II, iv, 1976, 49-50.

The Victoria History of the County of York: East Riding, II, ed. K.J. Allison, in *A.H.R.*, XXV, 1977, 59.

K.J. Allison, *The East Riding of Yorkshire Landscape*;
L.M. Munby, *The Hertfordshire Landscape*;
D.M. Palliser, *The Staffordshire Landscape*;
M. Williams, *The South Wales Landscape*, all in *J.Hist.Geog.*, IV, 1978, 398-399.

J.A. Chartres, *Internal Trade in England, 1500-1700*;
T.S. Willan, *The Inland Trade: Studies in English Internal Trade in the Sixteenth and Seventeenth Centuries*, both in *J.Hist.Geog.*, IV, 1978, 300-301.

Miners, Quarrymen, and Saltworkers, ed. R. Samuel;
R. Griffin, *The British Coalmining Industry: Retrospect and Prospect*, both in *E.M.L.H.B.*, XIII, 1978, 126-128.

A. MacFarlane, *Reconstructing Historical Communities;
Group Projects in Local History*, ed. A. Rogers, in *A.H.R.*, XXVI, 1978, 140-141.

S.M. Blumin, *The Urban Threshold: Growth and Change in a Nineteenth Century American Community*, in *U.H.Y.B.*, 1978, 128-129.

The Victoria History of the County of York: East Riding, III, ed. K.J. Allison, in *A.H.R.*, XXVI, 1978, 71.

Land and People in Nineteenth-Century Wales, in *A.H.R.*, XVII, 1979, 67.

V.Skipp, *Crisis and Development: an Ecological Case Study of the Forest of Arden, 1570-1674*, in *A.H.R.*, XVII, 1979, 61-2.

Mary Harvey, *The Morphological and Tenurial Structure of a Yorkshire Township: Preston in Holderness, 1066-1750*, in *A.H.R.*, XXVII, 1979, 60.

R.Fieldhouse and B.Jennings, *A History of Richmond and Swaledale*, in *A.H.R.*, XXVII, 1979, 142-43.

Masters and Journeymen: a Prehistory of Industrial Relations, 1717-1800, in *U.H.Y.B.*, 1981, 182-83.

HILL, T.G.
D.Gerhold, *Road Transport before the Railways: Russell's London Flying Waggons*, in R.H.E.S.C., 5, 1, April 1994, 113-4.

HOSKINS, W.G.
F.G. Thomas, *The Changing Village*;
F.J. Weaver, *The Material of English History*, both in *D.C.N.Q.*, XX, 1939, 332-334.

T.F.C. and H. Dexter, *Cornish Crosses: Christian and Pagan*, in *D.C.N.Q.*, XX, 1939, 189-190.

B.C. Spooner, *John Tregagle of Trevorder: Man and Ghost*, in *D.C.N.Q.*, XX, 1939, 143-144.

Proceedings of the West Cornwall Field Club (Archaeological), in *D.C.N.Q.*, XX, 1939, 237.

F.J.Weaver, *The Material of English History*, *D.C.N.Q.*, XX, 1939, 332-4.

M. Campbell, *The English Yeoman under Elizabeth and the Early Stuarts*, in *Ec.H.R.*, XIV, 1944, 193-196.

G.E. Fussell, *Farming Systems from Elizabethan to Victorian Days in the North and East Ridings of Yorkshire*, in *Ec.H.R.*, XVI, 1946, 79.

R. Pickard, *The Population and Epidemics of Exeter in Pre-Census Times*, in *D.C.N.Q.*, XXIII, 1947-49, 124-127.

E R. Delderfield, *The Raleigh Country*, in *D.C.N.Q.*, XXIII, 1947-49, 399-400.

A. W. Leyland, *The Story of Woodbury*, in *D.C.N.Q.*, XXIII, 1947-49, 127-128.

Bedfordshire Historical Record Society Publications, xxv, *Ec.H. R.*, 2nd ser.,1949, 104.

C.D.B. Ellis, *History in Leicester*, in *Ant.Jnl.*, XXIX, 1949, 99-100.

P. Stevens, *The Guildhall, Leicester*, in *T.L.A.S.*, XXVI, 1950, 142-143.

L. Fox, *Leicester Abbey*, in *T.L.A.S.*, XXVI, 1950, 142-143.

P. Stevens, *Roman Forum: Leicester*, in *T.L.A.S.*, XXVI, 1950, 142-143.

G.E. Fussell, *More old English Farming Books from Tull to the Board of Agriculture*, in *Ec.H.R.*, 2nd ser., III, 1950-51, 397-398.

Andrews and Dury's Map of Wiltshire, 1773, in *E.H.R.*, LXVIII, 1953, 487-488.

M.S. Briggs, *The English Farmhouse*, in *A.H.R.*, I, 1953, 54-55.

Guild Stewards Book of the Borough of Calne, 1561-1688, ed. A.W. Mabbs, in *E.H.R.*, LXVIII, 1953 640-641.

R. Douch, *A Handbook of Local History: Dorset*, in *E.H.R.*, LXVIII, 1953, 668-669.

R.C.H.M., *An Inventory of the Historical Monuments in Dorset*, I, in *E.H.R.*, LXVIII, 1953, 424-426.

O.Cook and E. Smith, *English Cottages and Farmhouses*, in *A.H.R.*, III, 1954, 50-52.

L. Redstone and F.W. Steer, *Local Records: their Nature and Care*, in *T.L.A.S.*, XXX, 1954, 134-135.

Sir William Savage, *The Making of our Towns*, in *H.*, XXXIX, 1954, 292-293.

The Manor of Etchingham cum Salehurst, ed. Sir Sylvanus P. Vivian, Sussex Record Society, in *E.H.R.*, LXIX, 1954, 150.

Miscellanea of the Yorkshire Archaeological Society, ed. C.E. Whiting, in *E.H.R.*, LXIX, 1954, 691.

Yorkshire Archaeological Journal, part 148 (1951), in *H.*, XXXIX, 312.
Sir Cyril Fox and Lord Raglan, *Monmouthshire Houses, III: Renaissance*, in *Arch. Jnl.*, CXI, 1954, 237-238.

A.T. Patterson, *Radical Leicester: a History of Leicester, 1780-1850*, in *T.L.A.S.*, XXX, 1954, 130-131.

L. Fox, *Stratford upon Avon*, in *E.H.R.*, LXIX, 1954, 141-142.

The Victoria History of the County of Sussex, IV, ed. L.F. Salzman;
The Victoria History of the County of Cambridge and the Isle of Ely, ed. R.B. Pugh, both in *E.H.R.*, LXIX, 1954, 350-351.

The Victoria History of the County of Wiltshire, VII, ed. R.B. Pugh, in *E.H.R.*, LXIX, 1954, 511.

B. Little, *The City and County of Bristol: Study in Atlantic Civilisation*, in *E.H.R.*, LXX, 1955, 473-474.

R. Fasnacht, *A History of the City of Oxford*, in *E.H.R.*, LXX, 1955, 474-475.

L.E. Elliott-Binns, *Medieval Cornwall*, in *E.H.R.*, LXX, 1955, 659-660.

Devon Monastic Lands: a Calendar of Particulars for Grants, 1536-1558, ed. J. Youings, in *D.C.N.Q.*, XXVII, 1956, 26-27.

The Leicestershire Archaeological Society, 1855-1955, in *E.H.R.*, LXXI, 1956, 682-683.

H.J. Randall, *Bridgend: the Story of a Market Town*;
J.M. Baines, *Historic Hastings*, both in *E.H.R.*, LXXII, 1957, 161.

A Catalogue of Inclosure Maps in the Berkshire Record Office, ed. P. Walne, in *E.H.R.*, LXXII, 1957, 207.

A. Raine, *Medieval York: a Topographical Survey Based on Original Sources*, in *E.H.R.*, LXXII, 1957, 351.

B. Garside, *People and Homes in Hampton-on-Thames in the Sixteenth and Seventeenth Centuries*, in *Ec.H.R.*, 2nd ser., X, 1957, 297-298.

Nottingham Corporation, *Records of the Borough of Nottingham, IX, 1836-1900*, in *E.H.R.*, LXXII, 1957, 382-383.

The Records of the Corporation of Leicester, ed. A.M. Woodcock, in *E.H.R.*, LXXII, 1957, 400.

W.M. Williams, *The Sociology of an English Village: Gosforth,* in *A.H.R.*, V, 1957, 107-110.

J.W.F. Hill, *Tudor and Stuart Lincoln,* in *Ec.H.R.*, 2nd ser., X, 1957, 142-144.

The Victoria History of the County of Essex, IV, ed. W.R. Powell, in *E.H.R.*, LXXII, 1957, 525-526.

Sir Matthew Nathan, *The Annals of West Coker,* ed. M.M. Postan, in *E.H.R.*, LXXIII, 1958, 342-343.

Devon Monastic Lands: Calendar of Particulars for Grants, 1536-1558, ed. J. Youings, in *D.C.N.Q.*, XXVII, 1958, 26-27.

Elizabethan Peterborough, ed. W.T. Mellows, in *E.H.R.*, LXXIII, 1958, 350-351.

The First Ledger Book of High Wycombe, ed. R.W. Greaves, in *E.H.R.*, LXXIII. 1958, 346.

R. Trow-Smith, *A History of British Livestock Husbandry to 1700,* in *Ec.H.R.*, 2nd ser., XI, 1958, 480-482.

M.W. Beresford, *History on the Ground,* in *Ec.H.R.*, 2nd ser., XI, 1958, 160-161.

M.W. Beresford and J.K. St Joseph, *Medieval England: an Aerial Survey,* in *The Listener,* LIX, 1958, 466.

Progress Notes of Warden Woodward, 1659-1675, ed. R.L. Rickard, in *E.H.R.*, LXXIII, 1958, 528.

The Victoria History of the County of Oxford, V, ed. M.D. Lobel, in *E.H.R.*, LXXIII, 1958, 512-513.

The Victoria History of the County of Wiltshire, V, ed. R.B. Pugh and E. Crittall, in *E.H.R.*, LXXIII, 1958, 133-134.

M.E. Finch, *The Wealth of Five Northamptonshire Families 1540-1640,* in *Ec.H.R.*, 2nd ser., XI, 1958, 163-164.

Essex Record Office, *Essex Homes, 1066-1850,* in *E.H.R.*, LXXIV, 1959, 759.

K. Cameron, *The Place-Names of Derbyshire,* in *The Listener,* LXI, 1959, 942.

The Local Collection Catalogue of Books and Maps relating to Berkshire, Reading Central Library, *E.H.R.*, LXXIV, 1959, 382-3.

J. Thirsk and J. Imray, *Suffolk Farming in the Nineteenth Century,* in *Ant.Jnl.*, XXXIX, 1959, 129.

N. Pevsner, *The Buildings of England: Leicestershire and Rutland*, and *Buckinghamshire*, in *The Listener*, LXIII, 1960, 854, 856.

A Guide to the Kent County Archives Office, ed. F. Hull, in *E.H.R.*, LXXV, 1960, 378.

A.E. Smailes, *North England*, in *The Listener*, LXIII, 1960, 314.

The Printed Maps of Warwickshire, 1576-1900, ed. P.D.A. Harvey and H. Thorpe, in *E.H.R.*, LXXV, 1960, 726.

T. Thomas and K.S. Woods, *Report on Country Town Industries of South-West England*, in *Ec.H.R.*, 2nd ser., XIII, 1960, 300-301.

N. Pevsner, *The Buildings of England: Suffolk*, in *The Listener*, LXV, 1961, 708.

K. Cameron, *English Place-Names*, in *D.C.N.Q.*, XXVIII, 1961, 330-331.

P. Russell, *A History of Torquay and the Famous Anchorage of Torbay*, in *D.C.N.Q.*, XXVIII, 1961, 295-297.

M.K. Ashby, *Joseph Ashby of Tysoe, 1859-1919*, in *The Listener*, LXV, 1961, 935.

E.A.G. Clark, *The Ports of the Exe Estuary*, in *Ec.H.R.*, 2nd ser., XIV, 1961, 150-151

R. Lennard, *Rural England, 1086-1135*, in *E.H.R.*, LXXVI, 1961, 319-324.

N.J. Williams, *Tradesmen in Early-Stuart Wiltshire: a Miscellany*, in *A.H.R.*, IX, 1961, 68.

The Victoria History of the County of Essex: Bibliography, ed. W.R. Powell, in *E.H.R.*, LXXVI, 1961, 189-190.

C.M.L. Bouch and G.P. Jones, *The Lake Counties, 1500-1830: a Social and Economic History*, in *The Listener*, LXVII, 1962, 652, 655.

A. Clifton-Taylor, *The Pattern of English Building*, in *The Listener*, LXVIII, 1962, 1057.

A.L. Rowse, *St Austell: Church: Town: Parish*, in *E.H.R.*, LXXVII, 1962, 139.

T.S. Willan, *A Tudor Book of Rates*, in *Ec.H.R.*, 2nd ser., XV, 1962, 373-375.

The Domesday Geography of South-East England, ed. H.C. Darby and E.M.J. Campbell;
The Domesday Geography of Northern England, ed. H.C. Darby and I.M. Maxwell, both in *The Listener*, LXX, 1963, 283-284.

Guide to the Nottinghamshire County Records Office, ed. P.A. Kennedy, in *E.H.R.*, LXXVIII, 1963, 206-207.

M.W. Barley, *The House and Home*, in *The Listener*, LXIX, 1963, 521-522.

HOSKINS, W. G.
K. Hudson, *Industrial Archaeology*, in *The Listener*, LXX, 1963, 759.

The Place-Names of the West Riding of Yorkshire , 8 vols., ed. A.H. Smith, in *The Listener*, LXIX, 1963, 607.

A. Briggs, *Victorian Cities*, in *The Listener*, LXX, 1963, 572.

L.R. Conisbee, *A Bedfordshire Bibliography*, in. *E.H.R.*, LXXIX, 1964, 221-222.

Worcestershire Historical Society, *Christopher Greenwood, County Map Maker, and the Worcestershire Map of 1822*, in *E.H.R.*, LXXIX, 1964, 872-873.

T. Atkinson, *Elizabethan Winchester*, in *H.*, XLIX, 1964, 69-70.

The Place-Names of Gloucestershire, 3 vols., ed. A.H. Smith, in *The Listener*, LXXII, 1964, 361.

K. Hudson, *The Industrial Archaeology of Southern England*, in *The Listener*, LXXIV, 1965, 502.

Terry Coleman, *The Railway Navvies*, in *The Listener*, LXXIV, 1965, 315.

Field Studies in the British Isles, ed. J.A. Steers, in *E.H.R.*, LXXXI, 1966, 221-222.

Sir Francis Hill, *Georgian Lincoln*, in *The Listener*, LXXVI, 1966, 360.

The Victoria History of the County of Gloucester, VI, ed. C.R. Elrington, in *H.*, LI, 1966, 394-395.

F.G. Emmison, *Archives and Local History*, in *H.*, LII, 1967, 413.

D. Portman, *Exeter Houses, 1400-1700*, in *Ec.H.R.*, 2nd ser., XX, 1967, 389.

The Agrarian History of England and Wales, IV, 1500-1640, ed. J. Thirsk, in *The Listener*, LXXIX, 1968, 478-479.

The Domesday Geography of South-West England, eD.H.C. Darby and R.W. Finn, in *Ec.H.R.*, 2nd ser., XXI, 1968, 383-384.

P. Jennings, *The Living Village*; R. Moreau, *The Departed Village*, in *The Listener*, LXXX, 1968, 832-833.

M.W. Beresford, *New Towns of the Middle Ages*, in *The Listener*, LXXIX, 1968, 215.

The Victoria History of the County of Leicester, V, ed. J.M. Lee and R.A. McKinley, in *A.H.R.*, XVI, 1968, 68-70.

Records of the Borough of Leicester, VI, The Chamberlain's Accounts, 1688-1835, ed. G.A. Chinnery, in *Ec.H.R.*, 2nd ser., XXII, 1969, 133-134.

J. Youings, *Tuckers Hall, Exeter: the History of a Provincial City Company through Five Centuries*, in *Ec.H.R.*, 2nd ser., XXII, 1969, 557.

The Devonshire Lay Subsidy of 1332, ed. A.M. Erskine, in *D.C.N.Q.*, XXXI, 1970, 195-196.

Land, Church, and People: Essays Presented to Professor H.P.R. Finberg, ed. J. Thirsk, in *L.H.*, IX, 1971, 362-363.

The Victoria History of the County of Oxford, VIII, ed. M.D. Lobel and A. Crossley, in *E.H.R.*, LXXXVI, 1971, 891-892.

H.P.R. Finberg, *West-Country Historical Studies*, in *E.H.R.*, LXXXVI, 1971, 156.

Industry and Society in the South-West, ed. R. Burt, in *D.C.N.Q.*, XXXII, 1971-73, 28-29.

The Geographical Interpretation of Historical Sources, ed. A.R.H. Baker, J.D. Hamshere, and J. Langton;
J.T. Coppock, *An Agricultural Geography of Great Britain*, both in *A.H.R.*, XX, 1972, 183.

R.C.H.M., *An Inventory of Historical Monuments in Dorset*, II: *South-East Dorset*, in *E.H.R.*, LXXXVII, 1972, 658-659.

R.C.H.M., *An Inventory of Historical Monuments in Dorset*, III: *Central Dorset*, in *E.H.R.*, LXXXVII, 1972, 911-912.

Murray's Handbook for Devon and Cornwall, 1859;
A.K. Hamilton Jenkin, *Cornwall and its People*;
B.D. Hughes, *Strong's Industries of N. Devon*;
H.M. Porter, *The Celtic Church in Somerset*;
R.H. Worth, *Worth's Dartmoor*;
C. Gill, *Dartmoor: a New Study*;
C.S. Orwin and R.J. Sellick, *The Reclamation of Exmoor Forest*;
L.V. Grinsell, *The Archaeology of Exmoor: Bideford Bay to Bridgwater*, all in *L.H.*, X, 1972, 39-41.

D. Sylvester, *The Rural Landscapes of the Welsh Borderland*, in *A.H.R.*, XX, 1972, 77-78.

The Victoria History of Shropshire, VIII, ed. A.T. Gaydon, in *A.H.R.*, XX, 1972, 78-80.

J.T.Coppock, *An Agricultural Geography of Great Britain*, in *A.H.R.*, XX 1972, 183.

The Devon Protestation Returns, 1641, ed. A.J. Howard, in *D.C.N.Q.*, XXXIII, 1974, 29-30.

The Certificates of Musters for Buckinghamshire in 1522, ed. A. C. Chibnall, in *Ec.H.R.*, 2nd ser., XXVIII, 1975, 709-710.

H.M. Spufford, *Contrasting Communities: English Villagers in the Sixteenth and Seventeenth Centuries*, in *Ec.H.R.*, 2nd ser., XXVIII, 1975, 711-712.

R.C.H.M., *An Inventory of Historical Monuments in Dorset, IV: North Dorset*; R.C.H.M., *An Inventory of Historical Monuments in Cambridgeshire, II: North-East Cambridgeshire*, both in *E.H.R.*, XC, 1975, 407.

HOWELL, C.A.H.
J.R. Ravensdale, *Liable to Floods: Village Landscapes on the edge of the Fens, A.D.450-1850*, in *J.P.S.*, II, 1975, 377-378.

IREDALE, D.A.
M. Cook, *Archives Administration*, in *Library Review*, 27, 1978, 10-13.

E.C.Kemp, *Manuscript Solicitation for Libraries, Special Collections, Museums and Archives*, in *Library Review*, 29, Spring 1980, 48.

KILBURN, T.
Joseph Whitworth, *Derbyshire Life and Countryside*, Oct. 1987, 65 & 69.

Joseph Whitworth, a Centenary Profile, Whitworth Centenary publications, 1987.

Joseph Whitworth, Toolmaker, Scarthin Books, 1987, 62pp.

KISSOCK, J.A.
H.S.A.Fox ed. *Seasonal Settlement*, in *Landscape History*, 18, 1996, 91.

LAITHWAITE, J.M.W.
R.B. Wood-Jones, *Traditional Domestic Architecture in the Banbury Region*, in *C.&C.*, II, 1964, 137-138.

The Topsham Society, *Topsham: an Account of its Streets and Buildings*, in *D.C.N.Q.*, XXXII, 1972, 190-191.

A. Quiney, *The Traditional Buildings of England*, in *Landscape History*, 12, 1990, 75-76.

Le Bois et la Ville du Moyen Age au Xxe Siècle, ed. J-L. Biget, J.Boissière and J-C. Hervé, in *Urban History*, 20, 2, Oct 1993, 242-3.

R.C.H.M., *Salisbury Cathedral: Perspectives on the Architectural History* and *Salisbury: The Houses of the Close*, in *Urban History*, 22, 2, Aug. 1995, 279-280.

R.Macin, *Rural Housing: an Historical Approach*, in *Landscape History*, 17, 1995, 81-82.

LORD, E.
The road to Wigan peers, in *T.H.E.S.*, 13th May 1994.

J.D.Marshall, *The Tyranny of the Discrete*, in *M.H.*, XXII, 1997.

McDERMOTT, M.B.
M. Aston and T. Rowley, *Landscape Archaeology*, in *S.A.N.H.*, CXIX, 1975, 79.

Somerset villages: the houses, cottages and farms of Chiselborough (Somerset and South Avon Vernacular Building Research Group), in *S.A.N.H.*, 137, 1993, 179-80.

Haselbury Plucknett, evolution and change of land, society and buildings (Somerset and South Avon Vernacular Building Research Group), in *S.A.N.H.*, 138, 1994, 202-204.

Topographical Writers in South-West England, ed. M.Brayshay, in *S.A.N.H.*, 139,1995,197-8.

Taunton: History, Archaeology and Development, ed. R.W. Dunning, in *S.A.N.H.* CXIX, 1975, 80.

Christianity in Somerset, ed. R.W. Dunning, in *S.A.N.H.*, CXX, 1976, 124-125.

R. Bush, *The Book of Taunton*, in *S.A.N.H.*, CXXI, 1977, 144-145.

McKINLEY, R.A.
M. James, *Family, Lineage, and Civil Society*, in *M.H.*, III, ii, 1975, 152-153.

S. Carlsson, *Studies in Middle English Local By-names in East Anglia*, in *Nomina*, XIV, 1990-91, 125-27

R.Bell, *The Book of Ulster Surnames*, in *Nomina*, XIV, 1990-91, 131-2.

G.W.Lasker, *Surnames and Genetic Structure*, in *E.H.R..*, 103, 1988, 279.

K. Forster, *Englische Familiennamen aus Ortsnamen*, in *Nomina*, III, 1979, 117.

Records of the Borough of Leicester, VII, ed. G.A. Chinnery, in *U.H.Y.B.*, 1975, 95-97.

MOIR, E.A.L.
A. Raistrick, *The Role of the Yorkshire Cistercian Monasteries in the History of the Wool Trade*, in *A.H.R.*, III, 1955, 127.

A. Fraser, *Sheep Husbandry and Wool Growing in Britain*, in *A.H.R.*, III, 1955, 127.

F.E. Halliday, *History of Cornwall*;

C.M. Matthews, *Haileybury since Roman Times*;

W.G. Hoskins, *Local History in England*, all in *H.T.*, IX, 1959, 637-638.

New Cambridge Modern History, II, ed. G.R. Elton, in *A.H.R.*, VII, 1959, 122-123.

MULLINS, S.

G.E. Calder, *The History of Eggington*;

S. Harrop, *Old Birkdale and Ainsdale: life on the south-west Lancashire coast, 1600-1851*;

R.C. Wilkes, The *Story of Penkridge*;

A.S. Nevens, *A History of North Weald Bassett and its people*;

A. Gill and G. Sargeant, *Village Within a City: the Hessle Road Fishing Community of Hull*, all in *L.H.*, 18,1, 1988, 28-29.

PAUL, E.D.

C. Lewis, *Particular Places. an Introduction to English Local History*, in *Library Review*, 39, 1, 1990, 63-64.

PAUL, E.D.

C.W. Holt, *Welsh Women: An Annotated Bibliography of Women in Wales and Women of Welsh Descent in America*, in *Reference Reviews*, VIII, 1, 11-12.

PEBERDY, R.B.

J.K.J. Thomson, *Clermont-de-Lodève, 1633-1789*;

C. Jones, *Charity and 'Bienfaisance'*, both in *L.H.*, XVI, 1985, 309-11.

S. Reynolds, *Kingdoms and Communities in Western Europe, 900-1300*;

M.J. Bennet, *Community, Class and Careerism*, both in *L .H.*, XVI, 1985, 434-6.

R.H. Britnell, *Growth and Decline in Colchester, 1300-1525*, in *L.H.*, XVII, 1986, 248-50.

The Register of William Edington, Bishop of Winchester 1346-1366, ed. Dom S.F. Hockey, in *L.H.*, XIX, 1989, 79-80.

A.G. Rosser, *Medieval Westminster, 1200-1500*, in *L.H.*, XXI, 1991, 31-2.

E. Acheson, *A Gentry Community: Leicestershire in the Fifteenth Century, c.1422-c.1485*, in *L.H.*, XXV, 1995, 248-9.

J. Goodacre, *The Transformation of a Peasant Economy*, in *L.H.*, XXVII, 1997, 183-5.

PHYTHIAN-ADAMS, C.V.

A.A. Dibben, *Coventry City Charters*, in *U.H.N.L.*, XIII, 1969, 18.

A.F.J. Brown, *Essex at Work 1700-1815*; F.G. Emmison, *Guide to the Essex Record Office*, in *Ec.H.R.*, 2nd ser., XXIII, 1970, 181-182.

J. Godber, *History of Bedfordshire 1066-1888*, in *E.H.R.*, LXXXVI, 1971, 889-890.

Studies in London History Presented to Philip Edmund Jones, ed. A.E.J. Hollaender and W. Kellaway, in *E.H.R.*, LXXXVI, 1971, 892-893.

J. Stow, *A Survey of London*, in *U.H.N.L.*, XVI, 1971, 8-9.

D.B. Rutman, *Winthrop's Boston: Portrait of a Puritan Town, 1630-1649*;
J. Demos, *A Little Commonwealth: Family Life in Plymouth Colony*;
P.J. Greven, jr, *Four Generations: Population, Land, and Family in Colonial Andover, Massachusetts*;
K.A. Lockridge, *A New England Town: the First Hundred Years*; all in *U.H.N.L.*, XV, 1971, 7-9.

E.A.L. Moir, *Local Government in Gloucestershire 1775-1800: Study of the Justices of the Peace*, in *E.H.R.*, LXXXVII, 1972, 435-436.

J.C. Russell, *Medieval Regions and their Cities*, in *U.H.N.L.*, XVII, 1972, 11.

A.D. Dyer, *The City of Worcester in the Sixteenth Century*;
J. Patten, *Rural-Urban Migration in Pre-Industrial England*, both in *U.H.Y.B.*, 1974, 63-64.

Exeter Freemen 1266-1967, ed. M.M. Rowe and A.M. Jackson, in *U.H.Y.B.*, 1974, 103.

Household and Family in Past Time, ed. P. Laslett and R. Wall, in *U.H.Y.B.*, 1974, 40-43.

Landscapes and Documents, ed. A. Rogers and T. Rowley, in *Arch.Jnl.*, CXXXII, 1975, 372-373.

J.S. Hartley and A. Rogers, *The Religious Foundations of Medieval Stamford*, in *U.H.Y.B.*, 1975, 65.

POSTLES, D.
The Agrarian History of England and Wales, III, *1348-1500*, ed. E. Miller,. in *E.H.R.* CVII, 1992, 388-90.

The Warwickshire Hundred Rolls of 1279-80. Stoneleigh and Kineton Hundreds, ed. T. John, in *E.H.R.*, CXI, 1996, 425-6.

The Black Death, ed. R. Horrox, in *Continuity and Change*, 11, 1996, 312-4.

Campagnes Médiévales. L'Homme et son Espace, Etudes Offertes à Robert Fossier, ed. E. Mornet, in *E.H.R.*, CXII, 1997, 706-7.

Law and Government in Medieval England and Normandy. Essays in Honour of Sir James Holt, ed. G. Garnett and J. Hudson, in *Law and History Review*, 15, 1997, 162-4.

Agriculture in the Middle Ages. Technology, Practice, and Representation, ed. D. Sweeney, in *Continuity and Change*, 12, 1997, 314-15.

S.H. Rigby, *English Society in the Late Middle Ages. Class, Status and Gender*, in *Continuity and Change*, 12, 1997, 148-9.

C. Platt, *King Death: The Black Death and its Aftermath in late Medieval England*, in *Albion*, 30, 1998, 90-1.

RAVENSDALE, J.R.

J. Godber, *A History of Bedfordshire, 1066-1888*, in *Arch.*, IX, 1970, 167.

C.C. Taylor, *The Cambridgeshire Landscape*, in *J.Hist.Geog.*, I, 1975, 113.

The Field Book of Walsham-le-Willows, 1577, ed. K.M. Dodd, in *Arch.*, XII, 1976, 145.

F.G. Emmison, *Elizabethan Life: Home, Work, and Land*, in *Arch.*, XIII, 1977, 93-94.

D. Summers, *The Great Level: a History of Drainage and Land Reclamation in the Fens*, in *J.Hist.Geog.*, III, 1977, 183-184.

A.J.L. Winchester, *Landscape and Society in Medieval Cumbria*, in *N.H.*, XXV, 1989, 310-11.

The Church in Town and Countryside: Papers Read at the 17th and 18th Meetings of the Ecclesiastical History Society, ed. D.Baker, in *U.H.Y.B.*, 1981, 179-80.

REED, M.A.

The English Landscape, Past, Present and Future, ed. S.R.J.Woodell, in *J. Hist Geog.*, 12, 1986, 331-332.

P. Borsay, *The English Urban Renaissance*, in *U.H.N.L.*, 2nd ser., 7, Autumn 1989, 9-10.

N.J. Williams, *The Maritime Trade of the East Anglian Ports, 1550-1590*, in *U.H.Y.B.*, 1990, 245-6.

J.F. Pound, *Tudor and Stuart Norwich*, in *U.H.Y.B.*, 1990, 246-8.

The Cambridge Guide to the Arts in Britain, 4, the Seventeenth Century, ed. B.Ford, in *Albion*, 23, 1991, 123-5.

C. Brown, *Northampton, 1835-1985*, and M.Miller, *Letchworth: The First Garden City*, in *Ec.H.R.*, 45, 1992, 432-3.

R.M. Berger, *The Most Necessary Luxuries: The Mercers' Company of Coventry, 1550-1680*, in *Urban History*, 22, 2, 1995, 292-3.

Rural Images: Estate Maps in the Old and New Worlds, ed. D. Buisseret, in *William and Mary Quarterly*, 1997.

SNELL, K.D.M.
M.W. Flinn, *The European Demographic System* 1981, in *History of Political Thought*, 1985.

Land, Kinship and Life-Cycle, ed. Richard Smith, in the *Ec.H.R.*, XXXIX, 1986, 309-311.

J.D. Marshall, *The Old Poor Law, 1795-1834*, 1985, in *Journal of Educational Administration and History*, 1986.

A. Howkins, *Poor Labouring Men: Rural Radicalism in Norfolk, 1870-1923*, 1985, in *J.Hist.Geog.*, 12, 2, 1986, 218-219.

Proletarianisation and Family Structure, ed. David Levine, 1984, in *Ec.H.R.*, XXXIX, 1986, 309-311.

Catarina Lis, *Social Change and the Labouring Poor: Antwerp, 1770-1860*, in *T.H.E.S.*, 10 Oct.1986, 28.

The World We Have Gained: Histories of Population and Social Structure ed. L. Bonfield, R. Smith and K. Wrightson, in *T.H.E.S.*, 25 July 1986.

People's history, *T.H.E.S.*, 25 July 1986.

Victims of change, *T.H.E.S.*, 10 Oct.1986.

A 'special theory' of English history, *T.H.E.S.*, 16 Oct. 1987, 19.

Gertrude Himmelfarb, *The Idea of Poverty: England in the Early Industrial Age*, in *History of Political Thought* 1987.

Alan Macfarlane, *The Culture of Capitalism*, in *T.H.E.S.*, 16 Oct. 1987, 19.

Howard Newby, *Country Life: a Social History of Rural England*, in *Social History*, 13, 1988, 240-242.

William Stafford, *Socialism, Radicalism, and Nostalgia: Social Criticism in Britain, 1775-1830*, in *Literature and History*, 14, 2, 1988, 249-250.

Alan Macfarlane, *The Family Life of Ralph Josselin*;
Witchcraft in Tudor and Stuart England;
Resources and Population: a Study of the Gurungs of Nepal;
The Diary of Ralph Josselin, 1616-1683;
Reconstructing Historical Communities;
The Origins of English Individualism;
The Justice and the Mare's Ale;
A Guide to English Historical Records;
The Culture of Capitalism;
Marriage and Love in England: Modes of Reproduction, 1300-1840;
all in *History Workshop*, 27, 1989, 154-163.

Margaret George, *Women in the First Capitalist Society: Experiences in Seventeenth-Century England*, in *T.H.E.S.*, 24 Mar.1989, 22.

English historical continuity and the culture of capitalism, in *History Workshop Journal*, 27, 1989, 154-164.

Sharers in calamity, *T.H.E.S.*, 24 Mar. 1989, 22.

Charles McGlinchey, *The Last of the Name*, in *R.H.E.S.C.*, 1, 2, 1990, 290-291.

Malcolm Chase, *The People's Farm: English Radical Agrarianism, 1775-1840*, in *Social History*, 15, 1990.

Alan Armstrong, *Farmworkers: a Social and Economic History, 1770-1980*, in *Social History*, 15, 1990, 120-122.

Class, Conflict, and Protest in the English Countryside, 1700-1880, ed. M. Reed and R. Wells, 1990;
Country matters, both in *T.H.E.S.*, 19 Oct.1990, 20.

J.S. Taylor, *Poverty, Migration, and Settlement in the Industrial Revolution: Sojourners' Narratives*, in *R.H.E.S.C.*, 2, 1, 1991, 119-120.

Barry Reay, *The Last Rising of the Agricultural Labourers: Rural Life and Protest in Nineteenth-Century Kent*, in *T.H.E.S.*, 8 Mar. 1991, 26.

J.E. Archer, *'By a Flash and a Scare': Arson, Animal Maiming, and Poaching in East Anglia, 1815-70*, in *T.H.E.S.*, 8 Mar.1991, 26.

Revolting behaviour, *T.H.E.S.*, 8 Mar. 1991, 26.

The Agrarian History of England and Wales, IV, 1750-1850, ed. G.E. Mingay, in *J.Hist.Geog.*, 17, 1991, 195-203.

David J.V. Jones, *Rebecca's Children: A Study of Rural Society, Crime, and Protest*, in *Social History*, 16, 1991.

G.R. Boyer, *An Economic History of the English Poor Law, 1750-1850*, in *Ec.H.R.*, 1992.

K.H. Jarausch and K.A. Hardy, *Quantitative Methods for Historians: a Guide to Research, Data, and Statistics*, in *R.H.E.S.C.*, 3, 1,1992, 127-128.

C.Stell, *An Inventory of Nonconformist Chapels and Meeting-Houses in South-West England*, in *R.H.E.S.C.*, 4, 2,1993, 236-37.

From Lancaster to the Lakes - the Region in Literature, ed. K.Hanley and A. Milbank, in *Social History Society Bulletin*, 18, 2, 1993, 21-22.

Rural studies in Britain and France, ed. P.Lowe and M. Bodiguel, in *R.H.E.S.C.*, 4, 1, 1993, 93-95.

N.J.Smelser, *Social Paralysis and Social Change: British Working-class Education in the Nineteenth Century*, in *Journal of the History of Behavioural Sciences*, 29, 1993, 75-76.

Victorian Village: the Diaries of the Reverend John Coker Egerton of Burwash, Sussex, 1857-1888, ed. R.A.E.Wells, in *L.H.*, 23, 4, 1993, 234-35.

I.Dyck, *William Cobbett and Rural Popular Culture*, in *Literature and History*, 2, 1, 1993, 118-120.

M.Sutton, `We didn't know aught': a Study of Sexuality, Superstition and Death in Women's Lives in Lincolnshire During the 1930s, 40s and 50s*, 1992, , in *L.H.*, 23, 2, 1993, 118. Review entitled 'All our yesterdays'.

The Deserted Village: the Diary of an Oxfordshire Rector, James Newton, of Nuneham Courtenay, 1736-1786, ed. Gavin Hannah,.in *L.H.*, 24, 2, May 1994, 119-120. Review entitled `Gone but not forgotten'.

Felix Driver, *Power and Pauperism: the Workhouse System, 1834-1884*, 1993, in *J.Hist.Geog.*, 20, 1, 1994, 97-99.

Georgina Boyes, *The Imagined Village: Culture, Ideology and the English Folk Revival*, 1993, in *R.H.E.S.C.*, 5, 2, 1994, 228-9.

Religious Dissent in East Anglia: Historical Perspectives, ed. Norma Virgoe and Tom Williamson, 1993, in *L.H.*, 24, 4 November, 1994, 245-6.

Leicestershire and Rutland Federation of Women's Institutes, *Leicestershire and Rutland Within Living Memory*, in *Leics.H.*, 4, 3, 1995, 33.

Bill Williams, *The Diary of a Working Man, 1872-1873*, in *L.H.*, 26, 2, May 1996, 21-2.

The World of Rural Dissenters, 1520-1725, ed. Margaret Spufford, in *R.H.E.S.C.*, 7, 1, 1996, 120-1;

W.B. Stephens, *Sources for English Local History*, 1994, in *J. Soc.Arch.*, Autumn, 1996.

Curwen Archives Trust, *The Rake's Diary: the Journal of George Hilton*, in *L.H.*, 26, 2, May 1996, 121-2.

Michael A. Williams, *Researching Local History: the Human Journey*, in *L.H.*, 28, 1, 1998.

S.J.D. Green, *Religion in the Age of Decline: Organisation and Experience in Industrial Yorkshire, 1870-1920*, in *L.H.*, 27, 4, 1998, 251-2.

SNELL, K.D.M. (with Houston, R.)
P. Kriedte, H. Medick, and J. Schlumbohm, *Industrialisation before Industrialisation*, 1981, first published as *Industrialisierung vor der Industrialisierung*, in *Historical Journal*, 27, 1984, 473-492.

SNELL, L.S.
Essays in Staffordshire History presented to S.A.H. Burne, ed. M.W. Greenslade, in *M.H.*, I, iii, 1972, 60-61.

Calendar of Cornish Glebe Terriers 1673-1735, ed. R. Potts, in *Ant.Jnl.*, LVI, 1976, 110-111.
The Southampton Terrier of 1454, ed. L.A. Burgess, in *Ant.Jnl.*, LXVII, 1977, 394.

SPUFFORD, H.M.
J. Sayers, *Estate documents at Lambeth Palace Library: a Short Catalogue*, in *Arch.* VII, 1966, 181.

A.C. Chibnall, *Sherington: Fiefs and Fields of a Buckinghamshire Village*, in *A.H.R.*, XVI, 1968, 71-72.

A.F.J. Brown, *Essex at Work, 1700-1815*, in *A.H.R.*, XXI, 1973, 71-72.

A. MacFarlane, *Reconstructing Historical Communities*, in *T.L.S.*, 1 Sept. 1978.

THIRSK, J.

A.R.B. Haldane, *The Drove Roads of Scotland*, in *A.H.R.*, I, 1953, 55-58.

M E. Seebohm, *The Evolution of the English Farm*, in *A.H.R.*, I, 1953, 60-61.

F.K. Riemann, *Ackerbau und Viehhaltung im vorindustriellen Deutschland*, in *A.H.R.*, II, 1954, 66.

C. Hole, *The English Housewife in the Seventeenth Century*, in *A.H.R.*, II, 1954, 61-62.

E. Kerridge, *Surveys of the Manors of Philip, First Earl of Pembroke and Montgomery, 1631-2*, in *Ec.H.R.*, 2nd ser., VI, 1954, 331.

A.E. Kirkby, *Humberstone: the Story of a Village*, in *A.H.R* , III, 1955, 57.

M.W. Beresford, *The Lost Villages of England*, in *A.H.R.*, III, 1955, 52-54.

Lord Leconfield, *Petworth Manor in the Seventeenth Century*, in *Ec.H.R.*, 2nd ser., VII, 1955, 392.

M.G. Davies, *The Enforcement of English Apprenticeship, 1563-1642*, in *Kyklos*, 2, 1957, 207-208.

R.C. Russell, *The 'Revolt of the Field' in Lincolnshire*, in *A.H.R.*, V, 1957, 116-117.

Lord Leconfield, *Sutton and Duncton Manors*, in *Ec.H.R.*, 2nd ser., X, 1957, 297.

J.W.F. Hill, *Tudor and Stuart Lincoln*, in *E.H.R.*, LXXII, 1957, 536-537.

R. Trow-Smith, *A History of British Livestock Husbandry to 1700*, in *A.H.R.*, VI, 1958, 54-55.

J.D. Chambers, *The Vale of Trent, 1670-1800*, in *E.H.R.*, LXXIII, 1958, 723-724.

F.W. Jessup, *A History of Kent*, in *E.H.R.*, LXXIV, 1959, 146.

W.G. Hoskins, *The Midland Peasant: an Economic and Social History of a Leicestershire Village*, in *E.H.R.*, LXXIV, 1959, 682-684.

R.C. Shaw, *The Royal Forest of Lancaster*, in *A.H.R.*, VII, 1959, 123-124.

D.R. Denman, *et al., Bibliography of Rural Land Economy and Landownership, 1900-1957*, in *E.H.R.*, LXXV, 1960, 552.

J.G. O'Leary, *Dagenham Place-Names*, in *E.H.R.*, LXXV, 1960, 146.

K. Cameron, *The Place Names of Derbyshire*, in *A.H.R.*, VIII, 1960, 120-121.

The Victoria History of the County of Stafford, V, ed. L.M. Midgley, in *Ec.H.R.*, XIII, 1960, 133-134.

The Victoria History of the County of Wiltshire, IV, ed. E. Crittall, in *Ec.H.R.*, 2nd ser., XIII, 1960, 299-300.

Court Rolls of the Manor of Tottenham. 1510-1531, and *Court Rolls of the Manor of Tottenham, 1547-1558*, ed. F.H. Fenton, in *A.H.R.*, IX, 1961, 126-127.

H. Grieve, *The Great Tide: the Story of the 1953 Flood Disaster in Essex*, in *E.H.R.*, LXXVI, 1961, 186-187.

G.H. Green, *Historical Account of the Ancient King's Mills (Castle Donington, Leics.)*, in *A.H.R.*, IX, 1961, 127.

J.M. Lambert *et al.*, *The Making of the Broads: a Reconstruction of their Origin*, in *E.H.R.*, LXXVI, 1961, 704-705.

M. Kirkus, *The Records of the Commissioners of Sewers in the Parts of Holland, 1547-1603*, in *E.H.R.*, LXXVI, 1961, 142-143.

The Sibton Abbey Estates, 1325-1509, ed. A.H. Denney, in *E.H.R.*, LXXVII, 1962, 140.

E. Juillard, *et al.*, *Structures Agraires et Paysages Ruraux*, 1957, and *Géographie et Histoire Agraires*, 1959, in *A.H.R.*, X, 1962, 57.

Victoria History of the County of Middlesex, III, and *Index* to II and III, ed. S. Reynolds, in *Ec.H.R.*, 2nd ser., XV, 1962, 535.

C.S. Davies, *The Agrarian History of Cheshire, 1750-1850*, in *A.H.R.*, XI, 1963, 50.

The Domesday Geography of Eastern England, ed.H.C. Darby and E.M.J. Campbell; *The Domesday Geography of Northern England*, ed.H.C. Darby and I.S. Maxwell, both in *H.*, XLVIII, 1963, 355-357.

Lord Ernle, *English Farming Past and Present*, in *E.H.R.,LXXVIII*, 1963, 590.

Hatfield Workers' Educational Association, *Hatfield and its People: Book 9, Farming Yesterday and Today*, in *A.H.R.*, XI, 1963, 60-61.

H.W. Brace, *A History of Seed Crushing*, in *A.H.R.*, XI, 1963, 53-54.

The Morphogenesis of the Agrarian Cultural Landscape, ed. S. Helmfrid, in *A.H.R.,*XI, 1963, 62-63.

S. Helmfrid, *Östergötland - `Västanstång' - Studien über die ältere Agrarlandschaft und ihre Genese*, in *A.H.R.*, XI, 1963, 58-59.

Thaxted in the Fourteenth Century, ed. K.C. Newton, in *E.H.R.*, LXXVIII, 1963, 367-368.

J. West, *Village Records*, in *Ec.H.R.*, 2nd ser., XVI, 1963, 161.

Court Rolls of the Manor of Tottenham, 1377-1399, and *Court Rolls of the Manor of Tottenham, 1558-1582*, ed. F.H. Fenton, in *A.H.R.*, XII, 1964, 61-62.

H.M. Heybroek, *Diseases and Lopping for Fodder as Possible Causes of a Prehistoric Decline of Ulmus*, *A.H.R.*, XII, 1964, 58-59.

W.G. Hoskins, *Provincial England*, in *Ec.H.R.*, 2nd ser., XVII, 1964, 401.

Deutsche Agrargeschichte, II, III, V, ed. Prof. Dr G. Franz, in *A.H.R.*, XIII, 1965, 69-72.

R.C. Russell, *The Enclosures of East Halton, 1801-1804, and North Kelsey, 1813-1840;*
R.C. Russell, *The Enclosures of Bottesford and Yaddlethorpe, 1794-97, Messingham, 1798-1804, and Ashby 1801-1809;*
V.H.T. Skipp and R.P. Hastings, *Discovering Bickenhill*, all in *A.H.R.*, XIII, 1965, 64-65.

M. Devèze, *La Vie de la Forêt Française au XVIe Siècle*, in *A.H.R.*, XIII, 1965, 68-69.

L.W. Hanson, *Contemporary Printed Sources for British and Irish Economic History, 1701-1750*, in *A.H.R.*, XIV, 1966, 136.

Sir Francis Hill, *Georgian Lincoln*, in *U.H.N.L.*, VI, 1966, 10-11.

J.D. Chambers, *Laxton: the Last English Open Field Village*, in *A.H.R.*, XIV, 1966, 135-136.

Devon Inventories of the Sixteenth and Seventeenth Centuries, ed. M. Cash, in *Arch.*, VIII, 1967, 98-99.

W. Abel, *Agrarkrisen und Agrarkonjunktur*, in *A.H.R.*, XVI, 1968, 77.

N. Sanchez-Albornoz, *Las Crisis de Subsistencias de España en el Siglo XIX*, in *A.H.R.*, XVI, 1968, 172.

D. Cromarty, *The Fields of Saffron Walden in 1400*, in *E.H.R.*, LXXXIII, 1968, 161.

F.W. Henning, *Herrschaft und Bauernuntertänigkeit. Beiträge zur Geschichte der Herrschaftsverhältnisse den ländlichen Bereichen Ostpreussens und des Fürstentums Paderborn vor 1800*, in *A.H.R.*, XVI, 1968, 78.

R.J. Forbes, *Notes on the History of Ancient Roads and their Construction*, in *A.H.R.*, XVI, 1968, 75-76.

Warwick County Records, IX: Quarter Sessions Records, Easter 1690 to Michaelmas 1696, eD.H.C. Johnson and N.J. Williams, in *Ec.H.R.,* 2nd ser., XXI, 1968, 171.

L. Symons, *Agricultural Geography,* in *A.H.R.,* XVII, 1969, 148-150.
P. and M. Spufford, *Eccleshall: the Story of a Staffordshire Market Town and its Dependent Villages,* in *A.H.R.,* XVII, 1969, 82.

W.E. Tate, *The English Village Community and the Enclosure Movement,* in *H.,* LIV, 1969, 159.

W. Abel, *Geschichte der Deutschen Landwirtschaft vom frühen Mittelalter bis zum 19 Jahrhundert;*

F. Lütge, *Geschichte der Deutschen Agrarverfassung vom frühen Mittelalter bis zum 19 Jahrhundert,* both in *Zeitschrift für Agrargeschichte und Agrarsoziologie,* Jahrgang 56, Heft 4, 1969.

G. Schröder-Lembke, *Martin Grosser, Anleitung zu der Landwirtschaft; Abraham von Thumbschirn, Oeconomia,* in *A.H.R.,* XVII, 1969, 154-155.

A.E. Chibnall, *Sherington: Fiefs and Fields of a Buckinghamshire Village,* in *H.,* LIV, 1969, 158.

H.-J. Schmitz, *Faktoren der Preisbildung für Getreide und Wein in der Zeit von 800 bis 1350,* in *A.H.R.,* XVIII, 1970, 79-80.

G. von Below, *Geschichte der deutschen Landwirtschaft des Mittelalters,* in *A.H.R.,* XVIII, 1970, 79.

H. Wiese and J. Bölts, *Rinderhaltung im Nordwesteuropäischen Küstengebiet vom 15 bis zum 19 Jahrhundert,* in *A.H.R.,* XVIII, 1970, 83-85.

Agrarian Change and Economic Development: the Historical Problems, ed. E.L. Jones and S.J. Woolf, in *E.H.R.,* LXXXVI, 1971, 894-895.

R.E.F. Smith, *The Enserfment of the Russian Peasantry,* in *A.H.R.,* XIX, 1971, 102-103.

E. Le Roy Ladurie, *Les Paysans de Languedoc,* in *A.H.R.,* XIX, 1971, 178-80.

P.A.J. Pettit, *The Royal Forests of Northamptonshire: a Study in their Economy, 1558-1714,* in *E.H.R.,* LXXXVI, 1971, 407-408.

Stability and Change: Some Aspects of North and South Rauceby in the Nineteenth Century, ed. A. Rogers, in *Ec.H.R.,* 2nd ser., XXIV, 1971, 147-148.

The Victoria History of the Counties of England: General Introduction, ed. R.B. Pugh, in *Ec.H.R.,* 2nd ser., XXIV, 1971, 483.

American Agricultural History; Eighteenth-Century Agriculture: a Symposium, in *E.H.R.*, LXXXVII, 1972, 191-192.

H. Mendras, *La Fin des Paysans. Changement et Innovations dans les Sociétés Rurales Françaises*, in *A.H.R.*, XX, 1972, 89-90.

Household and Family in Past Time, ed. P. Laslett, in *The Tablet*, 16 Dec. 1972, 1201.

The Victoria History of the County of Oxford, IX, ed. M.D. Lobel and A. Crossley, in *Ec.H.R.*, 2nd ser., XXV, 1972, 357-358.

D.M. Barratt, *Ecclesiastical Terriers of Warwickshire Parishes*, II, in *Ec.H.R.*, 2nd ser., XXVI, 1973, 342.

E. Wiest, *Die Entwicklung des Nürnberger Gewerbes zwischen 1648 und 1806*, in *A.H.R.*, XXI, 1973, 68-69.

The Victoria History of the County of Gloucester, X, ed. C.M. Elrington and N.M. Herbert, in *Ec.H.R.*, 2nd ser., XXVII, 1973, 472.

The Victoria History of the County of Oxford, X, ed. A. Crossley, *Ec.H.R.*, 2nd ser., XXVII, 1973, 683-684.

J.Z. Titow, *Winchester Yields: a Study in Medieval Agricultural Productivity*, in *Ant.Jnl.*, LIII, 1973, 128-129.

Abstracts of Wiltshire Inclosure Awards and Agreements, ed. R.E. Sandell, in *E.H.R.*, LXXXIX, 1974, 905-906.

M. Morineau, *Les Faux-Semblants d'un Démarrage Economique: Agriculture et Démographie en France à XVIIIe siècle*, in *A.H.R.*, XXII, 1974, 82-83.

Konrad Heresbach: Vier Bücher Über Landwirtschaft: Band I. Vom Landbau, ed. W. Abel and H. Dreitzel, in *A.H.R.*, XXII, 1974, 186-187.

Rufford Charters, I, ed. C.J. Holdsworth, in *M.H.*, II, iii, 1974, 197-200.

Early Records of the Bankes Family at Winstanley, ed. J. Bankes and E. Kerridge, in *E.H.R.*, LXXXX, 1975, 644-645.

J. Wake and D.C. Webster, *The Letters of Daniel Eaton to the Third Earl of Cardigan 1725-1732*, in *E.H.R.*, LXXXX, 1975, 653-654.

Rufford Charters, II, ed. C.J. Holdsworth, in *M.H.*, III, ii, 1975, 149.

Village Life and Labour, ed. R. Samuel, in *N.S.*, XXXII, 22 May 1975, 489-490.

J.R. Gillies, *Youth and History: Tradition and Change in European Age Relations, 1770 to the Present*, in *N.S.*, XXXIII, 17 July 1975, 150.

G. Ahrens, *Caspar Voght und sein Mustergut Flottbek: Englische Landwirtschaft in Deutschland am Ende des 18 Jahrhunderts*, in *A.H.R.*, XXIV, 1976, 80-82.

G.E. Mingay, *The Gentry: the Rise and Fall of a Ruling Class*, in *N.S.*, XXXVIII, 21 Oct. 1976, 155-156.

G.E. Fussell, *Jethro Tull: His Influence on Mechanized Agriculture*, in *A.H.R.*, XXIV, 1976, 161-162.

E.LeRoy Ladurie, *The Peasants of Languedoc*, in *The Listener*, 29 Jan., 1976.

L. Stone, *The Family, Sex, and Marriage in England, 1500-1800*, in *T.H.E.S.*, 28 Oct. 1977.

M.L. Bush, *The Government Policy of Protector Somerset*, in *Lit. Hist.*, VI, 1977, 256-258.

E. Le Roy Ladurie, *Times of Feast, Times of Famine: a History of Climate since the Year 1000*, in *H.*, LXII, 1977, 77-78.

Trade, Government, and Economy in Pre-Industrial England, ed. D.C. Coleman and A.H. John, in *The Magazine of the London School of Economics and Political Science*, 53, June 1977, 14-15.

B. Henrey, *British Botanical and Horticultural Literature before 1800*, in *A.H.R.*, XXVI, 1978, 59-61.

J. Blum, *The End of an Old Order in Rural Europe*, in *T.H.E.S.*, 27 Oct. 1978.

David Levine, *Family Formation in an Age of Nascent Capitalism*, in *William and Mary Quarterly*, 1978.

R. Mandrou, *Introduction to Modern France, 1500-1640*, in *Lit. Hist.*, VII, 1978, 113-115.

Medieval Settlement, ed. P. Sawyer, in *L.H.*, XIII, 1978, 50-52.

E. Le Roy Ladurie, *Montaillou, Village Occitan de 1294 à 1324*, in *J.Hist.Geog.*, IV, 1978, 301-302.

Paysannerie Française, Paysannerie Hongroise, XVIe-XXe Siècles, ed. B. Köpeczi and E.H. Balázs, in *A.H.R.*, XXVI, 1978, 58-59.

The Victoria History of Wiltshire, X, ed. E. Crittall, in *E.H.R.*, XCIII, 1978, 150-151

J.O.Appleby, *Economic Thought and Ideology in Seventeenth-century England*, in *Lit. Hist.*, VI, 1980, 260-61.

R.Ashton, *The English Civil War: Conservation and Revolution, 1603-49,* in *Ec.H.R.,* XXXIII, 1980, 276-77.

Ingomar Bog, Gunther Franz *et al., Wirtschaftliche und soziale Strukturen in saekularen Wandel. Festschrift fur Wilhelm Abel zum 70ten Geburtstag,* in *A.H.R.,* XXVIII, 190, 140-141.

The Court Rolls of the Manor of Wakefield 1639-1640, ed. C.M.Fraser and K.Emsley, in *E.H.R.,* XCV, 1980, 213-14.

J.Patten, *English Towns, 1500-1700,* in *A.H.R.,* XXVIII, 1980, 129-30.

Crisis in Cumbria - review of A.E.Appleby, *Famine in Tudor and Stuart England,* in *T.L.S.,* 11 Jan. 1980, 35.

G.Schroeder-Lembke, *Studien zur Agrargeschichte, Quellen und Forschungen zur Agrargeschichte,* in *A.H.R.,* XXVIII, 1980, 130-133.

K.P.Witney, *The Jutish Forest: a Study of the Weald of Kent from 450-1380 A.D.,* in *E.H.R.,* XCV, 1980, 390-400.

E.E.Rich and C.H.Wilson, *The Cambridge Economic History of Europe, V, The Economic Organization of Early-modern Europe,* in *A.H.R.,* XXIX, 1981, 58-60.

Change in the Countryside, eD.H.S.A.Fox and R.A.Butlin, in *J.Hist.Geog.,* VII, 1981, 311-12.

J.A.Yelling, *Common Fields and Enclosure in England, 1450-1850,* in *E.H.R.,* XCVI, 1981, 208-09.

R.A.Dodgshon and R.A.Butlin, *An Historical Geography of England and Wales,* in *U.H.Y.B.,* 1981, 177-8.

A Selection from the Records of Philip Foley's Stour Valley Ironworks, 1668-74, pt.1, in *E.H.R.,* XCVI, 1981, 912.

Ian Whyte, *Agriculture and Society in Seventeenth-Century Scotland,* in *Scottish Historical Review,* 1982, 61, 90-91.

I.J.Gentles and W.J.Sheils, *Confiscation and Restoration: the Archbishopric Estates and the Civil War,* in *A.H.R.,* XXX, 1982, 85-86.

John Bowle, *John Evelyn and his World: a Biography,* in *Ec.H.R.,* XXXV, 1982, 307.

M.Turner, *English Parliamentary Enclosure: its Historical Geography and Economic History,* in *E.H.R.,* XCVIII, 1983, 199-200.

The Lisle Letters, ed. M. St Clare Byrne, in *Lit. Hist.,* IX, 1983, 262-265.

Clifton and Westbury Probate Inventories, ed. J.S.Moore, in *M.H.*, 1984, IX, 131-2.

G.D.Ramsay, *The English Woollen Industry, 1500-1750*, in *Ec.H.R.*, XXXVII, 1984, 276-77.

J.G.L. Burnby and A.E.Robinson, `Now turned into fair Garden Plots', (Stow), in *A.H.R.*, XXXII, 1984,101-2.

The Origins of Open Field Agriculture, ed. T.Rowley, in *E.H.R.*, XCIX, 1984, 407.

Medieval Industry, ed. D.Crossley, in *E.H.R.*, C, 1985, 879.

P.D.A.Harvey, *The Peasant Land Market in Medieval England*, in *T.H.E.S.*, 1985.

D.B.Grigg, *Population Growth and Agrarian Change: an Historical Perspective*, in *E.H.R.*, C, 1985, 652-53.

E.Le Roy Ladurie and J.Gay, *Tithe and Agrarian History from the 14th to the 19th centuries: an Essay in Comparative History*, translated Susan Burke, in *E.H.R.*, C, 1985, 661-62.

R.J.P.Kain and H.C.Prince, *The Tithe Surveys of England and Wales*, in *T.L.S.*, 1985.

H.C.Darby, *The Changing Fenland*, in *E.H.R.*, CI, 1986, 500-01.

N. Evans, *The East Anglian Linen Industry: Rural Industry and Local Economy*, in *Textile History*, XVIII, 1986, 103.

N.Landau, *The Justices of the Peace, 1679-1760*, in *Ec.H.R.*, XXXIX, 1986, 298.

Alison Grant, *North Devon Pottery: the Seventeenth Century*, in *Southern History*, 8, 1986.

M.M.Rodriguez, *Pensamiento economic espanol sobre la Poblacion*, in *Ec.H.R.*, XXXIX, 1986, 151-52.

D.W.Sabean, *Power in the Blood: Popular Culture and Village Discourse in Early-modern Germany*, in *A.H.R.*, XXXIV, 1986, 213.

Helen M.Jewell *et al., Court Rolls of the Manor of Wakefield*, in *E.H.R.*, CII, 402, 1987.

Ellen Wedemeyer Moore, *The Fairs of Medieval England,*, in *Jnl of History*, 1987, 93-4.

Land, Kinship and Life Cycle, ed. R.Smith, in *A.H.R.*, XXXV, 1988, 108-9

Zur mittellaterlichen Siedlungsgeschichte in England, *Genetische Siedlungsforschung in Mitteleuropa und seinen Nachbarräumen*, ed. Klaus Fehn *et al.*, Verlag Siedlungsforschung, Bonn, 1988, 26, 57-69.

The Victoria County History of Wiltshire, XIII, South-west Wiltshire, Chalke and Dunworth Hundreds, ed. D.A.Crowley, in *E.H.R.*, CIV, 1988, 207.

C.M.Fraser, *Court Rolls of the Manor of Wakefield*, in *E.H.R.*, CIV, 410, 1989.

The Court Rolls of the Manor of Wakefield, 5: 1664-1665, ed. C.M.Fraser with K.Emsley, in *E.H.R.* 1989, 207.

A.Bermingham, *The English Rustic Tradition, 1740-1860*, in *Journal of Forest History*, XXXII, 1989, 222-3.

R.Lachmann, *From Manor to Market: Structural Change in England, 1536-1640*, in *Ec.H.R.*, 2nd ser., XLII, 1989, 406-7.

M.Schultz, *Paradise Preserved: Recreations of Eden in Eighteenth- and Nineteenth-Century England*, in *Journal of Forest History*, XXXII, 1989, 222-3.

Ann Kussmaul, *A General View of the Rural Economy of England, 1538-1840*, in *T.H.E.S.*, Nov. 18 and in *T.L.S.*, Dec. 7 1990.

H-H. Muller und Volker Klemm, *Im Dienste der Ceres. Streiflichter zu Leben und Werk bedeutender deutscher Landwirte und Wissenschaftler*, in *A.H.R.*, 39, 1, 1991.

Mark Bailey, *A Marginal Economy? East Anglian Breckland in the later Middle Ages*, in *A.H.R.*, 39, 2, 1991.

Victoria History of Wiltshire, XIII: South-West Wiltshire, ed. D.A.Crowley,. in *E.H.R.*, CVI, 418, 1991.

Rural History: Economy, Society and Culture, 1, 1, in *A.H.R.*, 39, 2, 1991.

Bridget Hill, *Women, Work, and Sexual Politics in Eighteenth-Century England;* Janet Todd, *The Sign of Angellica. Women, Writing and Fiction, 1660-1800*, both in *Lit.Hist.*, 2, 1, 1991, 103-4.

Karl Gunnar Persson, *Pre-industrial Economic Growth. Social Organization and Technological Progress in Europe*, in *E.H.R.*, 107, 1992, 476-7.

Jose Miguel Martínez Carrión, *La Ganadería en la Economía Murciana Contemporánea, 1860-1936*, in *A.H.R.*, 41, 2, 1993.

H.J. Yallop, *The History of the Honiton Lace Industry*, in *Business History*, 35, 4, 1993.

Philip Lyth, *The Pinfolds of Nottinghamshire. A Gazetteer*, in *A.H.R.*,. 41, 2, 1993.

Margaret L. King, *Women of the Renaissance*, in *Lit.Hist.* 3rd ser., 2, 2, 1993.

German Navarro, *El Despegue de la Industria Sedera en la Valencia del Siglo XV*, in *Textile History*, 25, 1, 1994.

Noticiario de Historia Agraria, I & 2, 1991, in *R.H.E.S.C.*, V, 1, 1994, 111-112.

Bridget Hill, *The Republican Virago. The Life and Times of Catharine Macaulay, Historian*, in *Women's History Review*, 3, 1, 1994.

Lucie Bolens, *L'Andalousie du Quotidien au Sacré, XIe-XIIIe siècles*; Lucie Bolens, *La Cuisine andalouse, un Art de Vivre, XIe-XIIIe-siècle*, both in *A.H.R.*, 43, 1, 1995.

E. Kerridge, *The Common Fields of England*, in *E.H.R.*, CX, 437, 1995.

Malcolm Kelsall, *The Great Good Place. The Country House and English Literature*, in *Lit.Hist.*, 412, 1995, 96-7.

Land, Labour and Livestock: Historical Studies in European Agricultural Productivity, ed. B.M.S.Campbell and Mark Overton, in *E.H.R.*, CX, 435, 1995.

N.W.Alcock, *People at Home. Living in a Warwickshire Village, 1500-1800*, in *Southern History*, 1995.

Clifford M. Foust, *Rhubarb. The Wondrous Drug*, in *E.H.R.*, CX, 438, 1995.

Amy L. Erickson, *Women and Property*, in *A.H.R.*, 43, 1, 1995.

Archivists and Researchers: Mutual Perceptions and Requirements, ed Helen Forde and Rosmary Seton, in *J.Soc.Arch.*, 16, 2, 250-1.

Laurence Wiedmer, *Pain Quotidien et Pain de Disette à Genève, XVIIe -XVIIIe Siècles*, in *A.H.R.*, 44, 2, 1996.

Francis Brumont, *Paysans de Vieille-Castille aux XVIe et XVIIe Siècles*, in *A.H.R.*, 44, 1, 1996.

Werner Rösener, *The Peasantry of Europe*, in *A.H.R.*, 44,2, 1996.

Robert von Friedeburg, *Sündenzucht und Sozialer Wandel. Earls Colne (England), Ipswich und Springfield (Neuengland), c.1524-1690 im Vergleich*, in *E.H.R.*, CXI, 4, 1996.

Jordan Goodman, *Tobacco in History. The Cultures of Dependence*, in *E.H.R.*, CXI, 1996, 441.

John Goodacre, *The Transformation of a Peasant Economy.Townspeople and Villagers in the Lutterworth Area, 1500-1700*, in *A.H.R.*, 44, 2, 1996.

Mark Overton, *Agricultural Revolution in England*, in *Ec.H.R.*, L, 1997, 378-9

Maxine Berg, *A Woman in History. Eileen Power, 1889-1940*, in *Gender and History*, 9, 2, August 1997, 416-8.

Guy de la Bedoyere, *The Writings of John Evelyn*, in *A.H.R.*, 45, 2,1997.

Margaret R.Hunt, *The Middling Sort. Commerce, Gender and the Family in England, 1680- 1780*, in *Business History*, 40, 1, 1998, 123-4.

Beverly Lemire, *Dress, Culture and Commerce. The English Clothing Trade before the Factory*, 1660-1800, in *Costume*, forthcoming.

Philip T.Hoffman, *Growth in a Traditional Society. The French Countryside, 1450-1815*, in *A.H.R.*, forthcoming.

David Cressy, *Birth, Marriage and Death. Ritual Religion and the Life Cycle in Tudor and Stuart England*, in *Lit.Hist.*, forthcoming.

J.D.Marshall, *The Tyranny of the Discrete. A Discussion of the Problems of Local History in England*, in *J.Hist.Geog.*, forthcoming.

THOMPSON, M.G.
C.Lewis, P.Mitchell-Fox and C.Dyer, *Village, Hamlet and Field: Changing Medieval Settlements in Central England*, in *R.H.E.S.C.*, 9, 2, October 1998.

TRANTER, E.M.
Robin Gill, *Competing Convictions*, S.C.M. Press, in *R.H.E.S.C.*, II, 1, 1991.

TRINDER, B.S.
H. Hanson, *The Canal Boatmen, 1760-1914;*

H. Fletcher, *A Life on the Humber: Keeling to Shipbuilding*, both in *L.H.* XII, 1976, 179-181.

K. Rodwell, *Historic Towns in Oxfordshire: a Survey of the New County*, in *C.& C.*, VI, 1976, 95.

M.B. Rowlands, *Masters and Men in the West Midland Metalware Trades before the Industrial Revolution*, in *M.H.*, III, iii, 1976, 236-238.

C.W. Chalklin, *The Provincial Towns of Georgian England*, in *L.H.*, XII, 1976, 111-112.

H. Lloyd, *The Quaker Lloyds*, in *L.H.*, XII, 1976, 181-182.

H.E. Meller, *Leisure and the Changing City*;
K. Barker, *Bristol at Play*, both in *L.H.*, XII, 1977, 376-377.

J. Obelkevich, *Religion and Rural Society: South Lindsey 1825-1875*, in *L.H.*, XII, 1977, 435-437.

The Works of Isambard Kingdom Brunel: an Engineering Appreciation, ed. Sir Alfred Pugsley, in *I.A.R.*, I, 1977, 194.

E. Pawson, *Transport and Economy: the Turnpike Roads of Eighteenth-Century Britain*, in *L.H.*, XIII, 1978, 170-172.

J.D.Porteous, *Canal Ports: The Urban Achievement of the Canal Age*, in *L.H.*, XIII,1979, 299-300.

F.Finnegan, *Poverty and Prostitution: a study of Victorian Prostitutes in York*, in *L.H.*, XIV, 1980, 48-53.

K.Hudson, *World of Industrial Archaeology*, in *I.A.R.*, V, 1980, 60-61.

L.Trottier, *Les Forges du Saint-Maurice: their Historiography*, in *I.A.R.*, VI, 1981-82, 65.

V.Berridge and G. Edwards, *Opium and the People: Opiate Use in Nineteenth-Century England*, in *L.H.*, XV, 1982, 181.

N.Wright, *Lincolnshire Towns and Industry 1700-1914*, in *I.A.R.*, VI, 1982,245.

M.Prior, *Fisher Row*, in *L.H.*, XV, 1983, 436-38.

R.Hewison, *The Heritage Industry - Britain in a Climate of Decline, 1992*, in *Landscape Studies*, III, 1988, 67.

D.Hempton, *Methodism and Politics in British Society, 1750-1850*;
M.Essex-Lopresti *Exploring the New River*, both in *L.H.*, 18, 1, 1988, 35.

The Crafts of the Blacksmith: Essays presented to R.F.Tylecote, ed. B.G.Scott & H.Cleere, in *Ant.*, LXII, 1988, 818.

C.J.Williams, *A Handlist of the Grosvenor (Halkyn) MSS*, in *Arch.*, XIX, 1989, 51.

I.Edwards, *Decorative Cast-Ironwork in Wales*, in *Transactions of the Denbighshire Historical Society*, XXXIX, 1990, 137-8.

D.Hey, *The Fiery Blades of Hallamshire*, in *L.H.*, XXII, 1992, 48-9.

H.Carter & C.R.Lewis, *An Urban Geography of England and Wales in the Nineteenth Century*, in *Planning Perspectives*, VII, 1992, 118-9.

A. Föhl, *Bauten der Industrie und Technik*, in *I.A.R.*, XVIII, 1995, 132.

The Potteries: Continuity and Change in a Staffordshire Conurbation,
ed. A.D.M.Phillips, in *Staffordshire Studies*, VI, 1994, 119-20.

R.B.Gordon & P.M.Malone, *The Texture of Industry: An Archaeological View of the Industrialization of North America*, in *Material History Review*, XLIII, 1996, 92-3.

WATKINSON, M.A.
W.G. Hoskins, *The Age of Plunder: the England of Henry VIII, 1500-1547*, in *Lincs.H.A.* XIII, 1978, 45-46.

WEST, F.
Sybil Marshall, *Fenland Chronicle*, in *A.H.R.*, XVI, 1968, 169-170.

WILLIAMS, M.I.
E. Hughes and A. Eames, *Porthmadog Ships*, in *W.H.R.*, VIII, 1976, 228-230.

Wales in the Eighteenth Century, ed. D. Moore, in *Arch.Camb.*, CXXXV,1976, 181-3

Names Index

CROSS, M.C., 47, 162
CROSSMAN, A.B., 98
CROUCH, P.J., 111
CUMMINS, H.A., 106

—D—

DAVENPORT, C., 111
DAVEY, B.J., 49, 106
DAVIES, R., 98
DAVIES, V.E.L., 143
DAVIS, D.K., 92
DE CLERCQ, P., 106
DE WAAL, E.A.L., 157 (also as Moir,
E.A.L.)
DEBNEY, C., 106
DeLONG, R.E., 151
DEXTER, J., 106 (also as Crompton, J.)
DOREE, S.G., 32, 37, 62, 77, 106, 142,
147, 154
DOWNER, S., 52, 77
DRAYCOTT, C., 77
DRINKALL, J.T., 147
DYER, C., 50, 92

—E—

EATON, M.D., 135
EDEN, P., 52, 60, 62, 63, 118, 184
EDWARDS, E., 126
EDWARDS, E.J.M., 106, 172, 173, 174
EDWARDS, H., 111, 151
EDWARDS, J., 73
EDWARDS, L.E., 135
EDWARDS, P.R., 37, 87, 111
ELL, P.S., 157
ELLIOTT, B., 111, 158
ELLIOTT, B.S., 63, 143, 174, 177
ENGLISH, S., 70, 87 (also as Wise, S.E.)
EVELEIGH, N.G., 52
EVERITT, A.M., 30, 32, 35, 42, 45, 48,
49, 50, 52, 73, 77, 84, 87, 98, 106, 118,
123, 126, 129, 144, 147, 158, 185

—F—

FAITH, R.J., 73, 77, 92, 148, 162, 178,
187
FARRELL, S., 98
FINBERG, H.P.R., 30, 37, 45, 47, 48, 52,
63, 73, 74, 77, 87, 93, 112, 123, 126,
148, 154, 187
FLEMING, A.J., 135
FLEMING, D., 85, 98, 135, 162, 170
FLETCHER, S.J.C., 135

FLETCHER, S.M., 52, 112, 118, 190
FORD, W.J., 79
FOX, A.W., 98
FOX, D.E., 88, 155
FOX, H.S.A., 32, 35, 42, 45, 52, 61, 79,
93, 98, 106, 111, 126, 142, 190
FREEBODY, N.K., 88, 162
FRIEL, I., 79, 118
FRYE, J., 143

—G—

GARRISON, L., 143
GARVEN, M., 95
GENT, F.J.R., 123
GENT, K.S., 167
GLADDEN, D.H., 158
GLASSON, M.O.J., 53, 70, 112, 135
GOODACRE, J.D., 45, 50, 63, 99, 112,
118, 130, 135, 148, 164, 193
GOODWIN, D., 107
GRAHAM, M., 32, 38, 63, 112, 118, 135,
162, 167, 178
GREENFIELD, E.M., 112
GREENWOOD, J.J., 130
GREWCOCK, C.E.S., 162

—H—

HADLEY A., 79
HAIGH, B., 99
HAIGH, D., 79, 80
HALEY, D., 130
HALL, J., 168
HALL, J.L., 107
HALL, T., 53, 80
HALLAM, H.E., 47, 95
HAMPTON, S.J.S., 119
HAMMOND, C., 112
HARRATT, S.R., 158, 162
HARRIS, K.S., 162
HARRISON, J.D., 95, 119
HART, C.E., 80, 88, 95, 112, 123, 181
HART, Clive R., 53, 54, 99, 124, 127, 194
HART, Cyril R., 32, 38, 42, 48, 49, 63,
80, 95, 127, 148, 155, 168, 181, 194
HAWKER, K., 112
HAYDON, E.S., 38, 88, 95, 99, 107, 194
HAYES, W.F.G., 139
HAYHURST, Y.M., 170
HEATH, J., 54
HEATHCOTE BALL, J., 168
HEMMING, A.C., 136
HENDY, S., 158

HEY, D.G., 32, 35, 38, 42, 45, 49, 50, 54, 64, 70, 74, 88, 99, 107, 112, 119, 124, 130, 136, 144, 148, 158, 194
HILL, T.G., 119, 136, 140, 196
HILLIER, K.A., 64, 124, 140, 162, 168, 181
HOARE, N.F., 140
HODGKINSON, J.S., 136
HOGAN, C.J., 159
HORTON, M., 81
HOSKINS, W.G., 30, 33, 35, 38, 48, 55, 64, 70, 74, 81, 85, 88, 89, 95, 99, 107, 113, 124, 127, 130, 136, 140, 142, 145, 148, 159, 163, 196
HOWELL, C.A.H., 89, 203
HUME, J.A., 144
HUNT, H.M.J., 131
HUNT, I.D.J., 107
HUTCHIN, J.D., 140

—I—

INDER, P.M., 140, 149, 151, 168, 181
INGLESANT, D., 113
IREDALE, D.A., 36, 39, 61, 64, 74, 100, 113, 149, 159, 163, 178, 203
IRONFIELD, C., 100

—J—

JACKSON, A.J.H., 85
JACKSON, P., 136
JAMES, T.M., 114, 124, 131, 155, 181
JENKINS, S.C., 57, 64, 65, 70, 74, 82, 107, 114, 119, 121, 124, 136, 142, 155, 167, 170, 178, 181
JONES, G.R., 155
JONES, K., 159
JOYCE, R., 85

—K—

KAYE, D., 70, 74, 122, 155, 163
KEEP, R.I., 82
KELLEY, J.W., 114
KENNEDY, P.J.B., 136
KILBURN, T., 36, 85, 167, 203
KING, J., 164, 168
KING, W., 100
KINGMAN, M.J., 137
KISSOCK, J.A., 39, 55, 56, 65, 74, 96, 114, 182, 203

—L—

LAITHWAITE, J.M.W., 65, 67, 131, 203

LANGWORTH, P.J., 96
LAUGHTON, J., 67, 100, 127, 151
LEWITT, G., 107
LEWITT, S.M., 82
LLOYD, P., 156, 159
LORD, E., 30, 36, 39, 85, 107, 125, 131, 137, 144, 149, 152, 178, 182, 204
LOWNDES, M., 137
LUXTON, S., 144
LYND-EVANS, P., 57

—M—

MALTON, P.N., 75
MARKS, R., 149
MARTIN, G.H., 47, 127
MASSAM, M., 178
McDERMOTT, M.B., 40, 67, 71, 141, 204
McHARG, G., 96
McINTOSH, T., 167
McKINLEY, R.A., 49, 75, 85, 96, 114, 125, 145, 163, 204
MERRALL, I., 168
MIDGLEY, L.M., 40, 75, 125
MILES, J., 137
MITCHELL, J.W., 114, 137
MITSON, A., 40, 68, 85, 89, 149
MOIR, E.A.L., 33, 85, 114, 159, 178, 204 (also as DeWaal, E.A.L.)
MOIR, J., 108
MOIR, M., 159 (also as Rogerson, M.)
MOORE, J.S., 48, 57
MOORE, M., 114
MOORE, P., 131
MORLEY, I.M., 142
MORRILL, J.S., 49, 86
MORRIS, C.I., 43, 61, 71, 122, 170
MORRIS, S.G., 115
MORTON-THORPE, A.M., 86
MOSS, C.A., 122
MOSS, S.R., 125
MOYLAN, P.A., 49, 86
MULLINS, S, 57
MULLINS, S., 205
MUSSON, E., 137

—N—

NAUGHTON, K.S., 49, 86
NEAVE, G.R., 159
NEILL, T.M., 100
NEWEY, R.G., 142
NEWMAN, E., 145
NEWTON, K.C., 40, 96, 127

STORM, A., 150
STUTTARD, R., 138
SURGEY, J.R., 138

T—

TEALL, D.G., 125
TENNANT, A.J., 102
TERRY,C., 59
TESTER, C.E., 102
THIRSK, J., 32, 34, 41, 43, 44, 47, 72, 75, 83, 90, 97, 102, 108, 116, 125, 133, 144, 150, 152, 179, 212
THOMAS, C.M., 150
THOMAS, K., 147
THOMPSON, M.G., 47, 69, 97, 142, 166, 222
THORNBOROW, P., 133, 143
THORNTON, C., 59, 97, 160
THORNTON, M., 152
TOOLE, S., 138
TOWNSEND, S.N., 169
TRANTER, E.M., 31, 36, 42, 44, 47, 59, 69, 72, 108, 123, 128, 160, 222
TRINDER, B.S., 36, 42, 60, 69, 72, 75, 116, 117, 123, 138, 171, 179, 222
TURNOCK, B.M., 83

—U—

UPTON, A.A., 133
UPTON, P., 60

—V—

VERDON, N., 152

—W—

WAINWRIGHT, J.A., 83
WALKEY, G., 117
WALLACE, J., 169
WARNER, P., 42, 50, 60, 75, 83, 164
WARREN, P., 104
WATKINSON, M.A., 104, 224
WATSON, A.F., 72, 83, 141, 150
WATSON, I.G., 128
WEEDON, R., 84, 92, 133
WEST, F, 42, 104, 143, 164, 224
WHITE, H.J., 117, 171
WICKES, M.J.L., 42, 72, 76, 104, 150, 161
WILCOX, P., 104
WILLARS, G., 169
WILLIAMS, M.I., 32, 34, 45, 60, 69, 92, 104, 117, 123, 133, 143, 144, 151, 164, 180, 224
WILLIAMS, N.K., 105
WILLIS, S.R., 161
WILLSHAW, E.M., 139
WISDOM, J., 139
WISE, R., 139
WISE, S.E., 139 (also as English, S.)
WOLFE, G., 86
WRIGHT, S., 92
WRIGHT, S.J., 42, 128, 151, 153, 161

Select Topographical Index
(England and Wales)

Longlevels, 60, 77
Loughborough, 31
Louth, 70
Ludlow, 151, 153
Lutterworth, 50, 63, 99, 130, 148, 164
Lydford, 63

—M—

Macclesfield hundred, 90
Maldon, 69, 131, 132
Manchester, 163
Mansfield, 138
Market Harborough, 53, 57, 92, 127,
   130, 135, 162
Medbourne, 107
Melton Mowbray, 98, 118, 137
Mersea, 38
MIDDLESEX, 41
Midlands, 37, 50, 55, 81, 82, 89, 94,
   99, 111, 117, 144, 159, 168. *also see*
   East Midlands
Milverton, 67
Minchinhampton, 100
moated sites, 52
Monk Bretton, 158
Montgomery, 110
moorlands, 58, 63, 66
Moreton, 127
Morton, 54
Myddle, 33, 88, 99

—N—

New South End, 132
Newark-on-Trent, 134, 158
Newcastle-upon-Tyne, 138
Newick, 105
Newport Pagnell, 135
Newton Poppleford, 133
NORFOLK, 49, 59, 61, 145, 159
North Leigh, 101
North Riding, 39, 155
Northampton, 109, 133, 136, 143, 154,
   161
NORTHAMPTONSHIRE, 48, 49, 51,
   80, 84, 86, 87, 92, 98, 101, 151
Northover, 71
NORTHUMBERLAND, 54, 111, 154
NORTHUMBRIA, 38

Northwich, 113
Norwich, 132, 140
Nottingham, 129, 139, 143, 152
NOTTINGHAMSHIRE, 74, 105, 112,
   122, 143, 149
Nuneaton, 133
Nuneham Courtenay, 167

—O—

Odsey hundred, 52
Offwell, 99
Oldbury, 136
Osney, 63
Otley, 142
Otterhampton, 71
Ottery St Mary, 62
Oundle, 81
Oxford, 38, 63, 135, 167
OXFORDSHIRE, 32, 48, 63, 74, 87,
   101, 107, 112, 118, 134, 135, 145,
   155, 162, 181, 182

—P—

Packington, 162
Padbury, 149
Paignton, 62
parks, 51, 54, 59, 62, 66, 68
pays, 51, 77, 94
Peak, the, 53, 70, 72
PEMBROKESHIRE, 56, 96
Pen-y-coed, 109
Peterborough, 38, 77, 81
Pickering, 133
Plymouth, 89
Portsmouth, 128, 138, 166, 168
Preston, 123, 162
Pyrford, 139

—R—

Radnor valley, 110
Radstock, 111
Ramsey, 38, 80, 96, 155
Reigate, 130
Rhuddlan, 110
Richmond, 39
Richmondshire, 107
Rimpton, 97
Ripon, 33, 86, 127, 131, 156, 182

Rippingale, 108
rivers and valleys, 53, 54, 57, 68, 76,
77, 79, 83, 98, 105, 106, 110, 114, 118,
122, 124, 169
Robin Hood's Bay, 150
Rochford hundred, 34
Rossendale, 100
Rothwell, 131
RUTLAND, 34, 37, 51, 70, 76, 82,
106, 114, 146

—S—

Saddleworth, 57, 61, 100
Salisbury, 151, 153
Sanders, 66, 67
Sawley, 136
Scarborough, 132, 168
Scartho, 104
Scilly, 52
Scraptoft, 88
Seavington, 71
Shapwick, 76
Shapwick with Moorlinch, 142
Sheffield, 49, 50, 53, 54, 113, 115,
124, 130, 136, 144, 145
Shelford, 63
Sherborne, 78
Shrewsbury, 138
SHROPSHIRE, 75, 99, 116, 117, 119,
123, 138, 140
Sidmouth, 168
Slaithwaite, 58
Sleaford, 33, 57, 75, 137
Smethwick, 136
Soar valley, 83
Solihull, 126
SOMERSET, 48, 67, 71, 73, 84, 98,
106, 119, 141, 154
Sompting, 62
SOUTH HUMBERSIDE, 89, 104
South Shields, 54
South Walsham, 104
South Zeal, 133
Southampton, 48, 126, 131
Sowton, 66
Sowy, 92
Spaxton, 67
St Helens, 117
St Ives, 71, 129

Stafford, 75, 125
STAFFORDSHIRE, 40, 53, 59, 63,
102, 125, 145, 151, 157, 168
Stamford, 125, 133
Stanstead, 106
Starcross, 89
Stocklinch Ottersey, 71
Stoke Canon, 64
Stokenham, 93
Stourbridge, 167
Stowe, 68
Stow-on-the-Wold, 139
Stratford-upon-Avon, 128
Stroud valley, 114
Stroudwater, 161
SUFFOLK, 38, 50, 60, 83, 84, 86, 90,
95, 101, 108, 128, 141, 145, 159
Sunderland, 54
SURREY, 63, 87, 114, 119,125, 139,
144, 149, 152
SUSSEX, 68, 82, 97, 145, 156
Sutton Mallet, 71
Swannington, 112
Swinford, 98

—T—

Tangmere, 108
Tavistock, 37, 78, 87, 112, 123, 126,
135, 148, 154
Taynton, 148
Telford, 42
Tewkesbury, 76
Thames valley, 76
Thaxted, 127
Thornbury, 133
Thorney, 38
Thorverton, 64, 95
Tidenham, 77
Torquay, 140
Totnes, 62, 66
Towcester, 125
towns, 40, 55, 61, 64, 66, 67, 73, 99,
111, 124, 126, 127, 128, 129, 130,
131, 132, 133, 134, 135, 137, 139,
151, 156, 163, 164
Towyn, 149
Trent valley, 68
Trull, 68
Tyburn, 59